FROM THE KITCHEN OF:

_____

_____

grist

grist

A PRACTICAL GUIDE TO COOKING GRAINS, BEANS, SEEDS, AND LEGUMES
140+ RECIPES AND 160+ VARIATIONS

by abra berens

PHOTOGRAPHS BY EE BERGER
ILLUSTRATIONS BY LUCY ENGELMAN
FOREWORD BY ADRIAN LIPSCOMBE

CHRONICLE BOOKS
SAN FRANCISCO

Library of Congress Cataloging-in-Publication Data

Names: Berens, Abra, author. | Berger, EE, photographer. | Engelman, Lucy, illustrator.
Title: Grist : a practical guide to cooking grains, beans, seeds, and legumes / by Abra Berens ; photographs by EE Berger ; illustrations by Lucy Engelman.
Description: San Francisco : Chronicle Books, 2021. | Includes index.
Identifiers: LCCN 2021018825 | ISBN 9781797207131 (hardcover)
Subjects: LCSH: Cooking (Cereals) | Cooking (Vegetables) | Cooking (Seeds) | Vegetarian cooking. | LCGFT: Cookbooks.
Classification: LCC TX808 .B39 2021 | DDC 641.6/31--dc23
LC record available at https://lccn .loc.gov/2021018825

Manufactured in China.

FSC
www.fsc.org

MIX
Paper from responsible sources
FSC™ C008047

Prop contributions from CGceramics, The Weaving Mill, Ruth + Rhoda, Laura Lou Pottery, Nicholas Newcomb Pottery, and Felt+Fat.

Prop and food styling by Mollie Hayward.

Design by Sara Schneider.

Typesetting by Frank Brayton.

10 9 8 7 6 5 4 3 2

Beano is a registered trademark of Medtech Products Inc.; Beyond Burger is a registered trademark of Beyond Meat, Inc.; Burger King is a registered trademark of Burger King Corporation; Drambuie is a registered trademark of William Grant & Sons Limited; Halsa is a registered trademark of Nothing But Real, Inc.; Impossible Burger is a registered trademark of Impossible Foods Inc.; Instagram is a registered trademark of Instagram, LLC; KitchenAid is a registered trademark of Whirlpool Properties, Inc.; Komo Mill is a registered trademark of Komo GMBH LLC; Mahatma is a registered trademark of Riviana Foods Inc.; Mockmill is a registered trademark of Wolfgang Mock GmbH; Morton's is a registered trademark of Morton Salt, Inc.; Quaker Oats is a registered trademark of The Quaker Oats Company; Rancho Gordo is a registered trademark of Rancho Gordo, Inc; Roundup is a registered trademark of Monsanto Technology LLC; Sqirl is a registered trademark of Sqirl LLC; Tajín is a registered trademark of Industrias Tajín, S.A. de C.V.; Uncle Ben's is a registered trademark of Mars, Incorporated; Whopper is a registered trademark of Burger King Corporation; Zingerman's Deli is a registered trademark of Dancing Sandwich Enterprises, Inc.

Chronicle books and gifts are available at special quantity discounts to corporations, professional associations, literacy programs, and other organizations. For details and discount information, please contact our premiums department at corporatesales@ chroniclebooks.com or at 1-800-759-0190.

Chronicle Books LLC
680 Second Street
San Francisco, California 94107
www.chroniclebooks.com

Quisieron enterrarnos. No sabian que eramos semillas.
They tried to bury us. They didn't know we were seeds.

This book is for everyone who turns the soil
to put food in our mouths.

foreword

It starts with the soil. Hands tend the soil that enriches the seed.

The seed nourishes the soil, body, and soul.

Throughout history, grains and legumes have been staples without cultural or ethnic boundaries. The omnipresent nature of these seeds and the sheer breadth of varietals in the cuisines around the world serves to unite distinct and separate groups, even if the names differ from region to region. My people were taken from afar and with them they carried seeds—the essence of their home, family, and livelihood. They brought too their deep knowledge of cultivation and harvesting techniques; their unique methods of preparation; and the tradition of passing down methods and recipes while establishing new ones via storytelling through the generations.

I can honestly say that my particular love for these ingredients has deep meaning and carries the stories of my ancestors. My Great-Grandmother James's loving hands dusted with wheat flour from morning biscuits. My great-grandfather imparting wisdom as he stirred a pot of his legendary pinto beans. The many past generations sowing green and golden fields with grains and legumes. These all made me who I am today. I have built all my recipes on their foundation. They are not just staples; they are means of survival. They are multidimensional and multipurpose, and serve as the underpinnings of meals from appetizers to desserts. It is impossible to deny their impact on our food world. As I get older, I have discovered a need to understand where they come from, their history, and how to grow them. It will take people like you and me to continue telling the stories of these essential ingredients.

It is with great enthusiasm that I write this foreword for Abra Berens's *Grist*. I myself was covered in Meadowlark wheat flour from baking when I received Abra's request. That same flour coated my computer keys as I quickly responded, "It would be an honor."

Although Abra and I have never met in person, reading *Grist* has given me the nostalgic feeling of childhood. It inspired me to look at my own labeled and cultivated collection of grains and legumes and ponder the evolution of the use of rice, wheat, grains, and seeds of all types. *Grist*'s thorough descriptions and admiration of these ingredients make me desire to hold and cherish them, to dive my hands among the many, and to feel them individually. My suggestion to you is to lose yourself in the pages of this book and imagine the endless possibilities of seeds. *Grist* will become a staple among the classics that respect these ancient ingredients and to the people who have brought them to us.

—**Adrian Lipscombe**

CONTENTS

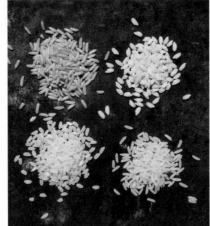

introduction

For me, the best meals come from ingredients I'm excited to prepare. Rarely am I enticed by a recipe and then seek out the things I need to make it. To be honest, I never took much notice of different grains or legumes. It wasn't until seeing the growth, in size and diversity, of the grain program at Granor Farm, where I work, that I started really thinking about how to utilize these often underappreciated staples. I started tasting the difference between wheats. Suddenly, I wanted to use oats for more than just porridge during brunch service. This book came about because, in a few short years, I got pumped on grains and legumes and wanted to create a resource for folks looking for that same sort of inspiration.

Grist guides you through the bulk section. It's your kitchen wing(wo)man, and, hopefully, a regular reminder to chuck a handful of cooked lentils over your salad.

We are told over and over again to eat a diet rich in whole grains and plant-based protein. The science is there—high in soluble fiber, low glycemic index, healthy fatted protein—but the perception of whole grains seems to still be of leaden health food, endless cooking times, and cud-like chewing at the end of it all. I have found my enthusiasm around grains and legumes by not trying to incorporate them into baked goods but instead celebrating them in their unprocessed (and often savory) state. Whole wheat berries add

pop and texture to a dish. Garlic-smashed chickpeas are simultaneously crispy and buttery. A simply stewed pot of beans often feels like a balm.

Cooking grains and legumes doesn't need to be a tricky affair. As with any ingredient, there are a variety of ways to prepare them that present differently on the plate, but simply boiling the grain in water as you would pasta, draining away the excess water, is my *desert island strategy*.

Grains and legumes are also perfect candidates for batch cooking—making larger amounts of any given recipe to have as leftovers for the rest of the week. There's a lot of back and forth about the benefits of batch cooking—maximum ease angel or bulk boredom devil. Traditionally, I've never taken to it. I would make a gallon of lentil soup and piously eat it every day, first marveling at my efficiency and then bemoaning the redundancy. Eventually it occurred to me, instead of making a big batch of lentil soup, cook a big batch of lentils and use them in different ways. Prep the ingredient instead of the finished dish so that ingredient can be used speedily while avoiding the dreaded "lentil soup fatigue." Throughout the book there are *a week without boredom grids* to illustrate how one pot of lentils can feed you throughout the week while eschewing boredom along the way.

Similarly, a lot of grains and legumes are somewhat interchangeable. A pot of stewed chickpeas is built the same way as a farro stew; fried buckwheat serves a similar textural purpose as fried bulgur. If the grain is the same, what goes into the pot or salad can change with whatever happens to be in your fridge. These seeds don't need to be handled with kid gloves—they can be conscripted into service when and how you need them. Like the grids, there are several *Flavor Formulas* studded throughout the book to show how to riff on a particular ingredient cooked in a particular way.

meat consumption

In thinking about this book, I debated about whether or not it should be completely vegetarian. Grains and legumes are standard stand-ins for animal proteins. There are many good reasons for minimizing and avoiding meat; you've probably heard a lot of them already. Health: A plant-based diet is linked to improved physical health and longevity. Environment: Agriculture accounts for 14 percent of domestic greenhouse gas emissions (right up there with fossil fuel travel); most of this is linked to intensive animal rearing—be it raising corn and soy as fodder or the runoff of toxic sewage lagoons used in confined feedlots. Animal rights: To eat meat is to take a life; to pretend otherwise is denial. Human rights: As we saw with the rampant COVID-19 infections at meat processing plants during 2020, the large slaughter houses that process 99 percent of this country's meat are operated with little regard for the people who work long, taxing days doing work that few of us can understand, let alone stomach.

The thing is, I eat meat.

I think that a plant-based diet does not need to be plant-exclusive and pinning all of our health woes on animal products is myopic. I think animals, when rotationally grazed, add value both to the soil and the profitability of diversified farms. Animals take time and space to rear; farmers need to be fairly compensated for that investment. Sustainability must include financial sustainability for farmers. I am also comfortable with the implicit agreement between a farmer and her animals. To eat meat with abandon abandons these issues.

I advocate eating meat deliberately; to eat less of it—either through portioning or frequency—and higher quality (that is, meat that does not negatively impact the animal, farmer, worker, or environmental health). This means knowing where you source your meat from and paying the true price of that ingredient.

Which leads us to cost. I believe that in an ideal society, we would spend more on food. In 1900, Americans spent, on average, 43 percent of their income on food. In 1950, 30 percent. In 2019, we spent 9.5 percent. These are percentages of total income, not disposable income. Food has gotten cheaper with the Green Revolution, and so we pay less for it. Factory farming made meat cost-competitive with beans and lentils. What was once the celebratory star of a holiday feast can now be had every day. Meat's ubiquity has led to a lot of banal consumption. It is simply there.

We cannot talk about cost without talking about issues of food access. Conversations about meat, let alone food as a whole, are both feckless and futile unless we assess our entire cultural and economic system. The ability for everyone to consume high-quality, time-intensive ingredients is inextricable from issues of class. If you, like me, have the ability to travel to a grocery store, can afford (and like) the food inside of it, have the time to prepare a meal, and can sit down with your family to enjoy it, you absolutely have the ability to effect change with your purchasing power. I encourage you to do so. It is wrong for "the haves" to demonize the choices someone less fortunate might make to get to the next day. Instead, let's focus on fixing the fact that in the wealthiest nation in the history of the earth, some of our fellow citizens aren't paid enough to afford basic living expenses like food.

Because of all of these issues, it felt disingenuous to exclude meat from this book. Many of these recipes are vegetarian or vegan and, where meat is included, it can easily be left out. I have often made the meat portions smaller than a traditional serving to give the featured ingredient top billing. I hope that this book makes you feel like you want (and have the tools) to skip a meaty meal once in a while. When you do, I hope it is from true want, instead of a feeling of "I should." There is enough to deal with without leveling "shoulds" at each other. Like my mom always said, "woulda, coulda, shoulda; you'll should all over yourself."

farmers and our food system

In *Ruffage*, I shared my stories of vegetable farming in hopes of connecting readers to the process of growing food. To shed a bit of light on the tremendous amount of work it takes to grow the most common of household ingredients. Today, the majority of American farmers are growing grains and legumes—two crops I've never grown and many of us won't grow in our gardens.

We don't grow these crops because, quite frankly, it doesn't make sense. It isn't sensible because of scale and infrastructure. It takes a good amount of space to grow enough wheat to make a pound of flour. That wheat then needs to be dried, cleaned, milled, and (often) sifted to make flour for our daily bread. That isn't something that works in a window box.

Additionally, dried grains and legumes are naturally shelf stable. The resources it takes to move them around the country are far fewer, because a pound of dried beans does not need to be refrigerated or frozen the way meat, dairy, or produce does. It makes sense to grow a lot of grain in areas well suited to that grain and then distribute it around the world in a way that growing a glut of cucumbers and then shipping those does not.

In my opinion, the problem is not the act of growing in large volume, but the lack of diversity in what we grow at that scale. Industrialization led to great advances in yields and efficiency, while transforming the agricultural landscape to one of fewer and larger farms growing more and more of fewer and fewer crops.

Earl Butz, the secretary of agriculture from 1971 to 1976, is famous for saying "get big or get out" and creating policies that incentivized just that. Agricultural policy over the last fifty years has helped create a food system based on monocultures and markets that seem to yield only less and less for farmers.

Short of sweeping food policy changes, I believe the best way to support growers is to create demand for a variety of grains and pulses (a term I use interchangeably with "legumes"), giving them more market access and financial incentive to make the switch. That starts in our own kitchen. As with just about any food, feeling confident cooking and excited about eating any ingredient will increase the likelihood that it shows up on our table. I believe that this demand for a variety of dried legumes and grains will make for a stronger food system by creating alternative, and profitable, markets for growers of all sizes.

In 1920, roughly 30 percent of the American population was made up of farmers; at the date of the last farm census in 2017, it was roughly 3 percent. Of that 3 percent, female farmers make up 27 percent of the total farm population. Only 2.8 percent of farms are Hispanic-owned, 1.6 percent are Indigenous-owned, and .05 percent are Black-owned. The average age of farmers in America is around 58 and many are looking toward retirement without clear succession plans. One consequence of the dwindling number of farmers is that we, as consumers, have less and less connection to the agricultural community and, thereby, have less and less knowledge of what it takes to grow food. The lack of grower diversity has broad implications for the food sovereignty of minority communities as well as the opportunity for building intergenerational wealth that has undergirded American agriculture for centuries.

I've included several conversations with different growers to share their stories and contextualize how an ingredient is cooked with how it is grown. It is trite, but true: no farms, no food. I believe the best way to support growers is to care about their work and the food that they grow. We should care not only because it affects our economy, environment, and national health, but also because we need to eat.

This book was written during the long-overdue social upheaval resulting from the COVID-19 pandemic and the deaths of Breonna Taylor and George Floyd (following so many before them). Throughout this reckoning, we saw how fragile our food system is—runs on supermarket flour, beans, and canned goods; cities on lockdown, necessitating emergency distribution of food into communities that are already held in food apartheids; produce abandoned in fields because there was no point in picking it, with schools and restaurants shuttered; meat processing facilities, due to the lack of care for workers, becoming hotbeds of infection and prompting the on-farm destruction of hogs and cattle; unprecedented demand on food pantries and food

banks to fill the gaps; and looming labor shortages due to the constraints on immigrant workers, who are critical to food production in this country.

In 2020, Americans got a crash course in how ruthlessly efficient our food system is when all is going according to plan, how unequal it is, and also how slow it is to pivot in an emergency. We must all be invested in the success, adaptability, and diversity of our food producers and supply chain as well as the physical and economic health of the workers who produce that food and get it to each and every table across this country.

Eating a more diverse array of grains and legumes is not a panacea for large-scale, structural problems in our food system and culture. But market shifts are nothing to sneeze at. So, if you're going to bemoan corn-soy monocultures, you best be doing something to create demand for what you do want to see.

Farmers, producers, and retailers are incredibly smart and adaptable, as we've seen. Give them the financial incentive they need to make the change you want to see, and tell the elected official who represents you to do the same. There's no more delicious activism than food activism—and no sovereignty can come without food sovereignty.

how to use this book— and some things to know

I firmly believe that great cooking comes from working with ingredients you are excited about, and the best meals come from bending recipes to showcase those ingredients instead of the other way around. Grains and legumes are perfect for this sort of cooking, because they are shelf stable and will wait at the ready until called into action. For me, the best way to not let them wither on the shelf is to be able to see them easily—consider transferring them to clear jars and displaying in a way that you will look at them regularly to get your creative gears turning.

This book is organized alphabetically, with legumes kicking off the list. For ease, I have grouped several large categories together as families—beans, rice, tiny grains, and wheat (berry grains). This is because in some ways any bean is a *bean* and any whole grain groat is roughly akin to a *wheat berry*. There is a subtle difference in flavor and texture within each family, but not enough difference in the cooking method to warrant a different chapter for every grain of sand.

The sheer volume of grains and legumes in the world and the subtlety in

their differences can be daunting. This entire book is your reference guide, and in turn each section has a *Notes Box*, which is effectively a quick cheat sheet for that particular ingredient: gluten free (or not), average cooking time, yield after cooking, ratio of water to grain, and so on. Included in the Notes Box is the point of origin for that particular item. I find that if you aren't sure what to do with an ingredient, it's best to start looking at the region that grew it originally; cooks there have the cultural understanding of what to do with it.

Because grains and legumes do not have seasonal swings in availability the way fruits, vegetables, and even some meat and fish do, I have included at least three seasonal variations for each recipe to give ideas for how to change the dish, prepared the same way, to best accommodate what else might be available at the market or in the garden.

Finally, unless otherwise noted, recipes in this book are scaled for four servings. Some of the recipes make a classic starch portion of a meal. Others are a meal unto themselves. The recipe notes will guide you.

how to store

As previously mentioned, dried grains and legumes are shelf stable, so you can pretty much store them wherever you want. Grains that have the germ and endosperm (see infographic on page 379) are more vulnerable to going rancid because of the volatile oils left intact; these should be kept in cold storage (fridge or freezer) to stave off that rancidity.

Additionally, like most foodstuffs, the best way to store them is to not. They are meant for eating, so gobble them up. I tend to keep seeds in jars on my pantry shelves, so that I can see what I have and remember to be excited about using them.

soaking

In short, it doesn't matter nutritionally whether you soak or not. Soaking does have benefits. It will always shorten the cooking time of a grain or legume, usually by about 50 percent. It also evens out the cooking time, especially in older beans, which need a substantially longer time and more cooking liquid to soften than beans that have been dried for only a year or so. Rehydrating beans before cooking also means that you will need less liquid during the cooking process because the beans will have already soaked up a good amount of liquid when rehydrating. All that said, if you forget or simply can't be bothered, you can cook any ingredient from dry and it will be fine—you'll just have to check on the simmering pot a bit more often to be sure the liquid hasn't been absorbed completely before the beans become tender.

canned

I prefer cooking grains and legumes from dried to opening a can but am not dogmatic about it. I like buying as unprocessed a product as possible. That said, I also like the convenience of popping a can open and having a meal ready in a matter of minutes. And if your family's small (one or two of you), the smaller amount in a can may be preferable to cooking a big batch and having some go to waste.

If using canned, I like to give the beans a rinse, because I find the slippery aquafaba unpleasant.

Canned beans can be used in a stew; simply expect that the stew will take far less time to cook, as the canned beans are already cooked, so you may need to cook off some of the excess liquid or start with a touch less and add as you go.

Additionally, look for cans labeled BPA free. Bisphenol A, an additive to the plastic that traditionally lined cans, has been linked to a whole host of health problems, so best to avoid.

salt and acid

I was taught to cook beans without salt or acid to keep from toughening the skins. As with most old wives' tales, there may be some element of truth, but not always. Dried beans on a traditional grocery store shelf have an average age of about five years, according to retail experts. I find when I add salt to those beans, the skins toughen. When I cook beans that I know have been dried within a year, they don't. To ensure tenderness (or out of habit), I generally wait to add salt and acid until the end of cooking dried beans, but not with other grains or legumes.

farts

If you assumed that you could get through a book full of bean, chickpea, lentil, and grain recipes without talking about farts, you're wrong. It's true: Whole grains and legumes tend to make people windy. Oligosaccharides are carbohydrates in most legumes that we lack the enzymes to digest. These carbohydrates feed bacteria in the lower intestine, resulting in gas that has to go somewhere.

There are about a million *science feels* for how to counteract it. I find simply eating more high-fiber ingredients more regularly helps lessen the swings in gas. It's like not having coffee for a month and then suddenly drinking a mega-venti espresso—you will feel the effects. Drink a bit of coffee every morning, you won't get the shakes. Same for the bacteria in your gut—if you starve them of sugar (carbohydrates) and then suddenly load them up, you'll kick them into overdrive.

Alternatively, adding the enzyme that we lack to help with digestion will minimize bacterial gas production. Joe Yonan recommends adding kombu to the boiling liquid. My neighbor, Mario Aranda, always adds some asafetida to his beans. My mom swore by Beano. In short, find what works for you. Me, I just think farts are funny, so I take no prophylactic.

protein

After questions about soaking and farting, the most frequent question I'm asked about grains and legumes concerns their protein content. Every single item in this book has some form of protein. I've included the average amount of protein per 100 g [3½ oz] in every Notes Box, mostly because I find it interesting. On the whole, I think that most consumers are overly concerned with protein and eat far more than the amount the body actually requires. Eating a balanced diet with any amount of whole grain or legume will provide you with a life-sustaining amount of protein and fiber, especially when combined with healthy fats and micronutrients found in fruits and vegetables.

glossary of terms

This section presents three types of information: general vocabulary, cooking techniques you may reference, and mini-recipes you'll want to come back to.

general vocabulary

ACIDULATED WATER

Water with an acid diluted in it and used either to keep vegetables from oxidizing or to poach eggs (vinegar makes the whites firm up faster). The traditional ratio is 1 qt [1 L] water to either the juice of 1 lemon (1½ oz [45 ml]), 2 Tbsp [30 ml] vinegar, or 1 cup [250 ml] white wine.

AQUAFABA

Water in which chickpeas or other pulses have been cooked, resulting in a viscous, protein-dense liquid often used to replace egg whites in vegan cooking.

CEREAL

Any grass cultivated for the edible components, such as wheat, rice, and corn.

DEGLAZE

To loosen browned bits of food from the pan bottom after searing or sautéing. You'll then pour off any excess fat, add ¼ to ½ cup [60 to 125 ml] of wine or hard cider to the pan, and with a flat wooden spoon vigorously scrape up the bits from the pan and continue cooking to reduce the liquid volume. This triple-duty method uses those very flavorful bits, adds acidity to a dish, and cleans the pan before washing.

DEGORGE

To salt a vegetable (commonly eggplant) before cooking to pull moisture from the flesh.

DESERT ISLAND STRATEGY

Term used to indicate that if you woke up on a desert island and came upon a random ingredient you would have at least one way of preparing it to make do while you sort out why you are on said desert island and what your next steps for rescue should be.

DIVVY

To divide a preparation equally among plates or platters.

FRESH

Seeds are edible in their green stage of life as well as their dried. Green or shelling beans will taste much more vegetal than dried beans and will cook in a quarter of the time. More and more fresh beans are available in the freezer section of grocery stores, especially soy, fava, and lima beans and green chickpeas.

GLUG

The amount of liquid poured from a container before air is pulled in past the "seal" formed by the flowing liquid in the neck of the container, creating a glug sound. An average glug measure is about 2 Tbsp to ¼ cup [30 to 60 ml]. It doesn't need to be exact—just splash it in there.

GRAIN

A small, hard, dry seed with or without an attached hull, grown for human or animal consumption. Most common grain crops are cereals or legumes.

HERB SALAD

A garnish of a mixture of picked herb leaves—the more diversity of herbs, the better; generally tender herbs, but rosemary and thyme have their place too.

LEGUME

A plant in the Fabaceae or Leguminosae family marked by high density of protein, dietary fiber, carbohydrates, and minerals.

MOJO

Pronounced "moe-hoe." A slightly thick and deeply flavorful sauce that can be spooned over any dish as a condiment. Translated from Spanish, it means "gravy" or "sauce." In English, the word "mojo" comes from the Creole mystic culture, meaning "spell" or "talisman." Either definition works here, as does the '70s slang usage of "getting one's mojo on."

PSUEDOCEREAL

Any nongrasses used in the same way as true cereal crops, such as amaranth and buckwheat.

PULSE

The seed of a legume grown agriculturally, primarily for human or livestock consumption but also for adding fertility to soil by fixing nitrogen in the roots of the plant.

RIG

A catchall phrase for a chunky, acidic relish that enhances everything it is spooned over. It is one part relish, one part vinaigrette, three parts awesome.

SCIENCE FEEL

A term my friends Heidi and Molly use for when you think there might be some science behind your opinion but don't have the facts (or the time to research it); it seems logical, and you really *feel* like there is science behind it.

cooking techniques

BLANCHED

This means to briefly cook an ingredient—usually a vegetable or green legume—by bringing a pot of salted water to a boil, reducing to a simmer, adding the ingredient, cooking quickly in the simmering water, and transferring to an ice-cold water bath to stop the cooking.

BOILED

Bring a pot of water to a boil—unsalted for beans, salted for everything else. Add the grains and return to a boil, reduce to a simmer and cook until tender, then drain away the excess cooking liquid and go forth. In general, the larger or denser a grain, the longer it will take. I find this the best method for tasting just the grain itself and the method for batch cooking that leaves you with the most unadulterated options. It's also the easiest to remember because, in short, just about anything can be cooked like pasta—no water-to-grain ratios to remember or even care about.

FRIED

Just about any seed can be crisped in hot oil after it has been cooked. Cooking the grain makes the interior tender. Frying it in hot oil makes the outside crunchy. Maybe not potato-chip crispy, but texturally different and (I find) pleasing. This is also my favorite way to use up the last scoop of batch-cooked grains. Fry it in several glugs of neutral oil, sprinkle with salt, and then scatter on any plate of roasted veg. As with all frying, excess moisture will cause the ingredient to spit when it hits the oil—so before you fry, consider giving the ingredient a pat with a towel or spreading it out on a baking sheet to dry out for a bit.

GROUND

All grains and legumes can be ground into flour, in textures ranging from coarse to fine. You can buy from the store or mill at home. I have had good success with both the Komo and Mockmill tabletop mills and the KitchenAid attachment for a stand mixer. Remember when baking that freshly milled whole-grain flour will behave differently from refined, so be prepared to tinker with your recipe. Remember too that whole-grain flour, which contains the germ and endosperm of the seed, also goes rancid more quickly, so mill in small batches and, if you're not using the whole batch, store the rest in the freezer. For very small batches, I also blitz some grains in a food processor or coffee/spice grinder. It works, but I wouldn't rely on this method for day-to-day use.

MARINATED

Less of a cooking technique and more of a way to dress a cooked grain. Cook the grain or legume fully and then, while still warm, dress in an acidic vinaigrette or sauce. As the seed cools, it will pull the flavor of the vinaigrette to the interior, yielding a very flavorful grain. I find this best for eating grains and legumes warm or at room temperature and especially in the summer. It's another good way to use batch cooking to make more than one meal at a time.

RISOTTO-ED

This is my term for grains that work well cooked in the style of risotto. It works best with short and starchy grains. To prepare, briefly fry the grain in hot oil to toast and then, stirring continuously, add a ladleful of hot liquid to the pan. Add the next ladle only after the liquid has been almost fully absorbed. The continuous agitation pulls the starch from the center of the grain, thickening the liquid as the grains absorb the liquid and tenderize. Risotto takes about 20 minutes from start to finish. Other grains vary in cooking time depending on their thickness and the accessibility of the starch. In general, the more polished or pearled a grain, the easier it is for the starch to release. For example, fully pearled barley will cook in a quarter of the time that a black barley with the hull intact will take. I suggest you make straight-ahead arborio or carnaroli rice risotto a couple of times to feel comfortable with the process (there's a recipe on page 334), then try out another pearled or polished grain and continue on from there.

SPROUTED

All grains and legumes are seeds. Sprouting tricks them into thinking it is time to grow the next season's plant. There are all sorts of ways (and things to buy) to sprout, but I've found simply soaking the seeds in body-temperature water for 5 minutes and then draining them twice a day until they unfurl works just fine. Remember that warmth and humidity will encourage the sprouting, so if it is the dead of winter, let the jar of just-soaked seeds sit in the warmest place in your kitchen. Sprouted grains have a 1:2 yield ratio, meaning that if you sprout 1 cup [about 200 g] of dried grain, you'll end up with 2 cups [about 400 g] of sprouted.

STEWED

Effectively a casserole for grains and legumes. Bloom some spices (optional), add aromatics (onion, garlic, hearty herbs), add the grain, add some liquid (water, stock, even beer), bring to a boil, lower to a simmer, and cook until tender and the liquid is mostly absorbed. This creates a dish that is more than the sum of its parts by intensifying all of the flavors used.

SWEATED

To gently cook (usually onions and garlic) over low heat until soft and translucent without coloring, generally 5 to 7 minutes.

cutting techniques/phrases

BATON

A cut traditionally ¼ by ¼ in by 1 to 2 in [6 by 6 mm by 2.5 to 5 cm] long. Make small sticks by slicing in one direction, flipping the slices, and slicing the other way to make long, thin rectangles. I use this cut over matchsticking when I want a bit more chew in the dish.

CHUNKS

Large, irregular pieces, cut for cooking, not for appearance. Generally about 1 in [2.5 cm] thick or so.

DICE

To cut into small(ish) squares by slicing in one direction, turning the slices 90 degrees, and slicing across at the same thickness. Small dice is generally ¼ by ¼ in [6 by 6 mm]; large is ¾ by ¾ in [2 by 2 cm].

MATCHSTICKS (JULIENNE)

Like a baton but a smaller cut, traditionally ⅛ by ⅛ in by 1 to 2 in [4 by 4 mm by 2.5 to 5 cm]. I use instead of a baton when I want a subtler mouthfeel.

RIBBONS (WIDE CHIFFONADE)

Cut at irregular lengths about ⅛ in [4 mm] thick. For greens, strip out the midribs, stack and roll into a log, and slice thinly, allowing the ribbons to unfurl as you go.

SHAVE

To cut into the thinnest possible slices with either a sharp knife or a mandoline. Think finely cut cabbage for coleslaw or very thinly sliced radishes for a salad.

THINLY SLICE

To cut into thin ⅒ in [2.5 mm] ribbons. Most commonly used for onions—tip and tail the onion, set the cut-side down, and then cut the onion in half from north to south pole. Peel and place each half, cut-side down, with one pole facing you, and cut across the onion very thinly from right to left (or opposite if you are left-handed), making thin ribbons or petals.

TIP AND TAIL

To cut off both ends of a vegetable, generally the stem and root end. This is usually the first step in preparing a vegetable.

vegetable cheat sheet

Vegetables are my favorite foods, and luckily, they pair well with every grain and legume. *Ruffage: A Practical Guide to Vegetables* is my tome dedicated to them. Consider this section your crib sheet for finding, storing, and using the vegetables that show up in the recipes throughout this book.

ASPARAGUS

Select: Look for bright, even coloring and avoid wrinkled stems. Buy asparagus that is all roughly the same size for evenness of storing and cooking.

Store: Refrigerate, wrapped in a protective layer. Eat as quickly as possible, because the sugars in the stalks convert to starch after harvesting.

Notes: To clean, snap the ends instead of cutting. Where they naturally give is where the stems are tender. Wash in plenty of water, because asparagus is often sandy, especially after a big rain.

BEANS: SNAP, STRING, GREEN, WAX, AND PURPLE

Select: Bright, even coloring with no obvious signs of browning. Some "rusty" coloring is OK but avoid any beans that have soft, squishy spots.

Store: Refrigerate, wrapped in a protective layer. Beans will last up to a couple of weeks.

Notes: Purple beans will turn a gray-green when cooked but are still tasty. To retain the lovely purple, either eat raw or gently cook by pouring boiling water over the beans to just take the raw edge off.

BEETS

Select: If the greens are attached, look for perky leaves with no obvious signs of rot. If just the roots, feel for firmness and avoid any overly soft beets or any with open gashes, as they won't store as long.

Store: Cut the greens from the roots, leaving about 1 in [2.5 cm] of stem at the root. If left attached, the leaves pull moisture from the roots quickly. Refrigerate the greens and use within a week or two. Roots can be stored in a cool, dry place for months. Avoid swings in temperature and freezing.

Notes: Remember that beets can color everything they touch, from hands to tongues to insides. Don't be surprised a few hours after eating beets. The lighter the beet color, the milder (less earthy) the flavor.

BROCCOLI, CAULIFLOWER, ROMANESCO

Select: Look for compact heads with no obvious signs of yellowing or rot.

Store: Refrigerate, wrapped in a protective layer. A healthy head will last a couple of weeks in the fridge.

Notes: The greens are edible and best cooked like kale or other hearty greens.

BRUSSELS SPROUTS, CABBAGE

Select: Look for heavy, compact heads with no black spots or undue yellowing.

Store: Refrigerate, wrapped in a protective layer. The larger and tighter the head, the longer the cabbage will store. Brussels sprouts have a higher tendency to dry out quickly, followed by loose cabbages like Napa, with head cabbage storing the longest—up to several months.

Notes: Cabbage will start to break down after being cut. Cut what you need from the head and store the rest in as large a piece as possible.

CARROTS

Select: Look for roots that are firm and not shriveled and free of little white hairlike roots or sprouted tops. If purchasing with the greens still attached, look for greens that are bright green with minimal yellowing.

Store: Separate the greens from the roots before storing, as the greens pull moisture from the roots quickly. Store only roots that are free from gashes or soft spots. Store the roots either protected in the refrigerator or in a dark, cool place free from temperature swings or freezing. Carrots will keep for months if stored properly.

Notes: The darker the carrot, the earthier the flavor.

CELERY

Select: Look for rigid, green stalks free from excessive browning. Avoid any celery that is squishy.

Store: Refrigerate, wrapped in a protective layer. The high moisture content of celery allows for easy rotting. If you see slimy brown spots start to appear, cut those bits away, as the bacteria will spread up the strings of celery, accelerating the breakdown.

Notes: The darker green the celery, the more tannic the flavor. Celery leaves are particularly flavorful—consider using them as an herb in any number of salads or garnishes.

CORN

Select: Look for ears that have bright, green husks and dry tassels. If you can peel back the husks, the kernels should be bright and firm. Small holes on either end of the ear are likely to indicate corn worms. If someone has munched a few kernels, you can cut the ends away, but corn that has had pests inside will not store well.

Store: Refrigerate if not using within several days. If using quickly, no need to refrigerate. The longer corn is off the stalk, the more the sugars convert to starch, so eat it up.

Notes: Most of the corn you can see growing from the road is field corn, not sweet corn. Do not pick it, for two reasons—one, it's theft; two, field corn is unpleasant to eat.

CUCUMBERS

Select: Look for plump, heavy cucumbers. Shriveled ends indicate moisture loss. If one side of the cucumber is pale, this is not a sign of under-ripeness; that side didn't receive as much sunlight.

Store: Cucumbers have a high moisture content and so should be refrigerated and used within a week or two.

Notes: Larger cucumbers will have larger seeds. The long, skinny English cucumbers have the thinnest skin and so are most pleasant for salads and eating raw.

EGGPLANTS

Select: Look for heavy fruits with tight, bright skin. Wrinkles occur most commonly at the stem end and are a sign of lost moisture and often a rubbery texture.

Store: Store at room temperature out of direct sunlight. Keeping in cold storage will cause pits in the eggplant as the cells break down.

Notes: There's a lot of to-do about degorging eggplant, to make them less bitter, by salting them ahead of cooking. I find that this makes the texture of the eggplant tough, and I rather like the slightly bitter interior of eggplant.

FENNEL

Select: Look for firm, heavy fennel with even coloring.

Store: Refrigerate, wrapped in a protective layer. If the fennel comes with its long fronds, separate the two and store the fronds separately.

Notes: Fennel oxidizes very quickly, so a bit of browning at any edge that is cut is OK. If that browning is wet or slippery, that is a sign of rot, and the fennel should be eaten quickly (after cutting away the brown bits).

GARLIC

Select: Look for garlic that has firm cloves and no signs of sprouting. If buying green garlic or garlic scapes, look for even coloring and firm skin.

Store: Head garlic is best stored at room temperature in a cool, dark place free from temperature swings or freezing. Green garlic or garlic scapes should be refrigerated, wrapped in a protective layer.

Notes: There are terrible stories of garlic being peeled by political prisoners in other parts of the world, so although it is slightly less convenient, please buy whole heads, ideally domestically grown.

GREENS, HEARTY (KALE, CHARD, MUSTARD, COLLARDS)

Select: Look for leaves that are rigid and vibrant green.

Store: Refrigerate, wrapped in a protective layer, or store at room temperature with stems in a jar of water like flowers in a vase.

Notes: Most hearty green stems are edible. Consider slicing them thinly and eating raw or sautéing them as part of the dish. If the greens are wilty, a 10- to 20-minute soak will often revive them. If they do not crisp back up, consider cooking the greens to wilt them even further. Be sure to distinguish between wilt and rot—wilting just indicates lost moisture; rot is actual decomposition.

GREENS, TENDER (SALAD GREENS, ARUGULA, SPINACH)

Select: Look for greens with bright color and crisp leaves. Avoid greens that have excessive browning, smell swampy, or are slimy.

Store: Refrigerate, wrapped in a protective layer, ideally in a crisper drawer or somewhere where the refrigerator fan cannot whip the greens excessively.

Notes: If the greens are wilty, give them a 10- to 20-minute soak in cool water to perk them back up.

KOHLRABI, TURNIP, RUTABAGA

Select: Look for heavy globes, free of shriveled ends or unhealed gashes or soft, brown-black spots.

Store: Refrigerate, wrapped in a protective layer. I've had luck storing each of these veg in a root cellar for several months, but they are more prone to going bad than other storage roots because they have more moisture in their cells.

Notes: The larger the root, the better it will store, because they will retain their moisture for longer. Small salad turnips should be eaten quickly. If you are lucky enough to buy any of these roots with their greens, be sure to cut these from the roots and use within a week or two of purchase.

LEEKS, SCALLIONS

Select: Look for long, even shafts with little to no yellowing on the leaves.

Store: Refrigerate, wrapped in a protective layer. Leeks generally store longer than scallions because they are thicker and have less moisture in their cells. If you buy leeks with excessively long leaves, trim them back if storing for more than a few days.

Notes: To clean either, slice the shaft and then soak in enough water that the pieces float with some clear water underneath. Agitate the water to loosen the dirt from within the layers. Then scoop the pieces from the top (as opposed to pouring the water out to drain) to keep the dirt from lodging in the pieces again.

ONIONS

Select: Look for onions that are firm when (gently) squeezed and without any sprouts coming out the top.

Store: Keep in a cool, dark place, avoiding large temperature swings or freezing.

Notes: Sweet onions have more moisture in their cells (diluting the sulfuric acid in the cells), making them taste sweeter, but they store for less time. To minimize your tears when cutting, wet your cutting board or place a dish of water nearby. It doesn't always do the trick entirely, but it often helps.

PEAS

Select: Look for peas with bright, even color. Avoid pea pods that are shriveled at either end or ones that have white fibers running the length of the pods (often an indication of age and toughness). When in doubt, frozen peas can be a cook's best friend.

Store: Peas don't store well, as their sugars quickly turn to starch after picking. So eat them up or freeze them quickly.

Notes: Shelling peas have plump peas inside and very fibrous pods (which are unpleasant to eat). Snap peas have plump internal peas and tender pods and should be eaten together. Snow peas have small internal peas and very tender pods.

POTATOES

Select: Look for potatoes that are firm and free of brown spots or greened skin. If you get a whiff of rot near the potato display, be sure that every single potato is firm when squeezed. The smell of a rotten potato is one of the worst, and longest lasting, smells on Earth.

Store: Keep potatoes in a dark, cool place, avoiding large temperature swings and freezing. Once a potato has started to sprout, use the potatoes quickly or discard.

Notes: Green skin is a chemical reaction to sunlight and is poisonous if consumed in large quantities. If you eat just a little bit, you'll be fine, but it is a larger sign of poor post-harvest care.

RADISHES

Select: Look for radishes with bright, even skin and perky green leaves. Avoid radishes that are dull or shriveled.

Store: Separate the greens from the roots and store each in the refrigerator wrapped in a protective layer. The greens should be used within the week. The roots will store for a bit longer.

Notes: If your radishes are either soft or extremely spicy, soak the roots or slices in cool water for 10 to 20 minutes. This will rehydrate the wilted radishes and wick away the mustard oil that gives the radish its characteristic bite. Radishes get spicier as a reaction to tough growing conditions—like drought or excessive heat—as a way of protecting the root from pest pressure on a weakened plant.

SQUASH, SUMMER

Select: Look for squash with bright, tight skin. The larger the squash, the larger the seeds. The smaller the squash, the more mild the flavor and creamy the texture.

Store: Store in a cool, dark place, avoiding large temperature swings. Storing in the refrigerator will encourage pocking in the skin.

SQUASH, WINTER

Select: Choose squash that feel heavy when you pick them up. The heavier the squash, the more moisture is still held inside. If a squash feels very light, the flesh will almost certainly be chalky and dry. Avoid squash with any obvious brown spots. Ideally, purchase the squash with the stem still intact. Once the stem is removed, the squash has to heal its "belly button" and it can easily become a place for bacteria to get in.

Store: Keep in a cool, dark place, avoiding freezing. The harder the skin, the longer the squash will store, as it will keep the moisture in for longer.

Notes: Acorn and delicata squash are technically summer squash, but their skin cures like a winter squash's, allowing for a longer shelf life. Eat these squash first, as they don't last as long as other squash. Their skin is also so thin that it is pleasant to eat.

SWEET POTATOES

Select: Look for tubers without any brown or soft spots. Also avoid sweet potatoes with wrinkly ends—a sign that the potato is starting to lose moisture.

Store: Store in a cool, dark place, avoiding temperature swings and freezing. The larger the sweet potato, the longer it will last.

Notes: Sweet potato leaves can be eaten; they are best treated like kale or chard.

TOMATOES

Select: Look for heavy orbs with tight skin. Avoid tomatoes with any clear soft spots.

Store: Keep at room temperature, out of direct sunlight. Refrigerating tomatoes kills the flavor. If you freeze whole tomatoes, when they thaw you can slip the flesh right out of the skin and cook the tomatoes down into a quick sauce. I find this much easier than blanching and peeling tomatoes for the freezer.

Notes: An heirloom tomato has traceable seed lineages. A hybrid is a modern cross between two different varieties. One is not better than the other, but a tomato that was harvested ripe and did not endure being shipped long distances is your best bet for great flavor.

PART 1

condiments

Condiments tie any meal together—and often, in my household, tie it together quickly. There is nothing better than coming home famished and finding some veg, some already boiled grains or legumes, and a couple of good sauces that let you create a meal with ruthless efficiency and maximum flavor. One quick note on salt: All of the recipes in this book were tested with Morton coarse kosher salt. It is saltier than other salts, so be sure to taste the finished dish and adjust the seasoning to your palette.

vinaigrettes, mayos, and dressings

All of these sauces should be stored, covered, in the fridge. In general, I don't have an expiration date in mind when I make a dressing. I have used anchovy vinaigrette several weeks after making it and was perfectly happy with its flavor. I have also used the mustard vinaigrette a week later and thought it tasted metallic. As a general rule of thumb, everything in this section should store for 1 week or so. After that, give it a taste and decide if you are happy with the flavor. If you have trouble remembering when something was made, do what restaurants everywhere do: Keep a roll of painter's tape (because it doesn't leave sticky goo behind when removed) and a marker in your kitchen, and label the container with the name of the sauce and the date it was made.

BASIC VINAIGRETTE	½ cup [125 ml] apple cider vinegar	2 Tbsp honey ½ tsp salt	1 cup [250 ml] olive oil
	Dissolve the vinegar, honey, and salt together, then whisk in the olive oil. Store at room temperature or in the fridge.		

| **ANCHOVY VINAIGRETTE** | 4 anchovy fillets, minced

1 shallot, minced | 2 Tbsp whole-grain or Dijon mustard

½ cup [125 ml] olive oil | ¼ cup [60 ml] sherry or red wine vinegar |

Combine all the ingredients together to make a slightly chunky vinaigrette. Store in the fridge.

| **BACON VINAIGRETTE** | 4 oz [120 g] bacon, cut into ¼ in [6 mm] strips

1 small red onion or shallot (about 4 oz [120 g]), minced | Salt

⅓ cup [90 ml] red wine vinegar (or any variety except balsamic, which is often too sweet) | ¼ cup [60 ml] olive oil |

In a frying pan, render the bacon and cook until brown and crispy. Pour the bacon and its fat over the onion with a pinch of salt and let sit for 5 minutes to soften the onion.

Add the vinegar and olive oil and whisk to combine. Adjust the seasoning as desired. Store in the fridge.

| **BROWN BUTTER VINAIGRETTE** | 4 Tbsp [60 g] butter

1 lemon (about 1½ oz [45 ml]), zest and juice | 1 orange (about 3 oz [90 ml]), zest and juice

1 Tbsp white wine or sherry vinegar | Salt

¼ cup [60 ml] olive oil |

This dressing needs to be served warm or on hot food; when it gets cold, the butter congeals and has an unpleasant mouthfeel.

To brown the butter: Place it in a stainless-steel sauté or saucepan over medium-low heat until it foams; the foam will eventually sink to the bottom and brown. Hold your nerve and let it get toasty brown. It will smell amazing.

Let the brown butter cool a bit. Combine the citrus zest and juice with the vinegar and season with a couple of pinches of salt. Whisk in the olive oil and browned butter, scraping the bottom of the pan to include the bits on the bottom. Store in the fridge.

GOAT CHEESE VINAIGRETTE

1 shallot or small onion (about 2 oz [60 g]), minced	1 lemon (about 1½ oz [45 ml]), zest and juice	¼ cup [60 ml] vinegar (any except balsamic)
	2 to 4 oz [60 to 120 g] fresh goat cheese	¼ cup [60 ml] olive oil
		Salt

Whisk together everything with a couple of big pinches of salt to make a loose and slightly chunky dressing. The more goat cheese you add, the thicker (and goat cheesier) the dressing will be. Store in the fridge.

LEMON TAHINI DRESSING

½ cup [125 ml] tahini	1 Tbsp olive oil	¼ tsp salt
2 lemons (about 3 oz [90 ml]), zest and juice	1 Tbsp honey	

Whisk together all the ingredients with ½ cup [125 ml] of water and adjust the seasoning as desired. Add more water, 1 Tbsp at a time, to thin as you like. Store in the fridge.

MUSTARD VINAIGRETTE

1 shallot (about 2 oz [60 g]), minced	¼ cup [60 ml] apple cider vinegar	¼ cup [80 g] whole-grain or Dijon mustard
½ cup [125 ml] olive oil		½ tsp salt

Whisk all the ingredients together and adjust the seasoning as desired. Store in the fridge.

VARIATION: CREAMY MUSTARD DRESSING

Replace half the olive oil with heavy cream or sour cream.

PICKLE LIQUID DRESSING

¼ cup [60 ml] pickle liquid from any nonsweet pickles

¼ cup [60 g] mayonnaise

Pinch of salt

Whisk all the ingredients together to make a loose dressing. If you want it more tart, add more pickle liquid (or a splash of vinegar). If you want it richer, add more mayo. If you want it saltier, add more salt. Store in the fridge.

SORGHUM VINAIGRETTE

¼ cup [60 ml] sorghum

¼ cup [60 ml] red wine or apple cider vinegar

1 shallot (about 2 oz [60 g]), minced

1 tsp whole-grain mustard

½ tsp salt

½ cup [125 ml] olive oil

Whisk together all the ingredients except the olive oil until the sorghum is fully dissolved. Whisk in the olive oil and adjust the seasoning. Store covered in the fridge or at room temperature.

BASIC MAYO

1 whole egg

1 Tbsp vinegar (anything except balsamic)

½ tsp salt

10 oz [300 ml] neutral oil

In a food processor, combine the egg, vinegar, and salt. With the processor running, slowly drizzle in the oil to make the mayo. Store in the fridge.

LEMON CAPER MAYO

1 whole egg

1 lemon (about 1½ oz [45 ml]), zest and juice

2 Tbsp capers

2 garlic cloves, peeled and smashed

½ tsp salt

10 oz [300 ml] neutral oil

In a food processor, combine all the ingredients except the oil. With the processor running, slowly drizzle in the oil. Adjust the seasoning as desired. Store in the fridge.

SPICY MAYO   ¼ cup [60 g] mayonnaise   1 Tbsp hot sauce, like sriracha or sambal

Mix the ingredients together. Store in the fridge.

TOMATO PAPRIKA MAYO

1 egg	1 tsp smoked paprika	¼ cup [60 g] Cherry Tomato Conserva (page 52) or 2 Tbsp tomato paste
1 lemon (about 1½ oz [45 ml]), zest and juice	½ tsp salt	
	12 oz [360 ml] neutral oil	

In a food processor, combine the egg, lemon zest and juice, paprika, and salt and whiz to blend.
    Drizzle in the oil to make a thick mayo.
    When the mayo is thick, add the tomato conserva and blend until smooth. Store in the fridge.

TRUE AIOLI   Make the Basic Mayo (page 37), but replace the vinegar with the zest and juice of 1 lemon and add 4 garlic cloves when whizzing the egg, salt, and lemon. Store in the fridge.

TUNA MAYO   Make the Basic Mayo (page 37). At the end, add one 5 oz [150 g] can of tuna (preferably packed in oil) and whiz to blend evenly. Store in the fridge.

spice oils and mixtures

Spices keep for a wonderfully long time at room temperature, but their flavors diminish with age. Nothing in this section will go bad; it will just be less robust and nuanced. Like with all things kitchen, it is helpful to date when you opened a jar of spices. This tells you a) how long you've had it, b) how quickly you are using it, and c) if you have two of the same spice, which one to use up first. All spices degrade more quickly if stored in high heat or direct sunlight, so it's best to keep them away from the stove and off of window sills and store in an airtight container.

CHAMOMILE LEMON OIL	¼ cup [60 ml] neutral oil	Zest of 1 lemon	¼ cup [60 ml] olive oil
	1 tsp chamomile blossoms or dried tea		

In a small saucepan, heat the neutral oil over medium-high heat until it begins to shimmer, about 1 minute. Add the chamomile and lemon zest, turn the heat to low, and allow them to bloom in the hot oil until fragrant, about 1 minute.

Remove from the heat and add the olive oil to cool the neutral oil. Allow to steep for 10 minutes before using.

VARIATION: CORIANDER LEMON OIL

Make the Chamomile Lemon Oil (preceding), but substitute 1 Tbsp of coriander seed and 1 Tbsp of fennel seed for the chamomile blossoms.

CHILI OIL	1 cup [250 ml] neutral oil	2 Tbsp chili flakes

In a medium sauce or frying pan, heat the oil over medium heat until it begins to shimmer, about 1 minute. Remove from the heat, add the chili flakes, and let steep for 5 minutes.

PAPRIKA CUMIN OIL

½ cup [125 ml] neutral oil   1 tsp cumin seed   ½ tsp chili flakes (optional)

1 tsp smoked paprika

Heat half of the oil in a small saucepan over medium-high heat until it begins to shimmer, about 1 minute. Add the spices and allow them to bloom in the hot oil until fragrant, about 1 minute.

Remove from the heat and add the rest of the oil to cool the mixture. Let steep for 10 minutes.

TAJÍN OIL

Make the basic Chili Oil (page 39), but substitute 2 Tbsp Tajín for the chili flakes.

ZA'ATAR CHILI OIL

Make the basic Chili Oil (page 39) and add ¼ cup [35 g] za'atar to the steeping mixture.

GARAM MASALA

1 Tbsp cumin seed   1 tsp ground cardamom   ½ tsp ground nutmeg

2 tsp black peppercorns   1 tsp cinnamon bark

1 tsp coriander seed   ½ tsp whole cloves

Mix and grind the seeds and spices as needed. The flavor will diminish with age.

| **MEDITERRANEAN SPICE MIX** | 2 tsp fennel seed | 1 tsp dried oregano or marjoram | ½ tsp dried rosemary |
| | | | ½ tsp chili flakes |

Mix the seeds and spices. The flavor will diminish with age.

RAS EL HANOUT	1 tsp cumin seed	1 tsp ground ginger	¼ tsp ground cloves
	1 tsp peppercorns	1 tsp salt	5 dried hibiscus flowers (optional)
	1 tsp coriander seed	½ tsp ground cinnamon	
	1 tsp chili flakes	½ tsp sweet paprika	

Combine all the ingredients and grind in a spice grinder until finely powdered. The flavor will diminish with age.

| **SMOKY SPICY MIX** | 2 Tbsp smoked paprika | 1 Tbsp brown sugar | 1 tsp ground cayenne |
| | 1 Tbsp sweet paprika | 2 tsp salt | |

Combine all the ingredients. The flavor will diminish with age.

YELLOW "CURRIED" SPICE MIX	3 bay leaves	1 Tbsp turmeric	1 tsp chili flakes
	2 Tbsp coriander seed	1 Tbsp ground ginger	2 whole cloves
	2 Tbsp cumin seed	1 tsp freshly ground black pepper	

Combine all the ingredients and grind in a spice grinder until finely powdered. The flavor will diminish with age.

| **ZA'ATAR** | 2 Tbsp dried thyme | 1 Tbsp sumac | 1 tsp salt |
| | 2 Tbsp dried oregano | 2 Tbsp sesame seed | |

Combine the thyme, oregano, and sumac in a spice grinder and pulse to grind. Add the sesame seed and salt. The flavor will diminish with age.

gussied-up dairy

Dairy should always be stored in the fridge. Often, it will store longer than recommended. I encourage you to taste it before you pitch it. At best, it is still fine and can be used. At worst, you'll have a sour milk taste in your mouth. Not so bad. Some items freeze well (noted within their individual boxes) but, in general, frozen dairy has a curdled texture when thawed, so I try to avoid it.

| **ANCHOVY BUTTER** | 4 oz [120 g] unsalted butter, softened | 1 shallot (about 2 oz [60 g]), minced | Zest of 1 lemon |
| | 4 anchovy fillets, minced | 5 sprigs parsley and/or dill, minced | ½ tsp salt |

Combine all the ingredients in a bowl and mash with a spoon (or the paddle attachment on a stand mixer) until evenly distributed.

Roll the butter into a log in parchment paper or plastic wrap and chill. Store in the fridge for up to 2 weeks or in the freezer indefinitely.

CITRUS RICOTTA	8 oz [225 g] ricotta ¼ cup [60 ml] heavy cream or sour cream	1 lemon (about 1½ oz [45 ml]), zest and juice Zest of 1 orange	½ tsp freshly ground black pepper ¼ tsp salt

Stir together all the ingredients and season with more salt as desired.

CREAMED MOZZARELLA	Two 6 oz [180 g] balls fresh mozzarella, torn into irregular chunks	¼ cup [60 ml] heavy or sour cream	Zest of 1 lemon Salt

Dress the torn mozzarella with the cream, zest, and a pinch of salt.

MORNAY SAUCE	1 oz [30 g] butter 1 oz [30 g] all-purpose flour	1½ cups [375 ml] whole milk 4 oz [120 g] Gruyère, grated	2 oz [60 g] Parmesan, grated 1 Tbsp Dijon mustard

In a medium saucepan, melt the butter over medium heat. Add the flour and stir to make a thick paste (roux). Cook the roux until it is golden and smells nutty, about 2 minutes.

Add in the milk in a steady stream, whisking the entire time. Stir continuously until the sauce bubbles and thickens, about 5 minutes. Lower the heat to low, add the cheeses and mustard, and stir until well melted and smooth. To rewarm, heat gently, stirring, over low heat.

MUSHROOM CREAM SAUCE

Neutral oil	Salt	½ cup [125 ml] white wine
1 small onion (about 4 oz [120 g]), thinly sliced	1 lb [450 g] mushrooms, any variety, sliced or pulled into thin strips	1½ cups [375 ml] heavy cream

In a sauce or frying pan over medium heat, heat a glug of neutral oil. Add the onion with a big pinch of salt and sweat until soft. Add the mushrooms and cook until they are starting to brown and are cooked through.

Add the wine to deglaze the pan and evaporate until almost dry. Add the cream, bring to a boil, lower the heat, and simmer until the sauce reduces by 10 percent, about 8 minutes.

SPICED MILK

3 cups [750 ml] milk (coconut, nut, oat, rice, or dairy)	1 tsp ground ginger	3 cardamom pods, slightly smashed
2 Tbsp brown sugar	1 tsp minced fresh ginger	½ tsp vanilla extract
1 tsp ground cinnamon	1 tsp ground turmeric	Pinch of salt
	1 tsp black peppercorns	

Combine all the ingredients in a large saucepan over medium heat and bring to the scalding point. Remove from the heat and let steep for 10 minutes. Strain out the black peppercorns and cardamom pods and discard.

YOGURT, CUMIN

¼ cup [60 ml] neutral oil	½ cup [125 ml] full-fat plain yogurt	½ tsp salt
1 tsp cumin seed		

In a small frying pan, heat the oil until it begins to shimmer, about 1 minute. Add the cumin seed and fry to bloom the flavor, about 30 seconds.

Remove from the heat and add to the yogurt along with the salt. Stir to combine.

**YOGURT,
GARAM MASALA**

¼ cup [60 ml] neutral oil

1 tsp garam masala or spice
    mixture of choice

½ cup [125 ml] full-fat
    plain yogurt

½ tsp salt

In a small frying pan, heat the oil until it begins to shimmer, about
1 minute. Add the spice mixture and fry to bloom the flavor,
about 30 seconds.

Remove from the heat and add to the yogurt along with the
salt. Stir to combine.

**YOGURT,
HERBED**

1 cup (2 oz [60 g])
    chopped mixed tender
    herbs (parsley, chervil,
    dill, chives, lovage,
    fennel fronds)

1 cup [250 ml] full-fat
    plain yogurt

½ cup [125 ml] olive oil

½ tsp salt

Whisk together all the ingredients. Adjust the seasoning as desired.

**YOGURT,
SMOKED**

1 cup [250 ml] plain
    yogurt

1 tsp smoked salt

1 tsp red wine vinegar

Olive oil (optional)

Whisk together all the ingredients; if too thick, add a couple of glugs of
olive oil.

herb relishes and flavorful rigs

As with the previous ingredients, there is no exact expiration date for these condiments. Any time herbs are added to something, the shelf life decreases because they either turn brown from the acid in the mixture or get slimy as their cells degrade after being chopped. Herb relishes are best used within 3 to 7 days. If there are nuts in the rig, they tend to last 7 to 10 days (assuming no herbs have been added) before they go soggy. Even when the nuts are soggy, it isn't bad, just not as texturally compelling as when it's fresh. Again, when in doubt, taste it.

GARLIC BREAD CRUMBS

¼ cup [60 ml] neutral oil

4 garlic cloves, minced

½ tsp salt

1 cup [140 g] bread crumbs or panko

In a large frying pan, heat the oil until shimmering. Add the garlic and salt. Remove from the heat and let sit for 10 minutes. Add the bread crumbs and stir to coat. Return to medium-low heat and toast the bread crumbs until golden brown and fragrant, about 3 minutes. Cool completely before storing in an airtight container.

GARLIC SCAPE RELISH

½ cup [125 ml] olive oil

¼ cup [60 ml] sherry or red wine vinegar

10 garlic scapes (2 oz [60 g]), any tough ends trimmed off, or 3 stalks green garlic (4 oz [120 g]) or 6 garlic cloves (1.2 oz [36 g]), thinly sliced

10 sprigs parsley, roughly chopped

1 tsp salt

Combine all the ingredients.

GRIBICHE

3 hard-cooked eggs, peeled and shredded on the largest holes of a box grater

1 shallot (about 2 oz [60 g]), minced

1 Tbsp capers, roughly chopped

1 Tbsp whole-grain mustard

6 sprigs dill, roughly chopped

¼ cup [60 ml] olive oil

Salt and freshly ground black pepper

Combine all the ingredients with a couple of pinches of salt and pepper to form a chunky, intense egg salad. Adjust the seasoning as desired.

HARISSA

¼ cup [60 ml] olive oil

10 chipotle or guajillo chilies (dried or canned), thinly sliced

1 dried cayenne chili or ½ tsp chili flakes

½ tsp cumin seed

½ tsp coriander seed

½ tsp fennel seed

1 red bell pepper (about 6 oz [180 g]), fresh or canned

¼ cup [60 ml] balsamic, red wine, or sherry vinegar

1 lemon (about 1½ oz [45 ml]), zest and juice

4 garlic cloves, minced

¾ tsp salt

In a frying pan, heat the olive oil over medium heat until shimmering hot but not smoking, about 1 minute.

Remove from the heat and add the dried (not canned) chilies and spices to toast for about 30 seconds.

If using canned chilies, combine with the spiced oil, bell pepper, vinegar, lemon zest and juice, garlic, and salt. Using a food processor or immersion blender, purée into a thick paste, adding a splash of water at a time if needed to keep it all moving. Store in the fridge.

HAZELNUT RIG

½ cup [65 g] hazelnuts, toasted, half the skins rubbed off, roughly chopped

¼ cup [75 g] dried tart cherries, roughly chopped

½ cup [125 ml] olive oil

¼ cup [60 ml] sherry or balsamic vinegar

Salt

Combine all the ingredients with a couple of pinches of salt and serve.

LEMON PARSLEY MOJO

1 cup [250 ml] olive oil

2 lemons (about 3 oz [90 ml]), zest and juice

10 sprigs parsley, about 2 oz [60 g], or 1 cup [60 g] chopped parsley

½ tsp salt

Combine all the ingredients to make a chunky, oily paste.

MINT ALMOND RELISH

½ cup [65 g] almonds, toasted and roughly chopped

1 shallot (about 2 oz [60 g]), minced

1 lemon (about 1½ oz [45 ml]), zest and juice

½ cup [125 ml] olive oil

Salt

5 sprigs mint, leaves picked and roughly chopped

10 sprigs parsley, roughly chopped

Combine the almonds, shallot, lemon zest and juice, and olive oil with a big pinch of salt and stir to combine.

Just before serving, add the herbs to the relish and toss.

MOJO DE AJO

1 cup [250 ml] neutral oil

20 garlic cloves (4 oz [120 g]), peeled and left whole

2 sprigs oregano

3 limes (about 4½ oz [135 ml]), zest and juice

1 orange (about 3 oz [90 ml]), zest and juice

Salt

Preheat the oven to 300°F [150°C]. Combine the olive oil, garlic cloves, and oregano in a small ovenproof pot. Bake for 45 minutes or until the garlic is soft and fragrant. Alternatively, stew on the stove over very low heat, checking on it regularly.

Allow to cool. Remove the oregano sprigs, squeezing any oil clinging to the leaves back into the pot. Add the citrus zest and juice and a couple of pinches of salt. Stir to combine, lightly smashing the garlic cloves with the back of the spoon to make a thick, oily sauce.

OLIVE RIG

8 oz [225 g] pitted olives (Kalamata, green, or a mix—just avoid canned black olives)

3 anchovy fillets (optional)

½ cup [125 ml] olive oil

1 shallot (about 2 oz [60 g]), minced

2 garlic cloves, minced

1 Tbsp capers, roughly chopped

Zest of 1 orange

Zest of 1 lemon

1 sprig rosemary, leaves picked and minced

¼ tsp chili flakes (optional)

In a food processor, quickly pulse the olives and anchovies (if using) until evenly chunky. Add the remaining ingredients and stir together.

RAS EL HANOUT APRICOT ALMOND RIG

1 cup [120 g] almonds, roughly chopped

1 cup [300 g] dried apricots, thinly sliced

½ cup [125 ml] olive oil

1 Tbsp Ras el Hanout (page 41)

1 lemon (about 1½ oz [45 ml]), zest and juice

10 sprigs parsley, roughly chopped

Salt

Combine all the ingredients with a couple of pinches of salt.

ROMESCO

1 cup [120 g] almonds, toasted

½ cup [125 ml] olive oil

1 red bell pepper (about 6 oz [180 g]), roasted, peeled, and seeded, or piquillo-style pepper from a jar, cut into rough strips

¼ cup [60 g] Cherry Tomato Conserva (page 52) or 2 Tbsp tomato paste

1 lemon (about 1½ oz [45 ml]), zest and juice

2 garlic cloves, roughly chopped

1 tsp smoked paprika

1 tsp salt

¼ tsp chili flakes (optional)

In a food processor, pulse the almonds until coarsely chopped. Add the rest of the ingredients and blend until chunky but evenly chopped.

ROSEMARY LEMON CHILI MOJO

| ½ cup [125 ml] olive oil | 4 garlic cloves, minced | 4 sprigs rosemary, leaves pulled and minced |
| 2 lemons (about 3 oz [90 ml]), zest and juice | ½ tsp chili flakes | |

In a small frying pan, warm the olive oil until it begins to shimmer, 1 minute.

Remove from the heat and add the lemon zest and juice, garlic, chili flakes, and rosemary. Set aside to steep for 10 minutes.

SAGE FRIED BROWN BUTTER

| 2 to 4 oz [60 to 120 g] butter | 10 sage leaves | Salt |

In a frying pan, heat the butter over medium heat until melted. Line a plate with paper towels.

Add the sage leaves and fry until dark green and no longer bubbling, 30 seconds to 1 minute. Remove from the heat. Lift the sage from the butter and drain on the paper towels. Sprinkle with salt.

Scrape out the butter, including the brown bits on the bottom of the frying pan, and reserve in an airtight container.

The butter will store in the fridge indefinitely. The sage leaves will stay crisp at room temperature for 1 to 2 days.

TARRAGON SUNFLOWER SEED RIG

½ cup [125 ml] olive oil	1 Tbsp minced shallot	¼ tsp salt
¼ cup [30 g] sunflower seeds, roughly chopped	10 sprigs tarragon, leaves picked and finely chopped	
1 lemon (about 1½ oz [45 ml]), zest and juice	1 tsp whole-grain mustard	

Combine all the ingredients to make a chunky relish.

WALNUT AILLADE

| 1 cup [130 g] walnuts, toasted | ½ cup [125 ml] olive oil | Zest of 1 orange |
| | 2 garlic cloves, minced | ½ tsp salt |

Process all the ingredients in a food processor or pound in a mortar and pestle to make a chunky, oily paste.

pickled/marinated vegetables

Salty, tangy marinated or pickled vegetables are another way to add a jolt to the traditionally mellow flavors of grains and legumes. They are called for in a handful of recipes throughout the book, but hopefully, you'll want to add them to dishes of your own creation in short order. All of the following recipes store in the fridge for a couple of weeks. Many also freeze well (noted in the individual recipes).

CHERRY TOMATO CONSERVA

5 lb [2.25 kg] cherry tomatoes (or any amount really, but here more is more, in that you can do this in very large batches and then you will want to eat it in very large batches)

Olive oil

Salt

Preheat the oven to 350°F [180°C]. Toss the tomatoes with several glugs of olive oil and pinches of salt.

Transfer to an ovenproof baking dish and bake the tomatoes, stirring every 20 minutes or so. The larger the baking dish, the more surface area you'll have to evaporate the liquid, so the faster they will cook, but truly any size dish will work. Bake until they burst and the liquid reduces until thick enough to drag a spoon across the baking dish and not have the liquid run into the path of the spoon, about 40 minutes.

Cherry tomato conserva freezes perfectly.

| **FRUIT COMPOTE** | ¼ cup [60 ml] neutral oil | 2 lb [900 g] any fruit *except* melon, pineapple, mango, or papaya, roughly chopped | Pinch of salt

Sugar (optional)

Freshly squeezed lemon juice (optional) |

In a large soup pot, heat the oil over medium heat until it begins to shimmer, about 1 minute. Add the fruit and salt and stir to coat. Lower the heat to low and half-cover the pot with its lid. Stir every 10 minutes or so, scraping the bottom.

When the fruit has started to release its juice, remove the lid. Cook until the fruit is soft, the liquid is mostly evaporated, and the mixture is the texture of chunky applesauce.

Remove from the heat and let cool. Add sugar if too tart and a squeeze of lemon if too sweet or bland.

Fruit compote freezes perfectly.

| **GIARDINIERA** | 1½ lb [675 g] cauliflower

1 lb [450 g] carrots

8 oz [225 g] celery

1 red bell pepper (about 6 oz [180 g])

1 cup [250 ml] red wine vinegar | 1 Tbsp salt

2 tsp sugar

8 oz [225 g] green olives, pitted and cut in half

10 pickled peppers or pepperoncini, sliced into rings

1 small onion (about 4 oz [120 g], thinly sliced | 6 garlic cloves, thinly sliced

2 tsp fennel seeds

4 sprigs oregano

4 sprigs thyme

2 bay leaves

½ cup [125 ml] olive oil |

Cut all the vegetables into bite-size pieces.

Bring a medium pot of salted water to a boil. Blanch the vegetables in batches until they are tender but crisp, about 2 minutes per batch; err on the side of undercooked.

Bring the vinegar, salt, sugar, and ½ cup [125 ml] of water to a boil and simmer until the sugar and salt are dissolved. Pour the hot liquid over the blanched vegetables. Add the olives, pickled peppers, onion, and garlic.

In a medium frying pan, toast the fennel seeds, oregano, thyme, and bay leaves until fragrant, about 2 minutes. Add these to the vegetable mix with the olive oil and stir to combine.

Allow to cool to room temperature and then store in the fridge.

This will keep for months on end as long as the vegetables are submerged in the liquid.

GINGERED APPLES	2 oz [60 g] fresh ginger root, peeled and grated	¼ tsp freshly ground black pepper	3 tart apples (about 1¼ lb [570 g]), medium diced
	½ tsp ground ginger	Pinch of salt	1 oz [30 g] butter
	1 tsp brown sugar	Neutral oil	

Combine the grated and ground ginger with the sugar, pepper, and salt.

In a large frying pan, heat a glug of neutral oil until almost smoking hot. Add the apples and pan fry until deeply caramelized, about 5 minutes.

Lower the heat to medium-low, flip the apples, and add the ginger mixture. Cook until the apples brown lightly on the bottom, then add the butter and remove from the heat.

Gingered apples freeze perfectly.

MARINATED EGGPLANT	2 medium eggplants, about 2 lb [900 g] total weight, cut in large chunks	Neutral oil	1 Tbsp capers, roughly chopped (optional)
		1 small onion (about 4 oz [120 g]), thinly sliced	¼ cup [60 ml] balsamic vinegar
	Salt	6 garlic cloves, minced	¼ cup [60 ml] olive oil

Heat a frying pan over medium high heat. Toss the eggplant with a few pinches of salt and several glugs of neutral oil to coat. Pan fry until the eggplant is golden brown on both sides and cooked through, flipping as needed, about 7 minutes. Lower the heat to low and add the onion, garlic, and capers (if using) and cook, stirring, until soft, about 3 minutes.

Transfer the mixture to a bowl. Immediately add the vinegar and olive oil and toss to combine. Marinated eggplant freezes perfectly.

MARINATED MUSHROOMS

2 lb [900 g] mushrooms, any variety, discarding excessively tough stems

6 Tbsp [90 ml] olive oil

¼ tsp chili flakes

¼ tsp fennel seed

Salt

4 garlic cloves, minced

4 sprigs thyme

2 sprigs rosemary

¼ cup [60 ml] red wine vinegar

Tear or cut the mushrooms into bite-size pieces. Toss them in 2 Tbsp [30 ml] of the olive oil, the chili flakes, fennel seed, and a couple of pinches of salt.

Pan roast the mushrooms over medium-high heat until they are cooked through and lightly caramelized. Immediately add the garlic, thyme, rosemary, vinegar, and remaining 4 Tbsp [60 ml] of olive oil and toss to coat evenly.

Allow to cool to room temperature before using.

Marinated mushrooms freeze perfectly.

MARINATED SUMMER SQUASH

3 lb [1.35 kg] summer squash or zucchini

2 cups [500 ml] Basic Vinaigrette (page 34)

Preheat the oven to 450°F [230°C]. Cut the squash into planks or wedges and arrange on a baking sheet. Roast until golden brown and cooked through, about 25 minutes.

Immediately after roasting, dress with the vinaigrette and let cool.

PEPERONATA

Olive oil

1 small onion (about 4 oz [120 g]), thinly sliced

4 garlic cloves, minced

Salt and freshly ground black pepper

1 cup [250 ml] white wine

5 lb [2.25 kg] bell peppers, any color except green, seeds removed and cut into strips

In a large sauté pan, heat a large glug of olive oil over medium heat. Add the onion and garlic with a couple of pinches of salt and black pepper, then sweat until soft. Add the white wine and deglaze the pan, allowing the wine to reduce by half, 4 minutes. Add the peppers and stew until soft, 20 minutes. Adjust the seasoning as desired. Peperonata freezes perfectly.

PICKLED DRIED FRUIT

½ cup [100 g] sugar

1 cup [250 ml] balsamic vinegar

2 cups [600 g] dried fruit

To make a gastrique, in a stainless-steel saucepan, heat the sugar over high heat until it starts to caramelize. Swirl the sugar until evenly brown and starting to smoke, about 5 minutes.

Remove from the heat and add the vinegar (it will bubble violently). Return the pan to low heat and cook until all the sugar has dissolved.

Put the fruit in a heatproof container and pour the hot gastrique over it. Let cool.

Store in the fridge indefinitely.

RATATOUILLE

Olive oil

1 tsp fennel seed (optional)

½ tsp chili flakes (optional)

3 onions (1½ lb [675 g]), thinly sliced

6 garlic cloves, minced

Salt and freshly ground black pepper

4 lb [1.8 kg] tomatoes, diced, or 2 cups [480 g] Cherry Tomato Conserva (page 52)

1 eggplant (about 1 lb [450 g]), cut into cubes

2 bell peppers (about 12 oz [340 g]), sliced

2 zucchini or summer squash (about 1¼ lb [600 g]), diced

In a Dutch oven or lidded pot, heat a glug of olive oil over medium heat. Fry the fennel seed and chili flakes (if using) in the hot oil for 30 seconds.

Add the onions and garlic with a big pinch of salt and turn down the heat to medium-low. Sweat the onions until soft, about 7 minutes. Add the diced tomatoes and cook until stewy, 7 to 10 minutes.

Add the eggplant, bell peppers, and zucchini and toss to coat. Cover and simmer until the eggplant and zucchini are soft but not mushy, about 15 minutes. Adjust the seasoning.

Ratatouille freezes perfectly.

PART 2

legumes

It is often the case that the most stalwart among us are the least celebrated. We saw throughout the early months of the pandemic that essential jobs are not the most glamorous or well paying. The things we miss the most when they are gone are not the glossiest, once-in-a-lifetime experiences, but the everyday things that knit society together—corner stores, neighborhood restaurants, greeting someone with a handshake or a hug. I think it is the same for ingredients. The cronut gets a million "likes," but in the face of trying times, it is the paper sack of black beans that brings stability. It's the bag of flour that allows us to bake bread when the grocery shelves are stripped bare.

This is true, maybe most of all, for the humble legume. Thankfully, pulses are receiving a bit of shine lately as people rediscover their wonder. In the same way that *vegetable* includes everything from asparagus to tomatoes to sweet potatoes, *legume* or *pulse* can mean anything from the ancient fava bean to the golden chickpea to the not-everyone's-darling green split pea to the onyx beluga lentil. Whatever color or texture you desire, you can find it in a legume.

This renewed interest has broad implications for their production. Beans and peas are farmed in every part of the world save Antarctica. They are grown at every scale from 10,000-acre farms to window boxes in backyard gardens. An increasing demand for beans gives farmers new markets and financial incentive to grow a diversity of crops, which has even broader positive implications for the overall health of our people, our food system, and our planet.

Pulses are regaining importance as we refocus on plant-based protein sources. They are all rich in protein and soluble fiber and have health benefits associated with their consumption. You can live on beans alone. This is not new. Pulses have supported life since ancient times across the planet. Beans found in caves in Peru have been carbon dated to several millennia BCE. Broad beans were important enough to end up in the tombs of pharaohs. Homer writes of beans in the *Iliad*.

Legumes, on whatever scale they are grown, enrich the soil. They, like a handful of other crops, improve soil fertility by fixing nitrogen through bacteria in their root system. This is why beans, which add nitrogen, are grown in tandem or rotation with corn and other grasses, which are heavy nitrogen feeders. Every acre that is planted with a nitrogen-fixing crop is one less acre requiring fertility inputs, decreasing the amount of nitrogen runoff that ends up in our waterways and eventually in the ocean, where it disrupts ecosystems, leading to a collapse in biological health and diversity.

Additionally, an uptick in demand for plant-based protein necessarily means a rebalancing in the volume of animals produced for meat. Industrial meat production is a heavy contributor to greenhouse gas emissions, so a reduction is an important part of preventing climate collapse. I do believe that animals and meat play an important role in a healthy agricultural system. Animals too add fertility to the soil, mitigate waste on biodiverse farms, and are a higher-margin product that increases financial solvency for many small and midsize farms. The problem is, we currently have an efficient but unsustainable food system in which farmers earn less and less for what they grow and thus are incentivized to grow more and more of fewer and fewer crops.

I admit, it is a tall order for a steaming bowl of stewy beans or lentils to turn that tide. Maybe I'm naive, but I am convinced it is worth working toward. Worst case, the world might still fall apart, but dinner will be good.

bean family

I felt dread tightening my throat the first time my Instagram feed had multiple images in a row of beans gently bubbling away. *Please, no. Don't do it to beans. We saw what happened to kale. Please don't let there be a celebrity sweatshirt emblazoned with the word BEANS across the front.*

And then came the ad for a dusty brown crewneck sweatshirt that said "BEANS." $37.

NOOOOOOOOO!!!!!!!!!

Not that beans don't deserve the fanfare. They are beautiful—take a look at varieties that are speckled or have golden eyes or are as black as the witchiest cat. They are life giving—protein and carbohydrates bundled together, waiting to be unlocked by our gut to feed our muscles and our blood. They are affordable enough that even the fanciest are egalitarian.

I don't trust us to be faithful lovers of beans. But I hope that beans will become a habit that is adopted. First tried because we were influenced, but then cooked regularly because they more than live up to the hype. Inevitably, the shine will dull. We'll stop harvesting Likes from a photo of beans cooking. But hopefully we'll still have a pot of beans on the stove, even when the sheer act isn't rad enough to warrant conversation.

beans, broad: lima, fava, soy

Sometimes I'm shocked to find out that ingredients I use interchangeably have no real genetic relation to one another. For
example, the beans listed in this section: fava, lima, and soy. One
time, I wanted to use fresh favas for a dish and couldn't find them
anywhere, not even in the frozen section. Not to be deterred, I
used baby lima beans that happened to be right next to where the
favas should have been on the store shelf. Everything turned out
great, but the next time I wanted to make it, no limas. Where the
lima bean tag still lingered, a bag of frozen edamame casually sat.
So I kept calm, blanched them, shucked them, and carried on.
Thus, the assumption that these wide beans were so alike they
deserved their own section in this book stayed firmly imprinted
on my mind. Then I come to find out they are a completely different genus and species. And if you actually look into the colloquial
naming, hold on to your boots. Broad beans are synonymous with
fava beans. Butter beans are limas. As of printing, soy beans have
yet to be given a nickname.

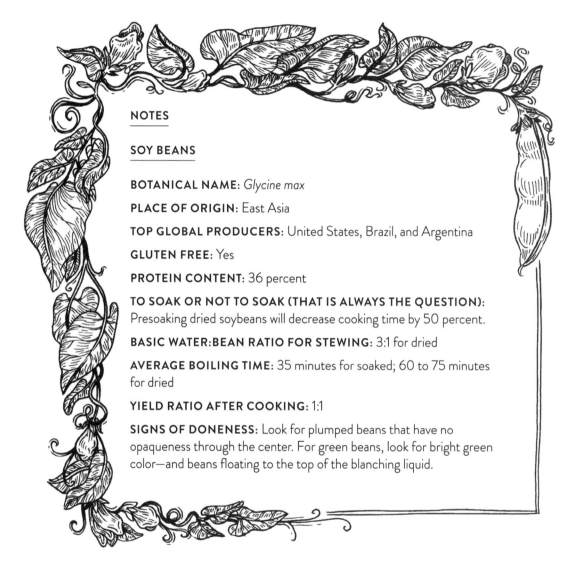

NOTES

SOY BEANS

BOTANICAL NAME: *Glycine max*

PLACE OF ORIGIN: East Asia

TOP GLOBAL PRODUCERS: United States, Brazil, and Argentina

GLUTEN FREE: Yes

PROTEIN CONTENT: 36 percent

TO SOAK OR NOT TO SOAK (THAT IS ALWAYS THE QUESTION): Presoaking dried soybeans will decrease cooking time by 50 percent.

BASIC WATER:BEAN RATIO FOR STEWING: 3:1 for dried

AVERAGE BOILING TIME: 35 minutes for soaked; 60 to 75 minutes for dried

YIELD RATIO AFTER COOKING: 1:1

SIGNS OF DONENESS: Look for plumped beans that have no opaqueness through the center. For green beans, look for bright green color—and beans floating to the top of the blanching liquid.

FAVA BEANS

BOTANICAL NAME: *Vicia faba*

PLACE OF ORIGIN: Fertile Crescent

TOP GLOBAL PRODUCERS: China, Ethiopia, and Australia

GLUTEN FREE: Yes

PROTEIN CONTENT: 26 percent

TO SOAK OR NOT TO SOAK (THAT IS ALWAYS THE QUESTION):
Soaking dried favas will decrease cooking time. Don't soak fresh favas.

BASIC WATER:BEAN RATIO FOR STEWING: 3:1 for dried

AVERAGE BOILING TIME: 35 minutes for soaked and peeled;
60 plus minutes for unsoaked and/or unpeeled

YIELD RATIO AFTER COOKING: 1:1 soaked; 1:2 unsoaked

SIGNS OF DONENESS: Beans will have almost doubled in size from
dried and will be tender when bitten, with even coloring throughout.
For fresh beans, look for a bright green color on the interior.

NOTE: There is a rare allergic intolerance to fava beans called favism,
so be sure to check with your guests before serving.

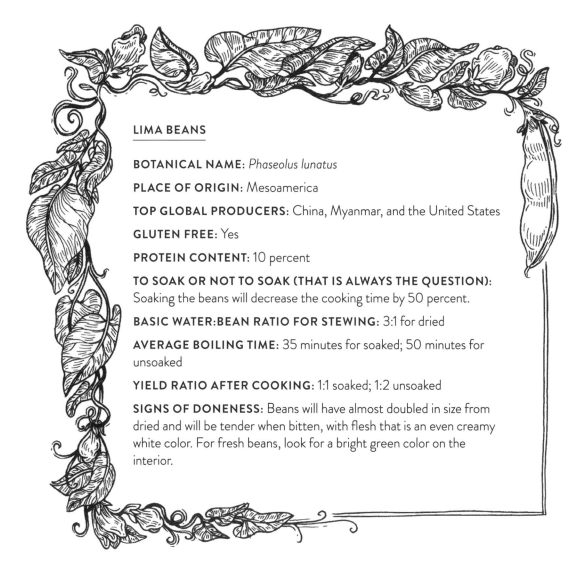

LIMA BEANS

BOTANICAL NAME: *Phaseolus lunatus*

PLACE OF ORIGIN: Mesoamerica

TOP GLOBAL PRODUCERS: China, Myanmar, and the United States

GLUTEN FREE: Yes

PROTEIN CONTENT: 10 percent

TO SOAK OR NOT TO SOAK (THAT IS ALWAYS THE QUESTION):
Soaking the beans will decrease the cooking time by 50 percent.

BASIC WATER:BEAN RATIO FOR STEWING: 3:1 for dried

AVERAGE BOILING TIME: 35 minutes for soaked; 50 minutes for
unsoaked

YIELD RATIO AFTER COOKING: 1:1 soaked; 1:2 unsoaked

SIGNS OF DONENESS: Beans will have almost doubled in size from
dried and will be tender when bitten, with flesh that is an even creamy
white color. For fresh beans, look for a bright green color on the
interior.

BOILED

Our starting point for preparing legumes and grains in this book is boiling in an abundance of water until tender, draining the liquid away, and then using that ingredient as the base for any number of meals. Ingredient + boiling + other stuff = dinner. Beans are no different, and by boiling a big pot full of beans simply, you can then use the beans in any number of different dishes throughout the week.

Similarly, most dishes can be thought of as an equation: This + this + this = delicious. What *this* is changes with the seasons or what you have on hand. For me, that Flavor Formula is: Start with 2 cups [400 g] of boiled beans (either warm or cool, up to you) + a vegetable (as much as you want) + fat (because it makes it satisfying and most micronutrients are fat-soluble, so it helps your body absorb them better) + an acidic relish or dressing + something crunchy for texture = the hearty bean salad of your dreams. The Flavor Formula coming up gives some suggestions, but there's no need to follow to the letter. Cook beyond the page and come up with your own combinations.

Cooking most grains and legumes by boiling is as simple as boiling a handful of pasta. Beans are no different. Bring a large pot of unsalted water to a boil, add the beans, turn down to a simmer, and boil until tender. When the beans are tender, add some salt to flavor the pot (adding it beforehand has the potential to toughen the beans). Adding some aromatics to the boiling liquid will add flavor, but it isn't necessary to achieving flavorful results. Soaking the beans overnight will cut cooking time in half. Using freshly dried beans also decreases cooking time and often minimizes the need to soak at all.

When cooking with dried fava beans, the outside hull may still be in place. If it is, soak or boil the beans for 3 minutes, then peel away the outer skin. You can leave the skin on, but be forewarned it can take 2 to 2½ hours to fully tenderize the bean skin. Most canned fava beans have already been peeled.

bean + vegetable + flavor + texture

Take 2 cups [400 g] of boiled beans (warm or cool, up to you) and . . .

1.	2.	3.
ADD A VEGETABLE, AS MUCH AS YOU WANT	**ADD FLAVOR**	**ADD EXTRA TEXTURE** Couple of scoops or pinches per person
Pan-roasted broccolini	Tuna Mayo (page 38) + Lemon Parsley Mojo (page 48)	Za'atar (page 42)
Pan-roasted or grilled asparagus	Gribiche (page 47)	Toasted sunflower seeds
Grilled green beans	Feta crumbles + Harissa (page 47)	Olive Rig (page 49)
Grilled peppers (skins and seeds removed) + Tomato chunks	Giardiniera (page 53) + Citrus Ricotta (page 43)	Garlic Bread Crumbs (page 46)

4.

TO SERVE

Toss the cooked broccolini and boiled beans together and then transfer to
a serving platter, dot the tuna mayo all over, top with several spoonfuls
of the lemon parsley mojo, and finish with a scattering of za'atar.

Heap boiled beans on a serving platter, top with the roasted asparagus,
spoon the gribiche all over, and finish with a handful of toasted
sunflower seeds.

Toss grilled green beans and boiled beans together with a spoonful of
harissa, then transfer to a serving platter. Crumble feta all over and finish
with dots of olive rig.

Toss the boiled beans with grilled peppers, fresh tomatoes, and giardiniera
and transfer to a serving platter. Dot the citrus ricotta all over and then
finish with a flurry of garlic bread crumbs.

STEWED

Someone once told me that hiking is just walking with terrain changes. It made it feel a lot less daunting. Similarly, stewing is just boiling but with other flavors cooked along with the beans. The only other real difference is using a specific amount of liquid instead of just a large pot of boiling water. Using a proportionate amount, in relationship to the volume of beans you're cooking, ensures that the liquid is absorbed or served along with the beans, and you won't drain away excess, sending all of that flavor down the pipes. Every ingredient chapter has a notes box with the ratio of liquid to ingredient to use when stewing.

1.

HEAT A GLUG OF NEUTRAL OIL OVER MEDIUM HEAT

2.

ADD 1 TBSP SPICE MIXTURE

(see pages 39 to 42 for inspiration) and fry for 30 seconds

3.

ADD AROMATICS (ANY OR ALL)

1 onion, thinly sliced

5 garlic cloves

3 carrots, diced

2 celery stalks, thinly sliced

4.

ADD 8 OZ [225 G] BEANS (IDEALLY SOAKED OVERNIGHT)

5.

ADD ENOUGH LIQUID TO COVER BY 2 IN [5 CM]

Water

Chicken stock

Vegetable stock

6.

BRING TO A BOIL, TURN DOWN TO A SIMMER, AND COOK FOR 25 MINUTES

7.

ADD 2 LB [900 G] STARCHY VEG

Potato

Sweet potato

Carrot

Parsnip

Pumpkin

Squash

Celery root

Cauliflower

8.

CONTINUE COOKING UNTIL VEG AND BEANS ARE TENDER

9.

ADD A BIG PINCH OF SALT, STIR, AND TASTE, ADJUSTING THE SEASONING AS DESIRED

10.

SERVE OVER 2 CUPS [400 G] COOKED GRAINS

See part 3, beginning on page 197, for inspiration

11.

TOP WITH A FLAVORFUL RIG, SAUCE, OR RELISH

See pages 46 to 50 for inspiration

12.

YUM!

PURÉED

All beans (or cooked pulses) can be blended to make a rich, creamy paste that, for me, often takes the place of a familiar sauce-catcher such as mashed potatoes or polenta. The purée stays the same; everything around it changes.

yemeni foul w/fry bread + harissa

Pronounced "fool," this fava bean dish holds many hearts in Yemen and beyond. Fava beans (with their skins on) are traditional, but you can substitute any other type of bean and make something similar. For dipping and sopping up the beans, also try pita, flatbread, garlic-rubbed toast, or even leftover pizza dough rolled and baked or pan fried.

I've left this foul unspiced (except for the cumin, which feels essential). Garnish with Chili Oil (page 39), or leave it as mild as mild can be, depending on your taste. Match this dish up with whatever vegetable you have on hand—try it raw and cut thinly, dressed with a squeeze of lemon and glug of olive oil—or really anything else you want to eat that day.

continued

8 oz [225 g] dried fava
beans, soaked overnight
(ideally)

¼ cup [60 ml] olive oil

4 garlic cloves, minced

1 tsp cumin seed

½ tsp salt

¼ cup [60 ml] Harissa
(page 47)

Fry Bread (recipe follows)

Place the fava beans in a pot and cover with water by 2 in [5 cm].
Bring to a boil, lower to a simmer, and cook until tender enough
to be mushed with a fork, about 2 hours (longer if unsoaked). Add
the olive oil, garlic, cumin seed, and salt and lightly purée the beans
and their liquid to make a chunky paste.

Transfer to a serving bowl and serve with any of the following
pairing options, a hearty spoonful of harissa, and the fry bread.

fry bread

Almost every culture has some sort of fried or griddled bread to round out a meal. This is the Oneida version that I first had at the Jane Addams Hull House in Chicago at an Indigenous Food Ways event.

1 cup [120 g] all-purpose flour

1½ tsp baking powder

¼ tsp salt

½ cup [125 ml] milk

½ cup [125 ml] neutral oil or animal fat

Whisk together the dry ingredients and then add the milk to make a soft dough. Divide into four equal pieces and roll into balls. Roll or stretch each ball into a circle about ½ in [12 mm] thick.

Heat the oil to 350°F [180°C] in a frying pan or deeper pot and fry the bread until golden brown, about 2 minutes. Flip and brown the other side. Transfer to a wire rack or paper towels on a sheet pan to let drain. Serve warm or at room temperature.

pairing options

Handful of spinach, kale, chard, or mustard greens
Shaved cabbage dressed with Mojo de Ajo (page 48)
Shaved cauliflower with Lemon Parsley Mojo (page 48)
Carrot ribbons with Mint Almond Relish (page 48)
Roasted squash or pumpkin chunks
Shaved summer squash and Herbed Yogurt (page 45)
Grilled eggplant
Marinated Mushrooms (page 56)
Peperonata (page 56)

FRESH

In the life cycle of a bean, a fresh bean is when the bean inside the pod is fully formed, but not dried. Before this stage, the bean is more like a traditional green bean. After it, the pod and the bean dry completely and are no longer perishable—ready to be stored for eating later or planted to start the cycle again. Fresh beans are both more vegetal and creamier than traditional dried beans. Plus, because they are not dried, they cook up lightning quick.
Fresh soy, lima, and fava beans are no different except that they are more widely available in grocery store freezers.

My favorite way to use these bright green darlings is to make big, hearty salads by pairing with other vegetables, some sort of fat, and a bit of dressing. Start with 2 cups [400 g] shucked fava, lima, or soy beans. Give them a quick blanch in salted water and then follow the Flavor Formula for exact suggestions, or riff your own combination to suit your preferences or what's in your larder.

how to build a myriad of fresh bean salads

Take 2 cups [400 g] blanched fresh fava, lima, or soybeans and . . .

1.	2.	3.
ADD A VEGETABLE, AS MUCH AS YOU WANT PER PERSON	**ADD A FAT, ABOUT 2 OZ [60 G] PER PERSON**	**ADD A SAUCE, A COUPLE OF SPOONFULS PER PERSON**
Shaved raw asparagus and thinly sliced radishes	Citrus Ricotta (page 43)	Tarragon Sunflower Seed Rig (page 50)
Roasted pumpkin wedges	Creamed Mozzarella (page 43)	Rosemary Lemon Chili Mojo (page 50)
Cucumbers cut into wide planks	Olive oil and dill	Walnut Aillade (page 50)
Spinach and orange segments	Feta	Mint Almond Relish (page 48)

4.

TO SERVE

In a bowl, combine the asparagus, radishes, and blanched beans with a glug of olive oil and pinch of salt. Then dot with the citrus ricotta and spoon on a liberal amount of tarragon sunflower seed rig.

On a serving platter, arrange the roasted pumpkin wedges. Nestle in the creamed mozzarella, scatter the blanched beans, and drizzle the rosemary lemon chili mojo all over.

On a serving platter, combine the cucumbers and beans, drizzle with olive oil, scatter the dill, then spoon the walnut aillade all over.

Cut the feta into rectangles. Arrange on serving plates. In a large bowl, toss the spinach, orange segments, and beans with a glug of olive oil and pinch of salt and pepper. Pile the salad on top of the feta and spoon a bit of the mint almond relish all over.

beans, common

Sometimes, the naming of a plant seems not nearly specific enough. The title Common Bean, *Phaseolus vulgaris*, encompasses everything from deep-dark black beans to stark-white gigante beans and all of the red, yellow, mottled, and speckled darlings in between. Some are runner beans; some are bush beans. I'm sure there is a genetic reason to lump them all together. Sadly, I'm not a botanist, and so it seems a bit unruly.

While each bean is dramatically different in color, texture, and flavor, they can all be prepared similarly. You will quickly start to see how one bean will present differently from another. A black bean pot liquor is thick and inky; one from cannellini beans is light in color and milky in texture. In the end, they are more alike than they are different, so swap with abandon.

In general, the larger the bean, the longer it will take to cook (remembering that older beans always take longer to tenderize and rehydrating them in advance will speed and equalize cooking times). The darker the bean, the darker the cooking liquid. If it matters to you how it lands on the plate, adjust your recipe or expectations.

NOTES

BOTANICAL NAME: *Phaseolus vulgaris*

PLACE OF ORIGIN: Americas—the oldest known domesticated bean was found in Peru's Guitarrero Cave

TOP GLOBAL PRODUCERS: Myanmar, India, and Brazil

GLUTEN FREE: Yes

PROTEIN CONTENT: Average 9.6 percent, but varies across bean varieties

TO SOAK OR NOT TO SOAK (THAT IS ALWAYS THE QUESTION): Soaking shortens and equalizes the cooking time of dried beans. Older dried beans (more than 2 years since harvest/drying) will cook at vastly different rates. Soaking helps equalize that cooking time by evenly hydrating before cooking.

BASIC WATER:BEAN RATIO FOR STEWING: 2:1, for dried

AVERAGE BOILING TIME: 30 minutes for unsoaked; 60 to 90 minutes for soaked for beans harvested and dried within the 2 years

YIELD RATIO AFTER COOKING: 1:2

SIGNS OF DONENESS: Beans will be tender and not mushy. You can cut into a bean to check for doneness: When done, the interior will be creamy and not chalky and the internal color will be even. A stark white center means it is undercooked.

MATT BERENS

Matt Berens and his brother, John, are third-generation farmers in Bentheim, Michigan (just east of Lake Michigan). They are also my cousins on my dad's side of the family. Together, they transitioned from farming cucumbers to radishes, turnips, and potatoes. Now they grow non-GMO corn and edible black beans on several hundred acres. Matt's experience typifies that of many midsize growers across the country. He talked with me late one evening in early April 2020 while doing some spring tilling.

Abra Berens: How did you get into farming?

Matt Berens: I grew up farming with my dad and enjoyed the lifestyle. I wanted to continue on with that family business.

AB: Growing up, our families grew pickles. Now you and John raise non-GMO corn and edible beans. How and why did you make that transition?

MB: There were a couple of reasons—mostly plant disease and then the processing plant in our town closed, which meant we had to haul the pickles farther to sell what we could harvest.

We had several years in a row of intense downy mildew, which meant that we had to spray way more than we wanted to keep it at bay. That is expensive in terms of both buying the spray and our time. At one point we had $1,100 per acre into the crop and had a total crop failure on over 60 acres.

It's hard to keep getting kicked like that and keep going. We had just bought a big piece of equipment, a $500,000 harvester, for a crop that was becoming less and less viable. So we sold the machine and started looking at what could be next.

Then we transitioned to soybeans for tofu. The first year it was a great contract, but we didn't get paid until April, which makes it hard to pay your bills for the whole year. The second year, we had a terrible fall and so lost a lot of what we could sell.

We transitioned to black beans because the market was good, and we had all the equipment we would need without having to buy anything else. Plus, we don't work with Roundup, for a number of reasons, but you can't use Roundup on an edible bean crop, so we felt confident that we could control weeds on a new crop.

Trouble is, every year the market value per hundred pounds of black beans goes down. We'll probably be on the hunt for something new shortly.

AB: It's April now; what is the trajectory for an average year for you?

MB: Well, right now as we talk, I'm driving a tractor, tilling in cover crop to get ready for planting as well as spreading manure and other fertilizer. This time of year, we also spend a lot of time working on equipment, making sure everything is ready as best we can.

May is busy, busy planting corn. One of the other reasons that edible beans work in our crop mix is because they plant later than everything else and are harvested before, so it works out well with timing to try to level out the workload.

June, we plant black beans and have corn maintenance. As soon as the corn comes up, we have to start controlling for weeds. Early weed prevention is critical. If weeds get established early, it's hard to manage all season—decreases yields, trouble harvesting, and on and on. Late June we'll start to side dress the corn with fertilizer. Corn is a big nitrogen feeder, so we have to add more fertility in mid-season.

In July, depending on the season, we'll start irrigation. It's best to irrigate at night—less evaporation and wind spread—so we'll be up all night managing the irrigators and then sleep a bit and get back to it the next day to spray fungicides and insecticides on the bean. Beans don't generally take as much irrigation. They are best when it is hot and dry— helps keep fungus down.

August is either busy or light depending on the rain. Good weather means we're able to get some sleep and maintain the crops. If it is dry, it's the constant push and pull of irrigation schedules.

September, we harvest the beans—when they're ready, they don't wait for us. The grain elevator wants beans at 17 percent hydration. We harvest at 19 percent hydration because when we've tried to let them dry down that last 2 percent in the field we get a lot more shattering and dropped beans at harvest. Plus, beans soak up an incredible amount of water. If we get a ¼ inch [6 mm] of rain overnight, the beans can swell and soak up 5 percent water. Then it takes two days for them to get back to where they were. Plus, you know this area: How many days in a row can you count on to be warm, sunny, and dry in September, especially late September? So we harvest them at as close to 19 percent as possible and take the dock [price reduction] at the processor.

October, we are harvesting corn and trucking the beans to Breckenridge, Michigan, over near the "thumb" [of the "mitten," extending into Lake Huron—about two hours each way], where there is more infrastructure for beans. Then it is just harvesting and trucking. Ideally, we are wrapped up with most everything by Thanksgiving. We should be totally done by middle of December. Then in January, February, and March our schedule is lighter—equipment maintenance, and we take on some other trucking work to pay bills.

AB: What does an average day look like for you?

MB: Well, I'm sure every farmer says this, but there isn't an average day. *[laughs]*

AB: Every single one! [laughs]

MB: Yeah, it really depends on the season and the weather and what needs to get done. It's one of the nice things about not having animals on our farm. Animals dictate a lot of the schedule because they are the priority—morning, afternoon, and evening chores. Because we don't have animals, we just have to do what the plants and soil need. I'm a night owl, always have been, so tonight I jumped on the tractor at 8 p.m. and will till until 2 a.m. and go home. You can't do that with animals. We also generally start a bit later in the day, because there's no point in getting out into beans before the dew dries.

AB: Why's that?

MB: The moisture spreads disease—same as rusty beans picked in a garden. Plus, if we try to harvest when the plants are wet, they just gum up the combine. So probably start about thirty minutes after first light. In September, that's what? Probably 7 a.m.

AB: Ha, late risers indeed. Starting at 7 a.m.! OK. So that's the rough schedule. What are the primary outlets for your crops?

MB: Our corn goes to local chicken farmers. In the last fifteen years or so, more and more animal farmers are making their own feed, so they aren't relying on a middleman. Plus milling it gives their workers something to do when not dealing with the animals. We sell direct to them.

AB: Does any of the corn end up as ethanol?

MB: No. With oil prices being so low and the mandated cap on the price of corn to keep ethanol competitive, there's no point.

AB: How about the beans?

MB: The beans are sold to a processer who cleans, grades, and polishes them. Most are sold to Mexico and Europe. I'd love to sell them domestically, but there isn't enough of a market, and there is only so much cold calling I can do. I was at our local grocery store—which advertises that they sell local ingredients, and they are a good mid-size regional chain, so should be moving some volume—and I said, "Hey, I'm a local bean grower. I can get them packaged for you, are you interested?" Never heard a word back.

If we could sell more around here it would solve a whole host of problems—I wouldn't be relying on Washington, DC, to solve the trade war or pass the USMCA [United States-Mexico-Canada Agreement] because I don't want to be anyone's political pawn. I wouldn't be relying on the Board of Trade to set prices for what I grow. We wouldn't have to drive them as far—and not just us, so much of what is grown in this country ends up on trucks. There's got to be a better way. We made this system, so we can unmake it, but it's hard to see how to do that and still make a living.

AB: Speaking of the processor: you mentioned getting docked for too high a hydration earlier. Can you explain that process?

MB: Yep. There's a price per hundred pounds for beans, or most commodity crops. That's the starting point. Then the processor will grade the crop and we will be docked from that starting price for things like too high a hydration, because it costs money for them to dry the beans down and there is shrinkage as they lose water weight, so we earn from that new pound weight at a lower price.

AB: What else docks from that starting price?

MB: Shattered or contaminated beans. That's why we don't grow soy at the same time as edible beans, the presence of soy—because people have allergies, etc.—cuts the price.

AB: What are the top three hurdles you face as a grower?

MB: Diseases—we are having more and more trouble controlling disease for all crops. We can pretty well control for drought, weeds, pests, and fertility; not for disease.

　　Input prices relative to sale prices—prices for inputs go way up when the commodity price is high, but they don't come down in tandem when the crop sale price is low. The market controls the sale price but not the price of what goes into producing the crop.

　　Lack of awareness of what goes into every meal—how much work it takes to grow everything we eat. There is an unending desire for cheap food. I want everyone to be able to eat—don't get me wrong—but when milk is $3 a gallon, it's like the world is ending, yet no one seems to know or care how much work goes into a gallon of milk or a bowl of beans. It's not like what Bloomberg said [on the campaign trail], "just sticking seeds in the ground, and anyone can do it." Anyone could do it, but not everyone does, and there's a lot more that goes into raising food.

　　I think that gets back to what we were talking about earlier—finding your market. Selling directly to consumers is the best price in part because it seems like the buyer is getting some sense of what it takes to grow the food or when it is in season—that we don't have strawberries year-round and so on. That's hard for a grower my size. We have too much to sell directly to people's homes, but we're too small to really hit the economy of scale that a commodity product requires.

AB: What are the top three successes from recent years?

MB: To be honest, there haven't been a lot lately. It's a struggle right now. Not to be negative, but it's a struggle.

If I think more about it, I'm proud of how we can pivot to a new crop seamlessly. John and I held on to some of the older ways of working that are more labor intensive but make us more flexible.

AB: How do you mean?

MB: Well, remember when I was saying we don't use Roundup? One of the primary benefits of Roundup to growers is that it is less volatile than other herbicides. You can spray it and it won't evaporate off. Instead, we still do things the way they did in the '70s and '80s, where we spray and immediately have to follow to till the spray into the soil so that it is effective and contained. If we wanted to go back to vegetable growing, there's a buffer time between the last spray of Roundup and when you can grow vegetables again. Because we do it the old way, we could grow pumpkins next year if the numbers worked for that crop. That takes skill, creativity, and hard work to have those options, and I'm proud of that.

In the same vein, I'm proud of the fact that we're able to raise a family on a mostly farm income. That's not easy in a tough agriculture economy, so I'm grateful for that.

AB: With all the struggles, why keep farming?

MB: Ha! Well, when you put it like that!

AB: [laughs] That's what every farmer has said!

MB: I don't doubt it. Truth is, I haven't really explored other options. This is what I grew up doing, it's what I've done my whole adult life. I'm a farmer.

But it's not just that I can't think of another way to earn a living. There's a lot to love about farming, even with the challenges. There's something about growing things—the planting and harvesting, working the land. Every year starting over again; I like the cycles of it. There's a bit of magic in the challenges—how to solve them. Plus, like any small business owner, I have a tremendous amount of independence, which I value.

AB: OK, last question and probably the hardest. Do you have a favorite way of cooking black beans?

MB: You know, I'm embarrassed to say it, but we don't eat beans that much. I don't know why, I like them, we just don't cook them that much. I've got a fifty-pound bag of our beans that the processor polished and packaged for us that has been in the garage for, oh, probably two years. If you want them, they're all yours!

AB: [laughs] That's funny, because I eat your black beans all the time. Every time I see my dad in the fall, he gives me like twenty pounds from your fields. I'll take that fifty-pound bag and bring you a copy of this cookbook when it's done!

MB: That sounds like a deal. Also, you could call Fawn over at the processor in Breckenridge. There is always a bean stew available when I drop off, and it is delicious. She might have the recipe.

A WEEK'S WORTH OF BLACK BEANS WITHOUT ANY BOREDOM

Cook 'em once; eat 'em five times. Stretch one big pot of black beans into a workweek's worth of distinct meals.

day one – basic black bean boiling recipe

¼ cup [60 ml] neutral oil

1 tsp smoked paprika

1 tsp cumin seed

½ tsp chili flakes (optional)

2 cups [400 g] dried black beans, soaked or not, depending on your state of mind

½ tsp salt

In a medium saucepan, heat the oil over medium heat. Add the spices and fry to bloom until fragrant (1 minute). Add the beans and toss to coat, then cover with cold water by 2 in [5 cm], bring to a boil, turn down to a simmer, and cook until tender, adding more water if needed.

When the beans are tender, add the salt and let the beans cool in the cooking liquid for at least 10 minutes (like soup, they get better the longer they sit—ideally, overnight). (You can reserve the cooking liquid for various uses, if you like.)

Make it more than just a pile of beans with one of these additions:

Add a starch: Combining protein and starch makes a complete meal. I usually assume half as much starch to the volume of beans I have on hand. Very optional, but a starch can also help flesh out a bowl of beans: rice, fonio (a millet-like grain), chickpea pancake, farro, bulgur, and on and on.

Add a vegetable: Adding a pile of roasted carrots and delicately dressed radicchio to a bowl of rice and beans lifts the dish from age-old staple to contemporary $14-small-plate status. Consider roasted carrots, sweet potatoes, stewed peppers, raw tomato, shaved radishes, roasted broccoli, shaved cauliflower, and *of course* greens, raw or cooked, in addition to any other veg or on their own.

Add some fat: Vitamins and micronutrients in beans are fat-soluble, so adding a dollop of sour cream or mashed avocado is not only delicious but also increases absorption of the healthful side of beans. Try sour cream, avocado, cheese, olive oil, Chili Oil (page 39), nuts, tahini, or vinaigrette.

Add something acidic: Beans are rich and provide the base of flavor for a great dish. That base is accentuated by an acidic foil. Top your bowl of beans with a spoonful of vinaigrette, spoonful of mustard, squeeze of lime, or spoonful of fermented vegetables to add dynamism and contrast.

Add something crunchy: Speaking of contrast, beans are often cooked until creamy and comforting. Adding a sprinkle of something crunchy means your mouth won't get too comfortable (read: bored). A handful of chopped nuts or a crumble of potato chips, tortilla chips, fried chickpeas, or crisped-up buckwheat will enliven the enveloping succor of a bowl of warm beans.

day two

Fill a quesadilla with a spoonful of black beans and serve with a cabbage salad dressed in Mojo de Ajo (page 48).

day three

Use reserved bean cooking liquid to make a soup (Black Bean Pot Licker w/Sweet Potato, page 110).

day four

Beans for breakfast! Warm a couple of big scoops of cooked beans and top with a soft-boiled egg and a handful of greens dressed with a spoonful of Lemon Parsley Mojo (page 48).

day five

Blend the last of the black beans with a couple glugs of olive oil to make hummus. Use that hummus to make any number of things: a BBLT (black bean, lettuce, and tomato) for lunch, or serve the purée with a dollop of Harissa (page 47) and any array of veg for a snack platter. Or schmear the hummus onto Chickpea Fritters (page 157) and top with some fresh greens for a light dinner, or transfer the purée to an ovenproof dish, cover evenly with a melty cheese, and bake until warm and bubbly, then serve with toast or chips for scooping, or . . . the options are endless.

BOILED

It doesn't get any simpler than putting a bunch of beans (maybe soaked, maybe not) in a pot, covering them with a good deal of water, and turning on the heat. You can add flavors in the form of spices or aromatics (onions, carrots, herbs). You can putter about, dipping in your spoon as you go. In the end, beans, water, heat, and some salt are all you need to make a delicious meal. Everything that goes with it is a matter of what you have on hand and how you want to dress up something that is already pretty great on its own.

cranberry bean salad w/roasted carrots + mojo de ajo

I came to know cranberry beans in the kitchen at Petersham Nurseries under the tutelage of Skye Gyngell. She called them by their Italian name, borlotti beans. Similar to a pinto bean, cranberry beans are a medium-size bean with mottled pink and white coloring. They can be cooked from dried or fresh, pulled straight from their long pods, and any bean can be substituted if you remember that the cooking time of the bean is directly correlated to the size and freshness of the bean at hand.

Note that this makes a good deal more Mojo de Ajo (page 48), which is a welcome addition to most any meal, including smashed beans on toast, in case you batch-cooked the beans.

continued

1 lb [450 g] dried
cranberry beans

1 onion (about 8 oz
[225 g]), cut into
chunks (optional)

10 sprigs thyme, tied in
a bundle (optional)

3 bay leaves (optional)

1 tsp salt, plus more for
the carrots

2 lb [900 g] carrots, cut
in half

Olive oil

Chili flakes (optional)

1 recipe Mojo de Ajo
(page 48)

10 sprigs cilantro, stems
and leaves roughly
chopped

½ cup [100 g] pepitas,
toasted

In a large pot, cover the beans with water by 2 in [5 cm]. Add the
onion, thyme, and bay leaves (if using). Bring to a boil, then turn
down to a simmer and cook until the beans are tender (anywhere
from 20 to 90 minutes, depending on whether the beans have
been soaked and their freshness). When the beans are tender, add
the salt and let sit for 10 minutes. Remove the herbs and discard.

Preheat the oven to 400°F [200°C]. Toss the carrots with a glug
of olive oil, a couple pinches of salt, and a pinch of chili flakes (if
using). Roast the carrots until deeply caramelized on the outside
and tender on the inside, about 40 minutes.

To serve, spoon a heaping serving of cooked beans per person
into a bowl and gently fold in ¼ cup [60 ml] of mojo de ajo per
serving. Transfer the beans into a serving dish or individual bowls,
portion the carrots evenly among the serving dishes, and garnish
with the chopped cilantro and a handful of pepitas.

variations

w/frozen peas, spinach + lemon tahini dressing

Heat ½ cup [125 ml] of water, ¼ cup [60 ml] of olive oil, and a big pinch of salt in a large frying pan over high heat until bubbling. Add ½ cup [100 g] of peas per person, cover, and cook until bright green, about 2 minutes. The water will fully evaporate; add more if the peas aren't cooked, and remove the lid to evaporate any additional liquid. Divide the beans into serving dishes and top each with a handful of fresh spinach (tear up any large leaves). Add 2 Tbsp or so Lemon Tahini Dressing (page 36) per person to the peas and toss to coat. Spoon the peas over the spinach and serve.

w/shaved summer squash + gribiche

Shave half a medium summer squash (per person) thinly with a sharp knife or mandoline. Dress the squash with a glug of olive oil, a pinch of salt, and a grind of black pepper just to coat. Divide the beans into serving dishes, top with a pile of the dressed summer squash, and finish with a ¼ cup [60 g] of Gribiche (page 47) per person spooned on top of each bowl.

w/peperonata + chard

Cut 3 chard leaves per person into thin ribbons. Heat 1 cup [250 ml] of Peperonata (page 56) per person in a small pot until hot. Divide the beans into serving dishes and top with a pile of the cut chard leaves. Spoon the peperonata on top to gently wilt the chard. For extra richness, top with a handful of chopped almonds or dots of goat cheese.

STEWED

If boiling a bunch of beans in plain water is as simple as it gets, these one-pot recipes add a lot of complexity of flavor with only a bit more work. Each version starts with a foundational sofrito—aromatics simmered in a fat. Garnish the beans with whatever you like, but of course, I've listed suggestions for what I would do.

cannellini beans w/saffron sofrito, shaved cauliflower + tomato paprika mayo

I learned this decadent sofrito from world-class cheesemonger Carlos Souffrant when we were making dozens of pans of paella over an open grill on the patio at Zingerman's Deli in Ann Arbor, Michigan. Carlos has an incredible palate, and when I was just starting I'd bring him little bites of what I was making just so he would describe the flavor to me. He gave me a language to articulate flavors and identify the tiny differences in taste, making me a stronger cook. I am forever grateful that he would always stop what he was doing to teach me something when he certainly had a million other more pressing things to do. Note: The sofrito will be delicious even without the saffron, but if you feel like splurging, it is *chef's kiss*!

½ cup [125 ml] olive oil, plus more for the cauliflower

5 threads saffron (optional)

1 sprig rosemary

1 onion (about 8 oz [225 g]), diced

6 garlic cloves, minced

Salt

4 canned plum tomatoes (about 14½ oz [410 g] total), roughly chopped,

1 red bell pepper (about 6 oz [180 g]), roughly chopped

1 lb [450 g] cannellini beans

½ cauliflower head (about 1 lb [450 g]), leaves removed

10 sprigs parsley, finely chopped

1 recipe Tomato Paprika Mayo (page 38)

continued

In a stockpot or Dutch oven, heat the olive oil over medium heat. Add the saffron (if using) and rosemary and fry for 30 seconds to bloom the flavor. Add the onion and garlic with a big pinch of salt and fry until just starting to turn golden brown, about 5 minutes. Add the tomatoes, their juice, and the chopped pepper. Turn down the heat to low and simmer until the tomatoes and pepper are very soft, 15 to 20 minutes.

Add the beans and just cover with cold water. Bring to a boil, then lower to a simmer, cover, and stew the beans until they are tender and cooked through, anywhere from 20 to 90 minutes, depending on whether the beans have been soaked and their freshness.

Remove from the heat and season with salt if needed. Let sit for 10 minutes.

With a sharp knife or mandoline, shave the cauliflower into wafer-thin cross sections. Combine the cauliflower and parsley with a glug of olive oil and a pinch of salt. To serve, portion the beans among serving dishes, top with a generous handful of the cauliflower parsley salad, and spoon several dollops of the mayo over the whole thing.

variations

summer beans w/fennel, orange + coriander sofrito, radicchio + goat cheese vinaigrette

½ cup [125 ml] olive oil

2 tsp coriander seed

1 onion (about 8 oz [225 g]), diced

1 head fennel (about 1 lb [450 g]), diced

Salt and freshly ground black pepper

1 orange (about 3 oz [90 ml]), zest and juice

¼ cup [60 ml] white wine

1 lb [450 g] medium beans, such as Jacob's cattle, tongue of fire, or scarlet runner

1 head radicchio or endive (about 4 oz [120 g]), cut into 2 in [5 cm] wide petals

1 recipe Goat Cheese Vinaigrette (page 36)

In a large stockpot or Dutch oven, heat the olive oil over medium heat. Add the coriander seed and fry briefly to bloom the flavor, 30 seconds to 1 minute. Add the onion and fennel with a big pinch of salt and fry until they are just starting to brown, about 4 minutes. Add the orange zest and juice and white wine to deglaze the pan and cook until the liquid is reduced by half.

Add the beans and cold water just to cover. Bring to a boil, lower to a simmer, cover, and stew until the beans are tender, anywhere from 20 minutes to 90 minutes depending on whether the beans have been soaked and their freshness. Remove from the heat and season with salt if needed. Let sit for 10 minutes.

Dress the radicchio leaves with the vinaigrette and a couple of grinds of black pepper. To serve, portion the beans among serving bowls and top with the radicchio salad.

continued

sofrito white beans w/mushroom + celery salad + creamy mustard dressing

4 Tbsp [60 g] butter

1 leek (4 oz [120 g]), trimmed, washed, and cut into thin half-moons

4 celery stalks (4 oz [120 g]), thinly sliced

10 garlic cloves (2 oz [60 g]), minced

4 sprigs thyme

Salt and freshly ground black pepper

1 lb [450 g] great northern beans or any other medium white bean

Neutral oil

2 lb [900 g] mushrooms, any variety, sliced or pulled into thin pieces

4 to 6 interior stalks celery (about 5 oz [150 g]) with the leaves attached, thinly sliced

5 sprigs parsley, roughly chopped

1 recipe Creamy Mustard Dressing (page 36)

In a stockpot or Dutch oven, heat the butter over medium-low heat. Add the leek, 4 stalks of celery, garlic, and thyme with a big pinch of salt and sweat until soft and tender, about 7 minutes. Add the beans and enough water to just cover.

Bring to a boil, lower to a simmer, and cook until the beans are tender and creamy, anywhere from 20 minutes to 90 minutes, depending on whether the beans have been soaked and their freshness. Remove from the heat and add a big pinch of salt if needed. Let sit for 10 minutes.

In a large frying pan, heat several glugs of neutral oil over medium-high heat and panfry the mushrooms, seasoning with salt and black pepper, until golden brown and cooked through with lightly crisped edges. Remove from the heat and let cool.

In a small bowl, combine the mushrooms, interior stalks of celery, and parsley with a couple of spoonfuls of the creamy mustard dressing, season with a pinch of salt, and toss to combine.

To serve, portion the beans among individual serving bowls and top with a generous serving of the mushroom and celery salad.

flageolet beans w/sofrito + fried artichoke

½ cup [125 ml] olive oil

4 sprigs thyme

1 lemon, peel cut into large strips with a vegetable peeler

2 stalks green garlic, thinly sliced

1 onion (about 8 oz [225 g], diced

1 lb [450 g] flageolet beans

Salt

1 cup [250 ml] neutral oil, for frying

Two 14 oz [392 g] cans artichoke hearts, drained and patted dry (the better you dry them, the less they will spit in the hot oil)

1 recipe Herbed Yogurt (page 45)

In a soup pot or Dutch oven, heat the olive oil over medium heat. Add the thyme and lemon peel and fry until they stop popping, about 30 seconds. Add the green garlic and onion and sweat until soft, 5 to 6 minutes.

Add the beans and just cover with cold water. Bring to a boil, lower to a simmer, and cook until tender, anywhere from 20 minutes to 90 minutes, depending on whether the beans have been soaked and their freshness.

Remove from the heat, season with salt if needed, and let sit for 10 minutes.

Line a plate with paper towels. In a large frying pan, heat the neutral oil and shallow fry the artichoke hearts until golden brown and crispy. Remove from the oil and let drain on the paper towels. Season liberally with salt.

To serve, portion the beans among individual serving bowls and top each with a generous spoonful of the yogurt and several fried artichoke hearts.

POT LICKER

Bean pot liquor is the extremely sumptuous and fortifying liquid left after cooking a pot of beans. When I first heard the phrase, I just assumed it was spelled "pot licker," thinking that it was a delightful way to describe something so delicious you just couldn't be stopped from licking the pot. Turns out if you put "pot licker" on a menu (or maybe in a book), some people will send you terse emails noting the misspellings and calling you a dummy. Sticks and stones, I still think the turn of phrase is funny (and true). Should you disagree, my email is potlickerlover@gmail.com. I look forward to hearing from you.

greens + bean pot licker

I tend to love greens and broccolini cooked just enough that it doesn't feel raw but is still a bit crisp. Not here. My friend Erin Stanley turned me on to cooking broccolini with some pasta cooking water until it is just about to fall apart. Swap pot liquor for pasta water and here we are. Feel free to add some pork or anchovy if you like, but honestly, I don't anymore.

Olive oil

1 onion (about 8 oz [225 g]), thinly sliced

4 garlic cloves, minced

Salt

2 bunches broccolini (about 1½ lb [675 g]), ends trimmed and stalks cut into 2 in [5 cm] pieces

1 bunch mustard greens or other hearty greens, such as kale or collards (about 8 oz [225 g]), rinsed and cut into 1 in [2.5 cm] ribbons

1 cup [200 g] boiled beans

2 cups [500 ml] bean pot liquor (from a previous bean session)

2 Tbsp [30 ml] vinegar, any variety (optional)

continued

In a large frying or sauté pan, heat 2 big glugs of olive oil over medium heat. Add the onions and garlic with a big pinch of salt and sweat until soft, 7 minutes or so. Add the broccolini and hearty greens and toss to coat.

Add the beans and their pot liquor. Increase the heat to high to bring to a boil, then lower to a low simmer and cook, uncovered, until the broccolini and greens are just about to fall apart, 15 to 20 minutes. If it starts to get dry along the way, add a bit of water.

Add the vinegar if the dish needs a bit of pep.

Serve with bread to soak up the liquid and several gratings of any hard cheese, if you like.

variations

black bean pot licker w/sweet potato

This is my favorite way to use up the inky black pot liquor from cooking black beans. I often remove the beans to use for something else, but you could also keep them in the soup to make it heartier. Feel free to substitute carrots, squash, or parsnips for the sweet potatoes. I've also added roasted corn to the mix. All of the vegetables can be cooked in the cooking liquid if you don't want to turn on the oven, but they tend to lack the textural difference and added caramelized complexity of flavor they gain when cooked in the broth.

2 lb [900 g] sweet potatoes, cut into chunks	1 onion (about 8 oz [225 g]), thinly sliced	4 to 6 cups [1 to 1.5 L] black bean pot liquor, all beans removed
Neutral oil	6 garlic cloves, minced	¼ cup [60 ml] sour cream
Salt		10 sprigs cilantro, chopped

Preheat the oven to 400°F [200°C]. Toss the sweet potatoes in a glug of neutral oil and a big pinch of salt, then roast until caramelized on the outside and tender on the inside, about 20 minutes.

In a medium stockpot, heat a glug of neutral oil over medium heat and sweat the onions and garlic with a pinch of salt until soft and tender, about 7 minutes.

Add the reserved pot liquor and thin with 2 cups [500 ml] of water or stock, then bring to a boil.

Add the roasted sweet potatoes.

To serve, portion the soup into serving bowls, top with a dollop of sour cream, and sprinkle on a handful of the chopped cilantro.

pot licker panade

Ribollita—the Italian bread, bean, and Parmesan rind soup—had a real moment a few years back. It is truly delicious, but I only ever make it when I have extra pot liquor around. One time I used more bread than was really sensible. Then I needed to free up a burner, so I finished it in the oven, and it made something more like the French *panade*. Now I just do it that way.

Olive oil or butter

4 sprigs thyme or 2 sprigs rosemary (optional; try both if you're up for it)

1 lb [450 g] mushrooms, any variety, roughly cut up

Salt and freshly ground black pepper

1 onion (about 8 oz [250 g]), thinly sliced

4 garlic cloves, minced

1 cup [250 ml] wine, any color, just not sweet

10 oz [280 g] stale bread, cut or torn into chunks

10 chard leaves and stems, cut into ½ in [12 mm] ribbons

2 qt [2 L] pot liquor

6 oz [180 g] hard cheese (Gruyère, Cheddar, Parmesan), grated

Preheat the oven to 350°F [180°C].

In a large ovenproof frying pan, heat a big glug of olive oil over medium heat. Fry the herbs (if using) until they stop popping, about 30 seconds. Add the mushrooms with a pinch of salt and grind of black pepper and pan fry until golden brown. Add the onions and garlic with a pinch of salt and sweat until tender, about 7 minutes.

continued

Add the wine to deglaze the pan and simmer until reduced by half. Add the bread and chard and stir to combine. Add the pot liquor and bring to a boil.

Transfer the pan to the oven and bake until the bread has soaked up the pot liquor and become like a loose casserole, about 25 minutes.

Top with the cheese and return to the oven to melt, about 10 minutes.

Remove from the oven and let sit for 10 minutes to avoid burning everyone's mouths and to let the bread set up a bit, then dish it up.

MARINATED

A pot of room-temperature beans, drained of their cooking liquor and immediately bathed in a piquant dressing (and given a chance to regain their wits), makes one of the most underappreciated dishes out there. Maybe it is because most three-bean deli salads are pretty terrible. Whatever the reason, I usually boil a couple extra cups of beans just to marinate and eat later in the week as a bean salad, and I hope it catches on.

anchovy-garlic marinated corona beans w/arugula + beets

My favorite bean salads are made with all those great big beans. I love the Royal Corona variety (often stocked by Rancho Gordo) or the Spanish gigante beans. Should you not take the time to seek these out, any bean can be boiled, drained, and marinated. There are precious, fiddly things in this world, but bean salad is not one of them.

1 recipe Anchovy Vinaigrette (page 35)	2 cups [400 g] just-boiled corona beans	Olive oil
Salt and freshly ground black pepper	2 to 4 oz [60 to 120 g] arugula	4 beets (1½ lb [675 g]), steam-roasted, peeled, and cut into chunks

Combine the vinaigrette with a pinch of salt and a grind of black pepper.

As soon as the beans are cooked through, lift them from their pot liquor, dress with the vinaigrette, and let sit for at least 10 minutes.

continued

Serve at room temperature or lightly chilled. To serve, dress the arugula and beets with a glug of olive oil and a pinch of salt. Dish up the beans and top with the arugula and several chunks of beet.

variations

mustard marinated beans w/shaved asparagus + parsley

Dress the just-cooked beans with ½ to 1 cup [125 to 250 ml] Mustard Vinaigrette (page 36) and let sit for at least 10 minutes. To serve, shave 8 oz [225 g] of asparagus into thin ribbons with a knife or mandoline. Combine the asparagus with some chopped parsley and a glug of olive oil and a pinch of salt. Dish up the beans and top with the asparagus.

buttermilk marinated beans on tomato slabs w/mint almond relish

Dress 2 cups [400 g] of just-cooked beans with 1 cup [250 ml] buttermilk and let sit for 10 minutes. Slice big tomatoes into ½ in [12 mm] thick rounds and top with the buttermilk marinated beans. Garnish with a spoonful of Mint Almond Relish (page 48). This is also good on top of toast, unlike most other things, which are not good on toast. (JK—almost everything is good on toast.)

w/bacon vinaigrette, acorn squash + spinach salad

Dress 2 cups [400 g] of just-cooked beans with ½ cup [125 ml] Bacon Vinaigrette (page 35) and let sit. Cut the squash in half, scoop out the seeds, and then cut into large claw-like wedges and roast in a 400°F [200°C] oven until tender and caramelized. To serve, toss the squash with a handful of baby spinach and the marinated beans.

peas, cow: black-eyed peas, crowder peas, field peas

Grains and legumes are so daunting, in part, because they are old and have long histories. Beans originating in western Africa were brought to the Americas by people who were enslaved. They were sewn into the hems of clothing or braided into locks of hair and then planted in the fertile soil of the Caribbean and American South. These seeds were a means of survival, and the names changed as they passed from one region or generation to the next.

I don't know why cowpeas, *Vigna unguiculata*, including the little brown crowder pea, the well-loved black-eyed pea, the murky-yellow pigeon pea, and field peas of all kinds, are called peas at all. They are scientifically designated as beans, but it isn't important. I learned them as peas. They are cooked like beans. It's confusing but doesn't really change that much.

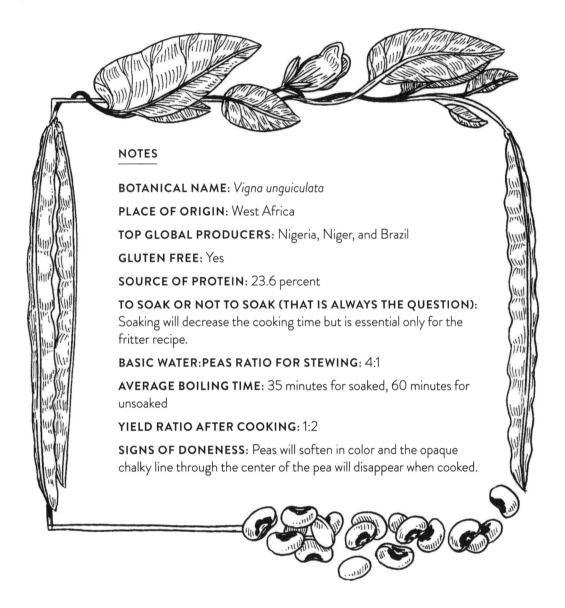

NOTES

BOTANICAL NAME: *Vigna unguiculata*

PLACE OF ORIGIN: West Africa

TOP GLOBAL PRODUCERS: Nigeria, Niger, and Brazil

GLUTEN FREE: Yes

SOURCE OF PROTEIN: 23.6 percent

TO SOAK OR NOT TO SOAK (THAT IS ALWAYS THE QUESTION): Soaking will decrease the cooking time but is essential only for the fritter recipe.

BASIC WATER:PEAS RATIO FOR STEWING: 4:1

AVERAGE BOILING TIME: 35 minutes for soaked, 60 minutes for unsoaked

YIELD RATIO AFTER COOKING: 1:2

SIGNS OF DONENESS: Peas will soften in color and the opaque chalky line through the center of the pea will disappear when cooked.

JERRY HEBRON

Jerry Hebron is the Executive Director at Northend Christian Community Development in Detroit, Michigan. She manages the Oakland Avenue Urban Farm, a nonprofit, community-based organization dedicated to cultivating healthy foods, sustainable economies, and active cultural environments. I called on Ms. Hebron because I wanted to learn more about the differences and similarities between rural and urban growers. Oakland Ave Farm has been growing crowder peas since 2013 at the request of several community members. She took several hours out of her Sunday afternoon in June 2020 to talk with me.

Abra Berens: Tell me about the history of your farm and how you came to farm.

Jerry Hebron: We've been here eleven years. We started over there where the guys are working. We are renovating that area and redesigning it to become a pollinator garden. That original footprint is now where we do more of our community engagement—our farmers' market is there—it is more of a gathering point.

AB: Yes, I saw the wood oven.

JH: Yeah, we are still working on that. We built that last year, but we had so much rain all of last year. We'd work on it one day; it would rain three. We'd work on it one day; it would rain four. We had one pizza party last September and it was fabulous. Then the farmers' market ended for the season, then holidays and winter; we were going to start working on it again this spring, then COVID. We will finish it this year. We need to. We have chefs chomping at the bit to use it. We built it to make pizza but also to bake bread using the old-fashioned recipes. Again, we have several chefs waiting for the opportunity to bake their bread. We have one partner who wants to work on his sourdough and send twenty-five loaves of bread out into the community.

AB: It sounds like this farm is really based around the people participating in it. The emphasis on community: bringing people together for a farmers' market, pizza parties, chef partners.

JH: In terms of community, we started this farm with bringing people together to talk about what to do with this space. Oakland was very desolate and dangerous, very uneventful when we came over in 2008 to think about what to do with these ten lots. There was a food movement going on. This community didn't have a grocery store—still doesn't to this day—and the health disparities are very high. So being a country girl, with a family from the South, we thought maybe we can grow some food and get people involved in that. We started inviting people to come in and meet with us, talk about the possibilities, and we found there was a huge interest in changing the perception of Oakland, and that the garden would be a good instigator for that to get people to understand the value of our commercial corridor—which isn't alive right now, but was alive and thriving when I was a child. There was some money that Greening of Detroit had; they didn't have a project, and they had two months left on the funding, and we said, "Hey, let's use it to help us do this work."

Our non-profit, Northend Christian Community Development, has always been about bringing resources to the community. That's what we do. That's how we started. We did the first garden space, and people thought, "They won't come back," because we didn't live in the neighborhood at the time. But it was a big success. Come fall, we went home, and in the spring, we came back. And people thought, "Oh, they must be crazy!" [*laughs*] We continue the work. The next year, in 2010, is when we opened the farmers' market and again, everyone thought it would be a big failure saying things like, "Who's going to come here, and who's going to buy your food?" But we found that a lot of people in this community came from the South, and they are used to growing food and eating healthy. They told us, "Grow greens, beans, and tomatoes," so that's what we did.

We tried the crowder pea the first year and it didn't do so well. The organic matter on the first site wasn't quite right. The next year, 2013, we had been building up the soil with organic matter, and the crowder peas had a bumper crop. Now people come to us for the crowder peas because they know they can buy them here.

AB: What is the life cycle or schedule of crowder peas?

JH: Typically we plant at the end of April, early May, and by end of July we'll be harvesting. Right now they are blooming, and there are a few pods on the plants. If we get a good rain—and it is supposed to rain this weekend—we'll be harvesting by next week.

AB: And are crowder peas like other beans, where if you keep picking they will keep producing, or are they more like a determinant crop where you get one big flush and they are done?

JH: No, they will keep producing. As long as we have heat and rain, they will keep going.

AB: And is that schedule, here in Michigan, the same as it is in the South?

JH: It's a little later. My mother said she would plant snap peas in late March and then come back and do crowders, black-eyed peas.

The variety that we use is called Mississippi Mud. We only bought the seeds once because we've been saving. This year, a couple of farmers asked if we would share seeds with them and we did, so next year there will be two other Black farmers growing the peas. Because we've been saving the seeds since 2014, the peas have adjusted. They are a drought-tolerant variety. This year it has been so frickin' hot and as you can see, we don't have a lot of shade trees, so they are getting full sun for twelve hours or so. As long as we water, they will do well.

What we are seeing is that the legumes have a substantial—how do I want to say this? They are filling. We want to grow things that help our families extend their dollars, their budget, but also get the nutritional value for their families. We know that beans and peas will do that.

This year, for the first time, in the hoop house we're doing an experiment with lady peas, another legume that my husband and I became very fond of because my husband is from Memphis and his mother, who is deceased now, would shell them and put them in the freezer for us to eat all winter. They are very tiny and easy to cook, and they are so good and so filling. It took us a while to find the seed, but we found them and now are testing them because Michigan is a different climate than Memphis. We haven't seen buds yet, but I'm hoping by August.

What we saw in our community is that people were unemployable because of the gaps to traditional employment. They either didn't have a high school diploma or GED, they had been out of the workforce for years, they had been incarcerated, they had substance abuse issues, they were dealing with homelessness, dysfunctional families, inadequate housing. We have identified about seventeen gaps that needed to be addressed so that they can move on to traditional employers, because traditional employers don't have the capacity to deal with people from a social impact position; that's not what they are looking for. For us, it's different—we are all about healing and helping people to become whole. Sometimes people are with us for a few months or several years. Sometimes they move on. We've had a couple of folks who went to Chrysler or Ford. We had one kid who now has his builder's license and his own company.

AB: *That's interesting that none of those are food-based businesses.*

JH: Well, that's true. We have one business, Afro Jam, that was run by a lady who was disabled and could not do traditional employment, but cooking was something that she loved doing. She started making the jam here. The problem was, she didn't have the capacity to go without an income, because you know before you make money you are putting money into the business. It may be a year or two before you start earning. She got frustrated and walked away. We took it on as a value-added product, and we're waiting to hand this off to someone else. I'll be here Tuesday making jam. We sell twenty jars of jam on Saturday at the market. That's the biggest part of our sales—the jam. We know that there's a market, but you have to be able to develop the business.

AB: It has been fascinating talking with all of these growers and hearing more about the financial weight of agriculture—getting paid only once a year, the dependency on loans—and then thinking about how that manifests with minority growers or those with unconventional farms who don't receive loans at the same rate as conventional growers. If your farm doesn't look like what a banker expects a farm to look like, it is more of a risk.

JH: Traditionally, we work with different organizations throughout the state, but it is interesting with COVID that there's this awareness of how essential this work is. We've gotten three or four small grants because of our work in emergency food distribution and because we are running an urban farm in a community without a grocery store and providing families access to healthy food. And that's helpful because it can go toward paying rent, utilities, labor, etc. But what's happening with COVID is that suddenly people understand that we are essential workers. We've been saying it for years, "People need food," and we're here doing this work, and they didn't want to sell us land. The response was, "An urban farm, who needs that? We need housing." Now all of a sudden people are looking at us and saying we're essential because people need to build up their immune systems. The breakdown in food distribution around the country—around the world, really—and it is like, wow! People are seeing it now.

AB: The pandemic has laid bare these things. Suddenly people are thinking about where the food is coming from because grocery store shelves are empty, and a lot of people have never been confronted with that before.

JH: It's shocking for a lot of people!

AB: Yes! And, I think equally, people are thinking about small businesses and wanting to spend their dollars where it will do the most good. I just hope that these inroads that the local food and food sovereignty movement have made take hold and people don't just go back after the pandemic.

JH: I don't think it will go back, because we are looking at fall and winter being scary, and then we come back to the spring. Actually, it depends on the growers. I tell the growers I work with, "It is up to us!" I've been telling them since 2013 that urban growing is connected to community development and economic development.

From the community development perspective, we are inside neighborhoods and we are sustaining these neighborhoods. We are taking abandoned lots and turning them into these beautiful, productive oases where people can gather and feel safe. We have no fences and people walk through here all the time. And it's OK.

The economic development aspect is when people spend money at our farmers' market; the vendors live in this neighborhood. The money goes back into our community—they get paid, they pay their rent, their light bill. What we have to offer is very necessary. Growers can't look at it like, "I've got tomatoes to sell; I've got squash to sell." No, you do more than that. We are holding down these neighborhoods.

I go to France every year. When I'm there I don't have a car, and the one thing I don't have to worry about is food. I can get a coffee, a croissant, ten steps from where I live. Then I come home, and the first thing I have to do is get in my car and drive to the grocery store. Oakland corridor used to be like France. I lived here as a kid; Oakland Avenue had everything we needed. Woodward is the next big street. I never went to Woodward. Didn't need to; there was a fish market on the corner where our greens are now. The bank, food, entertainment, beauty salon—it was all right here. We can do this again.

AB: As someone who isn't from Detroit and doesn't know the ins and outs of what you're facing with how Detroit, and other big cities, are changing: is it helpful to have people shop at your market who are not from the neighborhood, or is that depleting a resource that is better utilized by residents?

JH: Hmm, how do I want to say this? We built this farm and this market for our residents. If people not from the neighborhood want to come to shop, that's fine by me, and I believe that the people not in our community who shop with us are authentic in their desire to spend their dollars in a way that supports the market and the work we do. That's encouraging. We have never had an issue with people who don't know our neighborhood coming in and being disrespectful to anyone. Not our children, not our homeless people, anyone. The respect that I give to [the people in our community] I expect others to give as well. And if they don't, they'll be asked to leave. That said, we built this for the people who live here, and it is with those folks in mind that we make decisions for our future. That's who I'm worried about. I appreciate that those people want to come in and do good and feel good when they leave. I appreciate that.

peas, cow: black-eyed peas, crowder peas, field peas 123

AB: What are the top three hurdles you face as a grower?

JH: As we look at our succession plan, I'm troubled. That keeps me up at night. Our operational budget is about $200,000. I don't take a salary. My husband doesn't take a salary. Who are we going to find to continue without being paid for the work? That's why we are starting to look at some of the properties in our land trust to stabilize our income to offset the reliance on grant funding and allow for an executive director to be paid. That's one thing.

Another hurdle is tax exemption. I pay about $15,000 a year in taxes, and that could be someone's income. We'll get that resolved next year.

And another is the water. We are collecting data on how we use water and water runoff drainage. It's a huge problem. We know that farmers are necessary. We have to be sure that their expenses are manageable, so they can keep farming. Oakland County [just outside of Detroit] has an agricultural water rate.

AB: Seems pretty straightforward.

JH: Yeah! We have to get a handle on the rates for water usage and how the land is taxed. We want our farmers to be able to sustain their lives while they are feeding Detroit. The city has to value us and work with us on that.

AB: What are the top three successes from the past year?

JH: Our ability to acquire and manage land. The development of the land trust is huge. It is something we've been talking about for the last three years. We finally got it done.

I have to say, I'm very proud of the way that we engage people in our community. We are just continuing to honor them and remain respectful in the way that we do our work.

AB: How does that manifest for you?

JH: Just by being welcoming, informative. Everything that we do here, we take into consideration, "How's the community going to feel about this? Let's ask them."

AB: What do you wish nonfarmers knew about your work?

JH: Food is the tool through which we do this work. It touches everything.

BOILED

Like all grains and legumes, cowpeas can be cooked just like pasta in a big pot of boiling water. The larger the cowpea, the longer it will take to cook. Cowpeas, like beans, will flavor the cooking liquid and benefit from aromatics (onion scraps, garlic skins, carrot peels, herbs of all sorts) being added to the liquid. Consider saving the (strained) liquid to use as the base for a soup or to braise meats or greens.

crowder pea salad w/cucumbers, tomato, herbs + anchovy vinaigrette

This salad can be served warm—beans pulled straight from the pot and contrasting with the cold snap of cucumbers. It can be served cold with beans from the fridge several days after boiling. It can be served on its own. It can be served alongside an animal or fish protein. You can have it in a house. You can have it with a mouse. You can cook them in a pan. You can even use ones from a can.

2 cups [400 g] boiled crowder peas

2 medium cucumbers (10 oz [280 g]), half-peeled and cut into 2 in [5 cm] long wedges

2 large slicing tomatoes or 1 lb [450 g] cherry tomatoes, cut into chunks

1 cup [25 g] picked herb leaves, such as parsley, cilantro, mint, chives, chervil, basil, dill

1 recipe Anchovy Vinaigrette (page 35)

Add the cooked crowder peas, cucumbers, tomatoes, and herbs to the vinaigrette and toss to coat. Adjust the seasoning as desired.

continued

variations

w/butternut squash ribbons + gingered apples

Shave the neck of a butternut squash into thin ribbons with a vegetable peeler. Combine the squash ribbons with 1 cup [150 g] Gingered Apples (page 54) and 1 cup [200 g] cooked crowder peas, and dress with a glug of olive oil and a pinch of salt. Adjust the seasoning as desired.

w/celery root + gribiche

Cut 2 celery roots (about 1 lb [450 g]) into matchsticks. Dress the celery root and 2 cups [400 g] cooked crowder peas with a big glug of olive oil, a pinch of salt, and a couple grinds of black pepper. To serve, portion into serving bowls and top with ¼ cup [60 g] of Gribiche (page 47).

w/roasted radishes + mustard greens

In a large frying pan, heat a big glug of neutral oil and pan fry the radishes (5 or so per person) until well caramelized on all sides. Add mustard green leaves (4 per person) cut into wide ribbons and sauté until wilted. Add 1 cup [200 g] cooked crowder peas per person to warm through. Transfer to a serving bowl and garnish with a glug of olive oil and an extra pinch of salt.

STEWED

There is nothing especially innovative about this recipe; it's pork, beans, aromatics, and low-n-slow cooking. There is something about contrasting those heady flavors with the snap of raw or lightly cooked vegetables and the punch of a piquant relish spooned liberally over the top. In short, make a big pot of cowpeas and dish them up with any number of vegetable and sauce combinations.

black-eyed peas w/ham hocks and vegetables

I like to slice the onions, garlic, and celery as thin as can be, so they almost melt into the gravy of the peas. I like the carrots left larger for contrast. To be honest, 75 percent of the time I skip the pork because the whole thing is flavorful on its own. You can also always use Parmesan rinds, chunks of salted or smoked fish, or mushrooms for a different type of richness.

Neutral oil

2 bay leaves (optional)

4 thyme sprigs (optional)

1 onion (about 8 oz [225 g]), thinly sliced

4 garlic cloves, thinly sliced or minced

2 celery stalks, thinly sliced

2 carrots (about 4 oz [120 g]), cut into chunks

12 oz [360 ml] pilsner or wheat beer

1 lb [450 g] cowpeas of any sort

8 oz [225 g] ham hock or Parmesan rinds, mushrooms, or salted fish

Salt and freshly ground black pepper

In a Dutch oven, heat a glug of neutral oil over medium heat. Add the herbs (if using) and briefly fry to bloom, about 30 seconds. Add the onion, garlic, and celery and sweat until soft.

continued

Add the carrots and beer to deglaze and let reduce by half. Add the cowpeas and ham hock, then add enough water to cover by 2 in [5 cm] and bring to a boil.

Lower to a simmer and cook until the peas are tender and the ham hock pulls easily when probed with a fork, about 40 minutes.

Lift the ham hock from the pot and let cool until easy to handle. Pull the meat from the bone, discarding any skin, bone, or tendon. Return the meat to the pot and season with salt or pepper as desired.

pairing combinations

w/green beans + garlic scape relish

Sauté or grill 1 lb [450 g] of trimmed green beans. Dish the cowpeas onto a serving platter or individual bowls, top with the green beans, and spoon the Garlic Scape Relish (page 46) liberally over the top.

w/grilled bell peppers, roasted corn, basil + paprika cumin oil

Grill, skin, and seed 2 bell peppers (about 12 oz [340 g]), any color, and cut into strips. Pan roast sweet corn kernels (½ cup [75 g] per person) and add the peppers at the end. Portion the cowpeas into bowls and top with the corn/pepper salad, a few torn leaves of basil, and a healthy spoonful of Paprika Cumin Oil (page 40).

w/steamed bok choy + lemon parsley mojo

Cut 2 heads of bok choy (about 1 lb [450 g]) in half and steam. To serve, portion the cowpeas into individual bowls, top with a half of choy, and spoon Lemon Parsley Mojo (page 48) over the top.

FRIED

A fritter is just something fried. It can be made with any sort of batter, but the looser the batter, the more the fritter will spread; the thicker the batter, the more the fritter will stand up, but the longer it will take to cook through. Consider a slightly cooler temperature to avoid burning, or finish cooking by baking in a moderate oven.

accara black-eyed pea fritters

Accara are a beloved West African street food traditionally served with *kanni*, a tomato-based hot sauce. They are also great with any of the sauces listed below. Much like falafel, they can be served as a snack, an appetizer, or a side dish.

1 cup [200 g] dried black-eyed peas, soaked overnight	1 small red onion (about 4 oz [120 g]), minced	1 tsp salt, plus more for sprinkling Neutral oil

Drain the black-eyed peas and remove the outer skins by rubbing the peas back and forth in your hands. Blend the skinless peas in a food processor with a bit of water to make a fine paste. It should be stiff but cohesive. Add the onion and salt and pulse to combine.

Heat 2 in [5 cm] of neutral oil in a pot to about 375°F [190°C]. Cover a rack with paper towels and set on a tray. Spoon golf ball–size portions of the batter into the oil and fry until golden brown, about 3 minutes, then flip and brown the other side. Transfer to the paper towels to drain and sprinkle with salt.

Serve with a bowl of any of the following sauces for dipping: Lemon Caper Mayo (page 37); Tomato Paprika Mayo (page 38); ½ cup [120 g] Cherry Tomato Conserva (page 52) blended with ¼ cup [60 ml] Paprika Cumin Oil (page 40); Giardiniera (page 53); Creamy Mustard Dressing (page 36); or Tuna Mayo (page 38).

chickpeas

I was once adamant that chickpeas be cooked from dry. I wanted the long, slow process of soaking, simmering, and skimming. I wanted it to take all night. Something more than a fleeting fling. Something more than a thirty-minute meal.

Over the course of those long nights, I came to love chickpeas. Delicately dipping a spoon into the thickening water to pluck a single chickpea pearl from the lot. Testing it with my teeth to see if it resisted or had meltingly submitted to time and temperature. I got to know the pulse. I saw the beauty of a chickpea in any form—unadorned straight from the pot, dressed up with a bunch of butter and garlic, blended until creamy and spread across a slab of toast. Playing the star or the supporting role, a chickpea is the perfect kitchen partner.

After all these years, I've embraced the daily practicality of cracking open a can of chickpeas and having dinner ready 25 minutes later. I once thought our passion was only proved with hours and hours of fawning. Now I trust the deep love between us—practical convenience of making it, well-fed, through the day. Stealing a quick, satisfying spoonful between bath and bedtime has mostly replaced the all-night affair.

Our relationship has evolved, but I will never forsake it until death do us part.

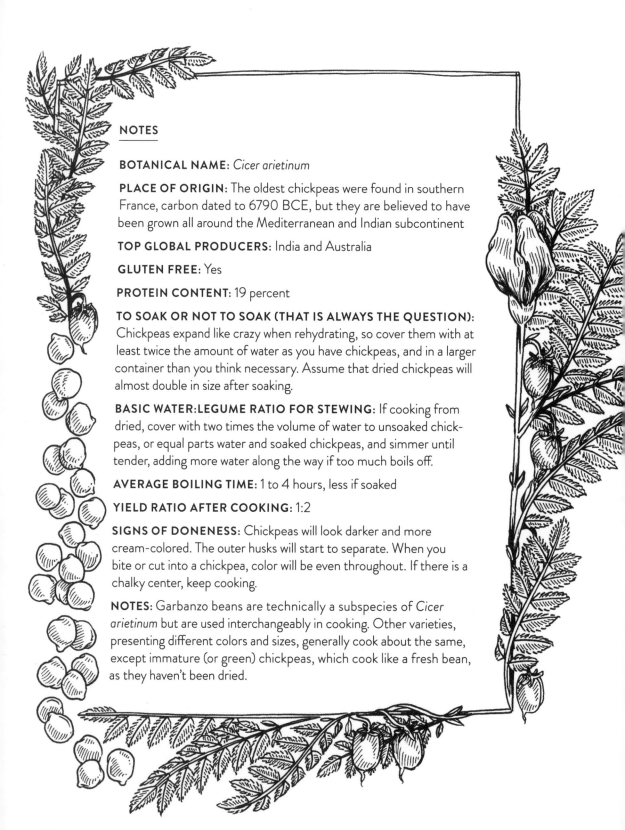

NOTES

BOTANICAL NAME: *Cicer arietinum*

PLACE OF ORIGIN: The oldest chickpeas were found in southern France, carbon dated to 6790 BCE, but they are believed to have been grown all around the Mediterranean and Indian subcontinent

TOP GLOBAL PRODUCERS: India and Australia

GLUTEN FREE: Yes

PROTEIN CONTENT: 19 percent

TO SOAK OR NOT TO SOAK (THAT IS ALWAYS THE QUESTION): Chickpeas expand like crazy when rehydrating, so cover them with at least twice the amount of water as you have chickpeas, and in a larger container than you think necessary. Assume that dried chickpeas will almost double in size after soaking.

BASIC WATER:LEGUME RATIO FOR STEWING: If cooking from dried, cover with two times the volume of water to unsoaked chickpeas, or equal parts water and soaked chickpeas, and simmer until tender, adding more water along the way if too much boils off.

AVERAGE BOILING TIME: 1 to 4 hours, less if soaked

YIELD RATIO AFTER COOKING: 1:2

SIGNS OF DONENESS: Chickpeas will look darker and more cream-colored. The outer husks will start to separate. When you bite or cut into a chickpea, color will be even throughout. If there is a chalky center, keep cooking.

NOTES: Garbanzo beans are technically a subspecies of *Cicer arietinum* but are used interchangeably in cooking. Other varieties, presenting different colors and sizes, generally cook about the same, except immature (or green) chickpeas, which cook like a fresh bean, as they haven't been dried.

BOILED

To boil a chickpea until it reaches a state of creamy, mind-melting wow takes a minimum of 1 hour and up to 4 hours. During cooking, chickpeas will initially kick off a very frothy scum—even if they have been soaked and their water changed diligently—requiring more attention than most cooking legumes. This is why I use canned, but to each her own. Find your own pleasure.

To boil a chickpea, soak the dried chickpeas overnight (or 6 to 8 hours), place in a large stockpot, and cover with water 1 to 2 in [2.5 to 5 cm] higher than the chickpeas. Add any aromatics that you like (onion, garlic, herbs, spices). Bring to a boil. Lower to a simmer. Skim off any foam. Cook until tender, checking after about 45 minutes but knowing that they could take hours. Add salt to season. Let chickpeas sit in that liquid for at least 10 minutes but ideally overnight.

whole roasted leeks w/chickpeas, lemon vinaigrette, ricotta + chard

After the long cooking time for chickpeas, the 35 minutes to slow roast whole leeks seems like just a second or two. This salad is also great without the whole leeks—between skipping the leeks and using canned chickpeas, it comes together very quickly. These leeks can also be made in large batches and served cool or at room temperature throughout the week.

4 large leeks (about 2 lb [900 g]), trimmed and cleaned of dirt

4 sprigs thyme (optional)

¼ tsp chili flakes (optional)

Salt and freshly ground black pepper

1 orange (about 3 oz [90 ml]), peel stripped, juiced, or ¼ cup [60 ml] white wine or hard cider

¾ cup [180 ml] olive oil

2 cups [540 g] cooked or canned chickpeas, rinsed

1 bunch chard (8 oz [225 g]), cut into ribbons (or spinach, kale, or arugula)

2 lemons (about 3 oz [90 ml]), zest and juice

4 oz [120 g] ricotta

Preheat the oven to 350°F [180°C]. Place the whole, cleaned leeks, side by side, in a roasting pan. Scatter the thyme (if using), chili flakes (if using), and 2 large pinches of salt evenly over the leeks. Scatter the orange peel strips over the leeks and drizzle them with the orange juice and ¼ cup [60 ml] of the olive oil to coat.

Cover with foil and bake until the leeks are tender, 35 to 45 minutes.

Combine the chickpeas, chard ribbons, lemon zest and juice, and remaining ½ cup [125 ml] of olive oil with a big pinch of salt and a couple of grinds of black pepper.

When the leeks are tender, transfer from the roasting pan to plates or a serving platter. Top with the chickpea and chard salad. Dot ricotta over the top and serve.

variations

w/roasted summer squash chunks + romesco

2 to 4 medium summer squash (1 to 2 lb [450 to 900 g]), cut lengthwise into quarters and then into 2 in [5 cm] pieces	Olive oil Salt 1 cup [200 g] cooked chickpeas	½ cup [115 g] Romesco (page 49) Fresh herbs—parsley, cilantro, or basil

Toss the cut summer squash in a couple of glugs of olive oil and a few pinches of salt. In a very hot pan or on a grill, sear the summer squash until well caramelized on the outside and tender but with some bite still in the center, about 4 minutes per side.

Lay the squash on a serving platter, scatter the chickpeas evenly over them, drizzle with the romesco, sprinkle with the herbs, and serve warm or at room temperature.

w/spring radishes, baby greens + smoked whitefish

4 to 6 radishes (about 8 oz [225 g]), cut into quarters or shaved thinly 1 cup [200 g] cooked chickpeas	4 oz [120 g] salad greens or any tender green 4 to 6 oz [120 to 180 g] smoked whitefish, flaked	½ cup [125 ml] Pickle Liquid Dressing (page 37)

Toss all the ingredients together to make a hearty salad.

w/winter red cabbage salad w/tuna mayo, tajín oil + cilantro

4 oz [120 g] red cabbage, cut into thin ribbons 1 cup [200 g] cooked chickpeas	2 Tbsp [30 ml] Tajín Oil (page 40) Salt	½ cup [115 g] Tuna Mayo (page 38) 10 sprigs cilantro, stems and leaves roughly chopped

Toss the cabbage, chickpeas, and Tajín oil together with a big pinch of salt. Transfer to a serving platter. Dollop with the tuna mayo and top with the cilantro.

SMASHED

Smashing the chickpeas with garlic-laden butter came about when we had several children over for dinner immediately after getting a new rug. There was some concern that if we left the chickpeas in their normally round and roly-poly state, the rug would never recover. Now we make it because we like it.

garlic-smashed chickpeas

Use any place you would want smashed potatoes or creamy beans. The only drawback is that the chickpeas won't soak up a sauce the way that polenta will, so best to not pair them with anything too loose. If reheating the next day, refry with a bit more olive oil until warm. Just be careful not to burn the garlic.

¼ cup [60 ml] olive oil	Salt	2 oz [60 g] butter
2 cups [400 g] cooked chickpeas, rinsed	4 to 8 garlic cloves, minced	

In a large frying pan, heat the olive oil over medium heat until warm. Add the chickpeas to the pan with a big pinch of salt and smash with the back of a spoon until evenly chunky.

Fry without stirring, allowing the chickpeas to start to crisp a bit on the edges, then add the garlic and butter. Toss to combine, then turn the heat to low. Cook gently, stirring every few minutes, until the garlic is soft but not browned. Remove from the heat and serve.

variations

w/seared whitefish, shaved fennel + tarragon sunflower seed rig

Shave the fennel (usually about half a bulb per person) and toss with a couple of spoonfuls of the Tarragon Sunflower Seed Rig (page 50). Then sear the fish and serve (crispy skin-side up) on top of the garlic chickpeas with the fennel salad on top.

w/grilled chicken + tomatoes in garam masala yogurt

Take 1 tomato per person, cut it into large chunks, and toss with several spoonfuls of Garam Masala Yogurt (page 45). Grill some chicken and serve it over the garlic chickpeas with the tomatoes on the side. Maybe top with some basil or cilantro if you have it.

w/poblano-corn salad + a fried egg

Cut ½ poblano pepper per person into long strips and sauté with some diced onion and a couple of pinches of salt. Add about ½ cup [100 g] of corn kernels per person to the pepper and sauté until cooked through. Fry 1 egg per person. To serve, scoop about ½ cup [100 g] of garlic chickpeas with the poblano-corn salad onto a plate and top with the fried egg. You could top the whole thing with a spoonful or two of Paprika Cumin Oil (page 40).

w/whole roasted carrots, broccoli rabe + ras el hanout apricot almond rig

Roast some whole carrots (2 or 3 per person) in a 450°F [230°C] oven until tender and caramelized, about 40 minutes. Sauté some broccoli rabe. Serve the garlic chickpeas on individual plates topped with the carrots and broccoli rabe and then spoon some of the Ras el Hanout Apricot Almond Rig (page 49) over each serving.

FRIED

In a restaurant scenario, I would deep-fry chickpeas until they are golden brown and crispy on the outside without being dry or too hard to crunch pleasantly. At home, I toss the chickpeas with a liberal amount of oil and bake or pan fry to achieve similar results. These chickpeas are not chruncy like a pretzel; rather, they're intended to have two distinct textures: a crisped exoskeleton and a tender, creamy interior. Either fried or baked, the chickpeas will crisp up some after they are removed from the heat and can be recrisped by returning to the heat as needed. If you want them to be fully dry, leave them in a low oven for several hours to dehydrate. Dehydrated chickpeas will hold their crisp texture for several days.

shaved summer squash w/greek yogurt, fried chickpeas + za'atar oil

Dousing the chickpeas in the za'atar oil after crisping ensures that they absorb some of that flavor without burning the spices during the crisping process. I tend to use these chickpeas more as a garnish than a full serving of protein, generally allowing for about ¼ cup [50 g] per person. I also like to cut the summer squash both in rounds and lengthwise for contrast in look and mouthfeel. This dish is a hearty salad and would go well with any sort of grilled meat. You could also add more vegetables like tomatoes or cucumber. The mild (some say bland) nature of summer squash is lifted by using a large variety of herbs. Feel free to add or subtract variety and quantity as desired.

continued

1 cup [200 g] cooked chickpeas	1 cup [250 ml] Greek yogurt	3 to 4 medium summer squash (about 1½ lb [675 g]), shaved thinly with either a knife or a mandoline
½ tsp chili flakes (optional)	10 sprigs parsley	
Salt	10 sprigs cilantro	
Olive oil	5 sprigs basil	
2 Tbsp Za'atar (page 42)	2 sprigs mint	

Preheat the oven to 400°F [200°C] and line a baking sheet with foil. Toss the chickpeas with the chili flakes (if using), a couple of pinches of salt, and several glugs of olive oil until well coated. Spread out on the prepared baking sheet and bake until the chickpeas are golden brown and slightly crisped on the outside, 15 to 20 minutes.

In a small frying pan, heat ¼ cup [60 ml] of olive oil over medium heat until it begins to shimmer. Then remove it from the heat, add the za'atar, and let it steep for at least 10 minutes.

Transfer the crisped chickpeas to a medium bowl and coat with the za'atar oil.

Whisk the yogurt until smooth and slightly fluffy.

Either chop the herbs or pick whole leaves. Toss these with the shaved summer squash, several glugs of olive oil, and a few pinches of salt. Adjust the seasoning as desired.

To serve, spoon the whipped yogurt onto a serving platter. Pile the herby squash on top of the yogurt and scatter the chickpeas all over. Drizzle any extra za'atar oil over the whole thing.

STEWED

Stewed chickpeas soak up the flavors they are paired with and don't tend to kick off starch and thicken a soup the way that rice or farro will. That said, I don't recommend stewing *dry* chickpeas, because of the long cooking time chickpeas require to soften and the foam they release. Plus, when you start with an already cooked ingredient these dishes don't take an intolerably long time to come together.

tomato + parsnip stew w/wilted kale

I like to finish these stews in the oven to slowly evaporate the liquid while creating a bit of a crust on top. It takes a little longer but requires less attention than the stovetop, though you could certainly do it that way too. Just give it a stir once in a while so it doesn't stick on the bottom.

Olive oil

½ tsp fennel seed

½ tsp chili flakes

1 onion (about 8 oz [225 g]), thinly sliced

3 garlic cloves, minced

Salt

One 14½ oz [410 g] can whole peeled tomatoes

8 parsnips (about 2 lb [900 g]), peeled and cut into medium chunks

2 cups [400 g] canned or cooked chickpeas

1 bunch kale (8 oz [225 g]), leaves stripped and cut into ribbons

1 lemon (about 1½ oz [45 ml]), zest and juice

Parmesan, for grating (optional)

Preheat the oven to 400°F [200°C]. In an ovenproof pot, heat a couple of glugs of olive oil over medium heat until shimmering hot, about 1 minute. Briefly fry the fennel seed and chili flakes until fragrant, 1 to 2 minutes.

Add the onion, garlic, and several big pinches of salt. Lower the heat to low and sweat the onion and garlic until soft, about 7 minutes.

continued

Add the tomatoes, juice and all, and cook until the liquid is reduced by half, about 5 minutes. Add the parsnips and chickpeas and stir to combine. Add 2 cups [500 ml] of water or chicken stock, bring to a boil, lower to a simmer, and cook for 10 minutes.

Remove from the heat and place uncovered in the oven. Cook until the parsnips are tender and the sauce is reduced and stewy, about 20 minutes.

Combine the kale, lemon zest and juice, and a pinch of salt.

Before serving, fold the kale into the parsnip chickpea stew and allow the heat of the stew to wilt the greens gently. If serving individually, add the kale to each bowl after doling out the stewed beans. Top with a hefty grating of Parmesan (if using) and serve.

variations

whitefish, tomato, zucchini + chickpea stew w/mint almond relish

Olive oil	1 lb [450 g] fresh tomatoes or one 14½ oz [410 g] can, cut into large chunks	Neutral oil
1 tsp Ras el Hanout (page 41)		2 sides (about 1½ lb [675 g]) of whitefish (or other light fish), cut into four portions
1 onion (about 8 oz [225 g]), thinly sliced	3 medium summer squash (about 1½ lb [675 g]), cut into 2 in [5 cm] long chunks	
5 garlic cloves, minced		1 cup [230 g] Mint Almond Relish (page 48)
Salt		
½ cup [125 ml] white wine	2 cups [400 g] cooked or canned chickpeas	

Preheat the oven to 400°F [200°C]. In an ovenproof pan or pot, heat several glugs of olive oil over medium heat. Briefly fry the ras el hanout until fragrant, 1 to 2 minutes. Add the onion, garlic, and a couple of pinches of salt. Lower the heat to low and sweat the onions until soft, about 7 minutes.

continued

Add the white wine and tomatoes and cook until the liquid starts to release, about 4 minutes. Add the summer squash pieces and chickpeas. Bring to a boil, then place in the oven and cook until the squash is tender and the liquid is reduced and flavorful, about 30 minutes.

In a large frying pan, heat several glugs of neutral oil over medium heat until smoking hot. Blot the skin of the fish dry and pan fry the fish, skin-side down, until it is golden brown and can be moved easily in the pan (indicating that the fish skin is fully seared and will no longer stick when removed from the pan).

Place the fish in the already hot oven to finish cooking, about 3 minutes.

To serve, divvy up the stew among serving dishes, place the fish skin-side up on top, and spoon the mint almond relish on top.

squash coconut stew w/raw cauliflower

Olive oil	Salt	½ head cauliflower (about 1 lb [450 g]), shaved thinly
1 Tbsp [12 g] Garam Masala (page 40)	1 butternut squash (about 3 lb [1.35 kg]), peeled and cut into 1 in [2.5 cm] cubes	¼ cup [50 g] Mojo de Ajo (page 48)
1 onion (about 8 oz [225 g]), thinly sliced		
5 garlic cloves, minced	2 cups [400 g] cooked or canned chickpeas	1 bunch cilantro, leaves and stems roughly chopped
1 in [2.5 cm] piece of ginger, peeled and minced or grated	One 12 oz [355 ml] can coconut milk	

Preheat the oven to 400°F [200°C]. In an ovenproof pan or pot, heat several glugs of olive oil over medium heat. Briefly fry the garam masala until fragrant, 1 to 2 minutes. Add the onion, garlic, and ginger and a couple of pinches of salt. Turn the heat to low and sweat the onions until soft, about 7 minutes.

Add the squash cubes, chickpeas, coconut milk, and a half can of water, both to add more liquid and to rinse out any lingering coconut milk. Bring to a boil, then place in the oven, uncovered, and cook until the squash is tender and the liquid is reduced and flavorful, about 30 minutes.

Combine the shaved cauliflower, mojo de ajo, and chopped cilantro.

To serve, dish up the stew and top with the cauliflower salad.

chick(en)peas stew

Olive oil or butter	2 cups [400 g] chickpeas, canned or cooked	2 cups (10 oz [280 g]) peas, fresh or frozen
1 onion (about 8 oz [225 g]), thinly sliced	3 cups [750 ml] chicken stock or water	10 sprigs dill, roughly chopped, including stems if they are tender
5 garlic cloves, minced	4 chicken breasts (about 1¼ lb [570 g]), sliced into ¼ in [6 mm] thick pieces	Parmesan for grating (optional)
Salt		
½ cup [125 ml] white wine		

In a medium stockpot, heat a glug of olive oil over medium heat until warm. Add the onion and garlic with a big pinch of salt and sweat until tender, about 7 minutes.

Add the white wine and cook until almost dry. Add the chickpeas and chicken stock and bring to a boil.

Add the chicken breast strips, separating them as you add them to the liquid. Lower the heat to a simmer and cook until the chicken breasts are cooked through, about 8 minutes. Adjust the salt as desired.

Remove from the heat, add the peas, and allow them to cook in the already hot broth until bright green, about 3 minutes.

Ladle the soup into serving bowls and top with the chopped dill, a glug of olive oil, and several gratings of Parmesan (if using).

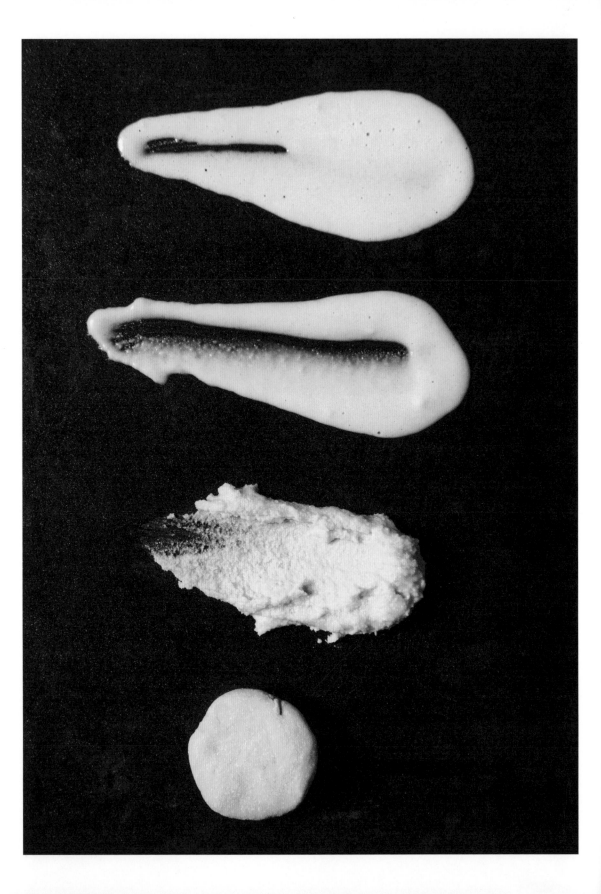

FLOUR

Chickpea flour is one of the most versatile ingredients I can think of because it can make everything from a shatteringly crisp (and gluten-free) batter to a firm, pupusa-like fritter by simply adjusting the texture of the mixture.

The thinnest batter (and the top example in the facing photo) will be thin enough to coat whatever you are frying, just like a traditional beer batter.

Socca and Farinata—individual rounds or one big baked pancake good for dipping—are two ways to make chickpea pancakes with a slightly thicker batter (the second smear from the top in the facing photo).

Panisse (aka panelle or chickpea fries) is a thicker-yet porridge that is set to cool, cut into rectangles, and fried for crispness (pictured third from the top in the facing photo).

Fritters are the thickest of all (pictured at bottom in the facing photo) and can be fried into individual cakes such as accara or arepa.

batter

To get the shatteringly crisp, just barely coated, not-clumpy texture of good tempura, the batter must be thick enough to coat the item you are dipping but not so thick as to distract from what's inside. The hydration of chickpea flour can vary from brand to brand, bag to bag, and season to season. To tell whether you have the right viscosity, dip your finger in the batter and hold your finger up vertically. The batter should coat your finger but be thin enough to see the contours of your nail through it. If it is so thick that you can't see the shape of your nail, add a bit more soda water. If it is so thin that the skin of your finger shows through, add a bit more flour.

1 cup [120 g] chickpea flour	¼ cup cornstarch	¼ tsp baking soda
	½ tsp salt	1 cup [250 ml] soda water

Whisk the dry ingredients together and add the soda water to make a thin batter. Do the finger test and adjust as needed.

In a deep pan, heat 4 in [10 cm] of frying oil to 375°F [190°C]. Dip any number of vegetables, chicken, fish, or shrimp in the batter and fry until golden brown and fully crisped.

variations

Summer Fritto Misto:

My favorite fritto mistos are not a fancy affair, just a big pile of perfectly battered and fried vegetables and a lot of True Aioli (page 38) for dipping. Heat an oven to 200°F [95°C]. Dip green beans, long batons of summer squash, petals of fennel, cauliflower florets, wedges of eggplant, and button mushrooms in the batter and gently drop them into the hot oil, being sure to not overload the pan. Fry until golden brown (about 3 minutes) and then lift and transfer to a rack set over a baking sheet or a plate lined with a paper towel. Transfer to the oven to hold. Continue to fry in batches, then pile onto a platter with a couple of lemon wedges and a big dish of aioli and feast.

Gluten-free chicken tenders:

Place the chicken tenders between two sheets of plastic wrap and pound until thin. Dredge in the batter and deep fry until cooked through and golden brown (6 minutes or so). Lift from the oil, sprinkle with salt, and serve with hot honey (2 parts honey, 1 part hot sauce stirred together).

Crispy shrimp:

Dip uncooked, peeled shrimp in the batter and deep fry until bright pink and cooked through (about 4 minutes). Serve with shaved red cabbage, chopped cilantro, and Tajín Oil (page 40).

Deep fry drizzles:

The batter itself makes great chickpea crunchies; garnish any salad or use as you would bread crumbs.

socca and farinata

Socca and farinata are two birds of a feather. The batter is the same texture; it is just cooked differently. Socca is cooked in individual pancakes, just as you would traditional flapjacks, and farinata is cooked as one giant pancake in the oven and cut into wedges to serve. Both can be served piled high with a fresh vegetable salad or with dipping sauces as an appetizer. The soda water gives the pancakes their bubbles. If you're in a pickle and don't have fizzy water, substitute beer or champagne (if that's the sort of pickle you're in). Just don't substitute any flavored seltzer—it gets real weird, real fast.

Socca and farinata can also be made with flat water, but in that case, I add a pinch of baking powder to give it some lift. Fry both in more olive oil than you might initially feel comfortable with; it adds flavor and the characteristic crunchy crust.

| 2 cups [240 g] chickpea flour | 2 cups [500 ml] club soda
½ tsp salt | ½ cup [125 ml] olive oil (more or less depending on desired amount for frying) |

For socca: Preheat the oven to 200°F [95°C] to keep the pancakes warm during frying. Set up a rack on a tray (you can use a tray without a rack, but the undersides of the pancakes will steam a bit).

Whisk the flour, club soda, and salt together until lump free.

Heat a medium or large frying pan over medium heat. Add two or three glugs of olive oil and heat until just about smoking.

Ladle the batter into the pan, just like making pancakes or crepes, adding more olive oil as needed and adjusting the temperature of the flame as the pan saturates with heat. When the bubbles in the center pop and hold their shape, flip the pancakes and brown the other side.

Transfer to the rack and keep warm in the oven.

For farinata: Heat the oven to 425°F [220°C] and preheat a medium to large frying pan in the oven for at least 10 minutes to fully warm through.

Remove the frying pan from the oven and add ¼ cup [60 ml] of olive oil to the pan.

Pour all of the batter in the pan and lightly swirl to spread evenly. Top with a handful of grated cheese if you like, but TBH I rarely do any more.

Bake until the pancake is springy when pressed in the center and pulled back from the sides of the pan, about 10 minutes.

Flip or lift out of the pan, cut into wedges, and serve with a vegetable salad or any number of dipping sauces. I like Spicy Mayo (page 38) the best.

variations

Spring—topped with spinach, goat cheese, and Tarragon Sunflower Seed Rig (page 50)

Summer—topped with chard, cucumber, and Cumin Yogurt page 44)

Fall—topped with shaved cauliflower and Peperonata (page 56)

Winter—topped with Mushroom Cream Sauce (page 44) and roasted broccoli

panisse (french), panelle (italian), chickpea fries (american)

Like chickpea pancakes, this recipe is as simple as combining chickpea flour, water, and salt. Only the process is different: cook into a porridge and set it before cutting and frying.

½ tsp salt, plus more for sprinkling

1 cup [120 g] chickpea flour

Olive oil, for frying

In a medium pot, bring 2 cups [500 ml] of water and the salt to a boil. Whisking continually, stream in the chickpea flour and cook until thickened, about 3 minutes.

Line a baking sheet with plastic wrap or parchment paper and spread the porridge evenly over it. Refrigerate until cold and firm.

Flip the mass out onto a cutting board, discarding the plastic wrap or parchment, and cut into small logs, about 2 to 3 in [5 to 7.5 cm] long.

In a medium frying pan, pour enough oil to fill about ½ in [12 mm] deep and heat over medium heat until a few drops of water bubble in it.

Gently fry the chickpea logs, in batches if necessary, until golden brown. Flip and fry the other sides, then remove to a paper towel–lined plate or baking tray.

Sprinkle with salt and serve with any of the dipping sauces listed with the socca, or cut into smaller cubes and toss into any salad like a crouton.

variations

Tomato Paprika Mayo (page 38)
Romesco (page 49)
Creamed Mozzarella (page 43) and Cherry Tomato Conserva (page 52)

chickpea fritters

This is the thickest batter, so it makes a fritter that is thick enough to form into a ball and pan fry. It can be flavored with spices (the Ras el Hanout or Smoky Spicy Mix are naturals) or left plain. The batter can be made ahead and fried when ready. The fritters can be fried ahead and served at room temperature or reheated in a hot oven just before serving. And like most fritters, these are good with any dipping sauce you could want. The texture is denser; it's not totally dissimilar to panisse but requires less prep time.

1 cup [120 g] chickpea flour

1½ tsp Ras el Hanout or Smoky Spicy Mix (page 41)

½ tsp salt, plus more for sprinkling

¼ tsp baking powder

Olive oil or neutral oil

Combine all the ingredients except the oil with ½ cup [125 ml] of water to make a batter the thickness of cookie dough.

Heat 1 in [2.5 cm] of oil in a large frying pan over medium heat. Line a plate with paper towels. Scoop the dough into the hot oil, just like you're scooping cookies. Dip a spoon in the oil and press down on each ball to form a patty.

Fry until the underside is golden brown, 2 to 3 minutes. Flip and brown the other side.

Remove from the pan with a slotted spoon and drain on the paper towels. Sprinkle with salt.

dipping sauce and topping ideas

Tuna Mayo (page 38)
Black bean purée (page 97, Day Five), and Marinated Summer Squash (page 56)
Harissa (page 47)
Herbed Yogurt (page 45)

FRESH

Fresh chickpeas are not a technique; they are the youngest, and more vegetal, stage of chickpeas, sharing the attributes of fresh favas, shelling beans, or peas. We don't grow chickpeas in any sort of quantity in Michigan, so I rely on the frozen green garbanzos from the grocery store. They are often in the same aisle as frozen soy and fava beans. Sometimes fresh beans, often still in the fuzzy ridged pods, pop up at specialty markets too.

I almost always cook them the same way—a quick blanch, straight from frozen, in heavily salted water and then pair them with the best of what is in season to make a fresh vegetable salad-y thing. If you find some fresh, blanch them in the pod (like edamame) or remove from the pod and cook like fava beans. Like favas, fresh green chickpeas have an exterior skin that can be peeled off, revealing the bright green interior seed, but I don't often bother except for looks.

If you don't have time to watch a pot come to a boil, green chickpeas (and favas or soybeans) can also be sautéed in a pan with a bit of olive oil and splash of water or wine until they are bright green. While the pods will never be pleasant to chew, they do provide a good barrier to the delicate beans inside if you want to grill or pan roast the podded chickpeas and then set them out like edamame for a starter.

tomato slabs w/green chickpeas, olive rig + fresh mozzarella

Again, for green chickpeas, I usually give a quick boil in heavily salted water for a few minutes and then toss with just about anything that is on hand. These are some of my favorite combinations for any point in the year.

continued

2 cups (10 oz [280 g])
green chickpeas

½ cup [200 g] Olive Rig
(page 49)

Olive oil

2 lb [900 g] large slicing
tomatoes, cut into ½ in
[12 mm] thick slabs

Salt and freshly ground
black pepper

1 to 2 balls [8 to 16 oz
[225 to 450 g]) fresh
mozzarella, torn into
chunks

5 sprigs basil, mint, or
parsley, or a combo,
torn or roughly chopped

Bring a medium pot of heavily salted water to a boil. Add the
chickpeas and cook until bright green, 3 to 5 minutes. Drain
and run under cold water to cool quickly.

Toss the chickpeas with the olive rig and an extra drizzle or two
of olive oil.

Lay the tomatoes on a serving platter and sprinkle with salt.
Scatter the torn mozzarella evenly over the top. Spoon the
chickpea and olive mixture over the cheese. Grind some black
pepper over the whole thing and top with the herbs.

variations

w/poached radishes, butter + tarragon sunflower seed rig

½ cup [125 ml] white wine

Salt

10 radishes (about 1 lb
[450 g]), any variety,
leaves removed and cut
in half if large

1 cup [150 g] green
chickpeas

2 Tbsp butter

¼ cup [60 g] Tarragon
Sunflower Seed Rig
(page 50)

In a small pot, bring 1 cup [250 ml] of water, the wine, and a couple
of pinches of salt to a boil. Add the radishes and poach until just
starting to mellow in color, about 3 minutes. Add the chickpeas
and cook until bright green, about 3 minutes. Add the butter to
the liquid to melt and coat the vegetables. Adjust the seasoning
as desired.

Spoon the tarragon sunflower seed rig over the whole thing
and serve.

w/roasted corn, peperonata + herb salad

Olive oil

1 cup (8 oz [225 g]) corn
kernels

Salt

1 cup (5 oz [150 g]) green
chickpeas

1 cup [225 g] Peperonata
(page 56)

1 cup [25 g] herb leaves
(parsley, basil, cilantro,
mint, tarragon, chives,
or a mix)

Heat a large glug of olive oil in a frying pan over high heat. Roast
the corn with a few pinches of salt until cooked and starting to
caramelize, about 7 minutes. Add the chickpeas and cook in the
pan with the corn until bright green, about 3 minutes. Adjust the
seasoning as desired.

Transfer to a serving dish. Top with the warm or room temperature
peperonata. Dress the herbs in a glug of olive oil and a pinch of salt
and scatter over the whole thing.

w/grapefruit, arugula + manchego ribbons

2 grapefruit (about 8 oz
[225 g]), ideally
different colors

1 cup (5 oz [150 g]) green
chickpeas, blanched and
chilled

2 oz [60 g] arugula leaves

Salt and freshly ground
black pepper

Olive oil

2 oz [60 g] Manchego,
peeled into ribbons with
a vegetable peeler

Peel and segment the grapefruit and lay the segments on a
serving platter. Scatter the chickpeas evenly over the grapefruit
and top with the arugula leaves.

To serve, sprinkle the whole thing with salt, black pepper, and
several glugs of olive oil and top with the Manchego ribbons.

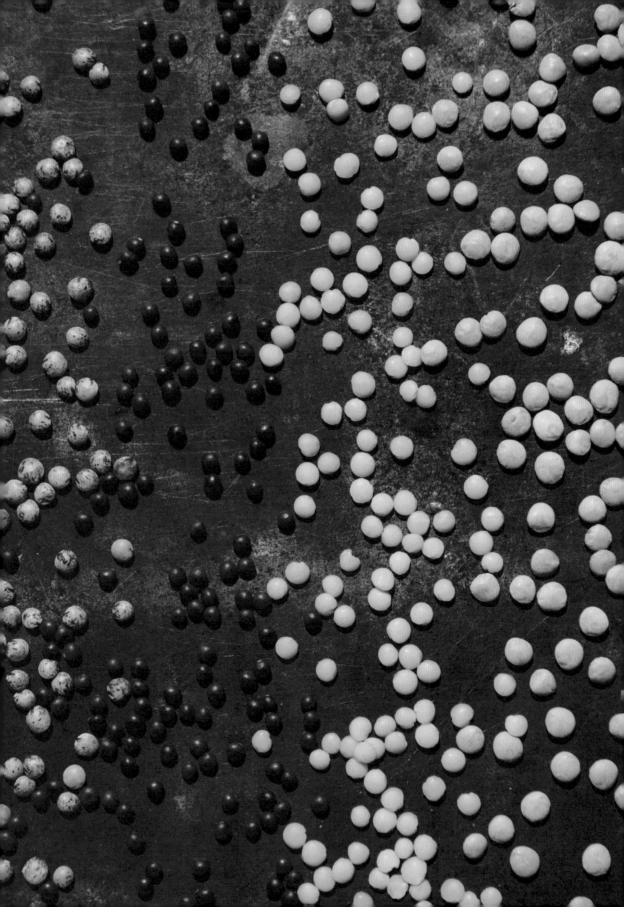

lentils

A few weeks ago, having read just shy of three hundred articles about fake meat, I couldn't stand not knowing what this tech meat tasted like. I went on a hunt for an Impossible Burger. Turns out, my hunt was not an epic odyssey: There was a Burger King twelve minutes away. I got in my car and hit the drive-thru, but I also had to get to my day job, so I took my takeout and headed to the organic vegetable farm where I work. As I unfurled the paper, my coworker said, "Whatcha got there?" and it seemed immediately silly to be eating fast food in the heart of slow food production.

I sheepishly explained that I wanted to try this plant-based meat and how I don't normally eat Burger King unless *excuse*, *excuse*, and so on. He smiled and said, "Yeah, I ate one of those on my drive home from Colorado. It was about as forgettable as a regular Whopper."

He was right. I dutifully ate my Imposs-opper, but I wasn't satisfied. It felt like a substitution, not a replacement for the burger I was now craving.

I just wanted a real burger—a griddled thing that makes me lick my lips and leaves me a little sleepy on the other side. Curiously, I also wanted a bowl full of lentils—spooned over buttered rice with maybe some roasted sweet potatoes and a thick slick of spicy (now) not-so-secret sauce (see the Harissa recipe on page 47).

I thought about lentils for the rest of the day and went home and put a pot on.

I crave lentils all the time (and not in a sanctimonious way); they are my comfort food. They simply make me feel good, so I eat them a lot. I love a pan-fried lentil fritter—mashed creamy and slightly smoky lentils binding together grated root vegetables and fried until golden brown nestled against a big spinach salad.

But I also love a skinny patty burger slick with grease crunching against ice-cold iceberg lettuce. Greasy burgers generally make me feel bad after I eat them, but I still want them now and again. More and more of my meals loaded with lentils and beans are overtaking meals with large portions of meat, because it feels good.

That's why I want replacements over substitutes. I don't want anything in between. A replacement isn't a hollow version of the thing you actually want. It becomes the thing that you seek out and that leaves you satisfied, maybe a little drowsy, after the hunt.

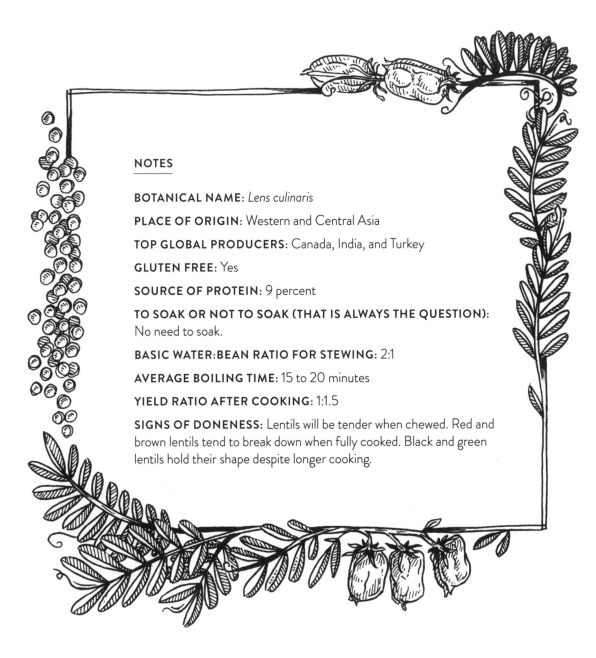

NOTES

BOTANICAL NAME: *Lens culinaris*

PLACE OF ORIGIN: Western and Central Asia

TOP GLOBAL PRODUCERS: Canada, India, and Turkey

GLUTEN FREE: Yes

SOURCE OF PROTEIN: 9 percent

TO SOAK OR NOT TO SOAK (THAT IS ALWAYS THE QUESTION): No need to soak.

BASIC WATER:BEAN RATIO FOR STEWING: 2:1

AVERAGE BOILING TIME: 15 to 20 minutes

YIELD RATIO AFTER COOKING: 1:1.5

SIGNS OF DONENESS: Lentils will be tender when chewed. Red and brown lentils tend to break down when fully cooked. Black and green lentils hold their shape despite longer cooking.

SPROUTED

Lentils are maybe my favorite legumes to sprout because they get these little tails shooting out from the side. All of the lentil varieties will sprout, but I like to use the everyday brown lentils because they are larger, and I like the extra chewiness.

sprouted lentils w/shaved brussels, parmesan + hazelnut rig

This dish goes to show that fall dishes don't need to be heavy to be comforting and filling. The hazelnuts and Parmesan add richness, and if you don't have time to sprout the lentils, you could certainly sub in boiled lentils (either warm or at room temperature). I also make this to take to work for lunch by layering the lentils, dressed sprouts, and hazelnut rig in a jar; just before eating, I give it a good shake.

1 lb [450 g] Brussels sprouts, trimmed of their outside leaves

2 cups (14 oz [400 g]) sprouted lentils (see page 26)

½ cup [125 ml] olive oil

1 lemon (about 1½ oz [45 ml]), zest and juice

4 oz [120 g] Parmesan or Manchego, shaved into ribbons with a vegetable peeler

Salt and freshly ground black pepper

½ cup [125 ml] Hazelnut Rig (page 47)

With a sharp knife or mandoline, shave the Brussels sprouts into thin ribbons. In a large bowl, combine the lentils, Brussels sprouts, olive oil, lemon zest and juice, and cheese ribbons. Season with salt and black pepper.

To serve, spoon the hazelnut rig over the top.

variations

lentil salad w/marinated mushrooms (page 56), radishes + arugula

w/marinated eggplant (page 54), creamed mozzarella (page 43) + basil salad (lots of types of basil)

sprouted lentil salad w/beets, radicchio, walnuts + brown butter vinaigrette (page 35)

A WEEK'S WORTH OF LENTILS WITHOUT ANY BOREDOM

Boil a big pot of lentils and use them several different ways: in salads, soup, puréed, and fried. Combined with a variety of other vegetables and flavorings, and achieving a range of textures by applying different cooking methods, lentils provide health, happiness, and ease for days.

day one

Boil more lentils than needed. Cut 3 Swiss chard leaves (and stems) per person into thin ribbons. When the lentils are tender, toss ¾ cup [150 g] lentils per person with the cut Swiss chard and dress with several spoonfuls of Bacon Vinaigrette (page 35). Serve with a poached egg on top.

Cool the rest of the lentils and refrigerate.

day two

In a large frying pan, sear a chicken thigh per person. Remove from the frying pan and toss ½ cup [100 g] per person of the rice and lentils together in the frying pan to warm quickly (maybe add a couple of pats of butter or glugs of olive oil). Maybe roast some carrots or sweet potatoes. Serve with a green salad. (Could also use sprouted lentils.)

day three

Take 1 cup [200 g] of the boiled lentils and allow them to dry (using a kitchen or paper towel as needed). Fry the lentils in a good deal of oil in a medium-size frying pan until crisp—they will pop a bit, so be warned. Sprinkle over any number of combinations—some are suggested on pages 175–176.

day four

Blend 1 cup [200 g] of the boiled lentils in a food processor with ½ cup [125 ml] olive oil, 1 garlic clove, and a few pinches of salt. Shave or thinly slice a handful of vegetables (carrots, cauliflower, radishes, cabbage, beets) and toss with a handful of herbs (like parsley, cilantro, mint, and/or basil) and several glugs of olive oil and pinches of salt. To serve, spoon the purée onto a plate, top with the shaved salad, and then spoon Paprika Cumin Oil (page 40) over the whole thing.

day five

¼ cup [60 ml] olive oil

½ tsp cumin seed

1 tsp smoked paprika

1 small onion (about 4 oz [120 g]), thinly sliced

3 garlic cloves, minced

Salt

1 cup [200 g] cooked lentils or lentil purée

1 egg (or more if needed)

¼ cup [40 g] cornmeal (to thicken if necessary)

1 cup [200 g] grated root vegetables like carrot, rutabaga, beet, parsnip (optional)

Neutral oil

In a medium frying pan, heat the olive oil over medium heat until it begins to shimmer, about 1 minute. Add the cumin seed and paprika and fry until fragrant. Add the onion, garlic, and a big pinch of salt and lower the heat to low. Sweat the onion until translucent, about 7 minutes. Add the lentils and warm them.

continued

Remove from the heat and then, using the back of a spoon, mash until the lentils are slightly broken up. Add the egg, cornmeal, and grated vegetables (if using).

Mash together until the mixture is the texture of oatmeal—if too thin, add more cornmeal; too thick, another egg.

Heat several glugs of neutral oil in a medium frying pan over high heat until it starts to shimmer. Lower the heat to medium. Scoop about ¼ cup [50 g] of the lentil mixture into the pan and press to make a patty.

Repeat with the rest of the mixture until the pan is full. Fry the lentil fritters until golden brown, about 3 minutes, then flip and brown the other side. Repeat with the remaining lentil mixture.

Serve warm with any vegetable sides, such as a cucumber tomato salad with Lemon Tahini Dressing (page 36), green salad, shaved cauliflower dressed with Rosemary Lemon Chili Mojo (page 50), shaved carrots with Mint Almond Relish (page 48), or roasted parsnips with Paprika Cumin Oil (page 40).

day six

And if you can't eat any more lentils, make the soup on page 177 and freeze it for another day.

BOILED

At its most basic, boiling lentils is just that: boiling lentils with twice as much water (and some salt) until they are tender. Adding (any or all) onion, garlic, white wine, and/or herbs will make the lentils even more flavorful, which is why I've included them in the base recipe. That said, if your cupboard is bare of onions or white wine, it's OK; lentils alone will be just fine (especially paired with such flavorful components).

lentil + pecan filled acorn squash w/sage fried brown butter

This wintertime classic can be made ahead and either frozen or kept in the fridge until you are ready. Simply rewarm in an uncovered roasting pan and serve with a green salad on the side.

2 to 3 acorn squash (or carnival, sweet dumpling, kabocha), about 1 lb [450 g] each, cut in half and seeded

Neutral oil

1 small onion (about 4 oz [120 g]), diced or thinly sliced

4 garlic cloves, minced

5 sprigs thyme, leaves picked

Salt and freshly ground black pepper

½ cup [125 ml] white wine or hard cider

1 cup (7½ oz [210 g]) lentils, any color except red

½ cup pecans (2 oz [60 g]), toasted and roughly chopped

1 orange (about 3 oz [90 ml]), zest and juice

1 recipe Sage Fried Brown Butter (page 50)

Parmesan or Cheddar for grating over the top (optional)

Preheat the oven to 350°F [180°C]. Place the squash halves, cut-side down, on a baking sheet lined with parchment paper or foil and bake until tender, about 25 minutes.

continued

While the squash is cooking, heat a glug of neutral oil in a medium saucepan over medium heat. Add the onion, garlic, thyme leaves, and a big pinch of salt. Sweat until tender, about 7 minutes. Add the white wine and reduce until almost dry. Add the lentils and briefly sauté in the onion mixture, about 2 minutes.

Add 2 cups [500 ml] of water and bring to a boil over high heat, then lower to a simmer and cook until the lentils are tender, about 20 minutes.

When the squash is cooked, remove from the oven but leave the heat on. Let the squash cool until you can handle it easily. Using a spoon, scoop most of the flesh from the squash into a large bowl, leaving a thin layer next to the skin so the squash shell stays intact.

Add the cooked lentils, pecans, orange zest and juice, and the brown butter to the squash pulp and season with a pinch or two of salt and a couple of grinds of black pepper. Mix until well blended; adjust the seasoning as desired.

Scoop the squash filling into the squash shells, top with several gratings of Parmesan or Cheddar (if using), and rewarm, uncovered, in the heated oven until warm throughout, 10 to 15 minutes.

To serve, garnish with the fried sage by either placing whole leaves on top or gently crumbling to scatter evenly.

variation

w/rice, grilled green beans + walnut aillade

Snap the green beans (I plan on about a handful per person), douse them with olive oil and a big pinch of salt, and grill. To serve, spoon the rice and lentils into a serving bowl, top with the green beans, and spoon the Walnut Aillade (page 50) all over.

FRIED

You can fry or simply crisp any grain or legume after it is cooked, transforming it from something soft and comforting to something crunchy and new. This is also a good way to use canned pulses.

seared eggplant + cherry tomatoes w/fried lentils + tahini dressing

Tahini is having a bit of a moment in the food world—with the added benefit that it is moving from the often dusty and unspecific "ethnic food" aisle in small grocery stores to the center of the displays. Fine by me. For this dish, I prefer the long, skinny eggplants for the visual effect. If using the more traditional globe eggplants, probably half an eggplant per person is just fine.

4 to 6 small eggplants, 1 to 2 lb [450 to 900 g] total

Neutral oil

1 cup [200 g] cooked lentils

Salt

8 oz [225 g] cherry tomatoes, halved

½ cup [125 ml] Lemon Tahini Dressing (page 36)

5 sprigs basil, cilantro, or parsley (or a mixture, ideally)

Preheat the oven to 400°F [200°C]. Halve the eggplants lengthwise.

In a large frying pan, heat several glugs of neutral oil over high heat until smoking. Add the lentils, season with a pinch of salt, and fry, stirring occasionally, until crisped, about 3 minutes. Remove from the heat and spoon the lentils from the pan, leaving the oil behind.

continued

Return the pan to the heat, season the eggplant liberally with salt, and sear, cut-side down. When all the eggplants are in the pan and seared, transfer to the oven and roast until the eggplants are tender throughout, 15 to 25 minutes depending on size.

When the eggplant is cooked, transfer from the frying pan to a serving platter. Scatter the tomatoes over the eggplant and drizzle with the tahini dressing. Top with the herbs and serve.

variations

scattered over roast carrots w/za'atar chili oil (page 40), parsley + cumin yogurt (page 44)

w/spicy bratwurst, cauliflower + rosemary lemon chili mojo (page 50)

w/fresh radishes + anchovy butter (page 42)

SOUP

Lentil soup often epitomizes the tedium that large batch cooking can create. You make a giant batch of lentil soup and then have to eat lentil soup over and over until you never want to eat lentil soup again. This makes a big enough batch that you will have soup for a few days, but not all week. Alternatively, cook a lot of lentils and then at the end of the week add any lentils that you haven't eaten in other things to the soup in place of the uncooked lentils. When the liquid comes to a boil, the lentils are done and you can proceed with the rest of the recipe—a nice, quick way to finish off the rest of your lentils, sans tedium!

lentil soup w/cumin, garlic, lemon + pine nuts

This soup is an amalgamation of my favorite lentil soups I've had over the years. My friend Hitoko was the first person I knew to combine lentils and cumin—and serve it for breakfast. I had a delicious lentil soup, topped with pine nuts, with dear friends Nikki and Karl at a small restaurant in Red Hook a couple of years ago. The garlic-lemon-parsley sauce is my own, but I'm sure it came from someone else along the way. I like to do the partial blending too, but it's not a must. And for the sausage variation, I like a spicy fennel sausage. I hope you'll take this amalgam of lentil soups from friends and make it your own.

1 Tbsp cumin seed

1 small onion (about 4 oz [120 g]), thinly sliced

Salt

1 cup [250 ml] white wine

8 oz [225 g] brown lentils (other colors will work, but the texture will be different)

8 cups [2 L] chicken stock or water

2 garlic cloves

½ bunch parsley, roughly chopped

1 lemon (about 1½ oz [45 ml]), zest and juice

½ cup [125 ml] olive oil, plus more as needed

4 oz [120 g] pine nuts or sunflower seeds, toasted

continued

In a large pot, heat a glug of olive or neutral oil over medium heat. Add the cumin seed and briefly fry, about 30 seconds. Add the onions and 1 Tbsp of salt and stir to coat. Lower the heat and sweat the onions until soft, about 7 minutes.

Add the white wine and cook until reduced by half, about 4 minutes. Add the lentils and briefly toast, about 3 minutes.

Add the stock and increase the heat to bring to a boil. Turn down to a simmer and cook until the lentils are very tender, about 40 minutes.

Mince and smash the garlic with a pinch of salt to make a rough paste. In a medium bowl, combine the garlic, parsley, lemon zest and juice, olive oil, pine nuts, and big pinch of salt to make a very lemony, oily sauce. Reserve.

When the lentils are cooked through, blend briefly with an immersion/stick blender to make it a loosely chunky, slightly thickened soup. Adjust the seasoning as desired.

To serve, portion into serving bowls and top with a heavy slick of the sauce.

variations

lentil + sausage soup w/harissa

1 lb [450 g] pork sausage	1 Tbsp salt	8 cups [2 L] chicken stock or water
1 small onion (about 4 oz [120 g]), thinly sliced	1 cup [250 ml] apple cider or white wine	¼ cup [60 ml] Harissa (page 47)
4 garlic cloves, minced	8 oz [225 g] brown lentils	

In a large pot, brown the sausage, breaking it up into chunks as you go. Add the onion, garlic, and salt and sweat with the pork until soft, about 7 minutes.

Add the apple cider and cook until reduced by half, about 4 minutes. Add the lentils and toast for about 3 minutes.

continued

Add the stock and increase the heat to bring to a boil. Turn down to a simmer and cook until the lentils are soft, about 40 minutes. Adjust the seasoning as desired.

To serve, portion into bowls and top each with a hefty spoonful of harissa.

carrot, tomato + lentil soup w/garam masala yogurt

Olive oil or coconut oil	4 garlic cloves, minced	8 oz [225 g] lentils
4 carrots (about 12 oz [340 g]), cut into chunks	2 Tbsp [40 g] salt	½ cup [125 ml] Garam Masala Yogurt (page 45)
	One 12 oz [355 g] can peeled whole tomatoes, squeezed apart into rough pieces	
1 small onion (about 4 oz [120 g]), thinly sliced		½ bunch cilantro, leaves picked (optional)

In a large pot, heat a glug of olive oil over medium heat. Add the carrots, onion, garlic, and salt and sweat until soft, about 7 minutes.

Add the tomatoes and lentils and stew together, about 3 minutes. Add 8 cups [2 L] of water or chicken stock and increase the heat to bring to a boil. Lower to a simmer and cook until the lentils are soft, about 40 minutes. Adjust the seasoning as desired.

To serve, portion into bowls, top each with a hefty spoonful of the yogurt, and sprinkle with cilantro (if using).

parsnip + lentil soup w/parmesan + rosemary lemon chili mojo

Olive oil

4 parsnips (about 12 oz [340 g]), cut into chunks

1 small onion (about 4 oz [120 g]), thinly sliced

4 garlic cloves, minced

2 Tbsp salt

1 cup [225 ml] red or white wine

8 oz [225 g] lentils

4 oz [120 g] Parmesan, grated or shaved into ribbons with a vegetable peeler

¼ cup [60 ml] Rosemary Lemon Chili Mojo (page 50)

In a large pot, heat a glug of olive oil over medium heat. Add the parsnips, onion, garlic, and salt and sweat until soft, about 7 minutes.

Add the wine and cook until reduced by half, about 4 minutes. Add the lentils and toast for about 3 minutes.

Add 8 cups [2 L] of water or chicken stock and increase the heat to bring to a boil. Lower to a simmer and cook until the lentils are soft, about 40 minutes. Adjust the seasoning as desired.

To serve, portion into bowls and top each with Parmesan and a hefty spoonful of the mojo.

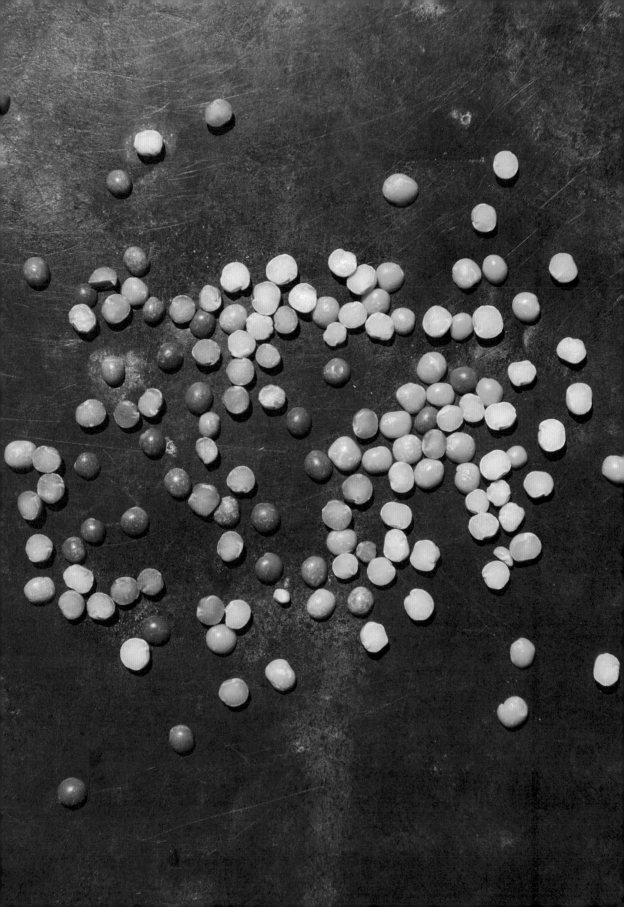

peas, split field

We instinctively ask each other, "How are you doing?" as a greeting. Recently I've begun answering, "Pea soup." It started because I thought someone asked me what I was eating, which was, in fact, split pea soup. Nowadays I just like it because it is a stand-in for a general murky, muddy, downtrodden feeling in the face of the health and economic repercussions of the COVID-19 pandemic, combined with confronting four hundred years of systemic racism in our country and ourselves. The lurking fear that, while there is tangible work that can be (and needs to be) done, it may never get any better. Can we ever transcend our own shortcomings? Can split peas ever be more than an unflatteringly green obligation?

The sheer volume of pea soup I was eating came about as I worked to eat through my pantry—clearing out the items that had languished too long in the back of the cupboard. I'm not sure why I bought ten pounds in the first place. For those of you who read *Ruffage*, it will come as no surprise that I don't actually care much for peas in general, let alone split peas in particular. I find the flavor muddy and unexciting. Lentils, harbinger of joy; split peas, ennui. But I had bought them, so now lack of desire didn't disallow the need to eat them up. My husband, skilled at eschewing burdens that needn't be borne, stopped eating the pea soup quite a while back, and said to me—I'd argue maybe a bit too pointedly—"If you don't like the soup, maybe try something else, Abra."

Turns out, he was right. Usually is.

Like a lunatic, I was trying to cultivate an appreciation for an ingredient by just eating it the same way enough times. I pulled myself out of my murk and looked to find a way to actually play to the split peas' strengths instead of highlighting their shortcomings—a good way to be, across the board. I started marinating them just after boiling them. And just about anything is good fried, so I tried that. I even stopped and thought about the soup—what did I like? What was tedium? After a few weeks of not-pea soup, surprise, surprise! I ended up craving the nemesis soup, now tinkered up with anchovies in the base, a heavy slick of chili oil, and sour cream on the top.

There you go. Ten pounds of split peas and a mood change later, I found other things to make besides soup, even though now the soup is pretty darn good, too. OK, it may seem stupid to compare working to right the world's wrongs with struggling through an unreasonably large bag of split peas. But for me, the pea episode was a weird side current that happened at the same time and was a good reminder that just moping around doesn't do anyone any good. Figure it out. Do better. Do more. Turn the murk into something better than you thought it could be. I still don't love split peas. The world is still unjust and working to heal. Improvement is the goal, and the work.

Are you excited to eat split peas now?

NOTES

BOTANICAL NAME: *Pisum sativum*

PLACE OF ORIGIN: Fertile Crescent

TOP GLOBAL PRODUCERS: Canada, France, and China

GLUTEN FREE: Yes

SOURCE OF PROTEIN: 25 percent

TO SOAK OR NOT TO SOAK (THAT IS ALWAYS THE QUESTION): Not necessary.

BASIC WATER:PEA RATIO FOR STEWING: 2:1

AVERAGE BOILING TIME: 15 to 20 minutes

YIELD RATIO AFTER COOKING: 1:2

SIGNS OF DONENESS: Peas will be tender when bitten or pushed and the centers will not look chalky—coloring will be even throughout.

FRIED

Like falafel and accara, these fritters are made by blending soaked but uncooked legumes into a rough paste and then frying to cook through. I prefer the look of these when made with yellow split peas, but the green will work A-OK too. You can, of course, serve them just as you would falafel or accara, but I've been liking them pressed flat into the pan and then used as a vehicle for other vegetables.

pea breakfast fritters w/fried egg, greens + smoked yogurt

If I were really cute and fancy, I'd make these with fried quail eggs and microgreens for an early morning soirée. Turns out I'm neither of those two things, so I make the fritters in big batches and then freeze the leftovers to repurpose when I need something to hold down an all-vegetable meal. They also work well fried and then cut into smaller pieces and used in place of croutons in a salad. The pickles add brightness and a subtle, can't-quite-put-my-finger-on-that-flavor tang, but can of course be left out if you don't have any on hand.

2 cups [400 g] split peas, preferably yellow but not critical, soaked for at least 4 hours

2 onions (about 1 lb [450 g]), thinly sliced

4 garlic cloves, smashed

4 pickle spears (2 oz [60 g]), roughly chopped

5 sprigs parsley, roughly chopped

5 sprigs dill, roughly chopped

2 tsp cumin

1 tsp coriander

1½ tsp salt, plus more as needed

Neutral oil

4 oz [125 ml] plain yogurt

1 Tbsp balsamic vinegar

1 tsp smoked salt (or 1 tsp salt and 3 drops liquid smoke)

2 oz [60 g] spinach, kale, chard, or other hearty green per person

1 egg per person

Freshly ground black pepper

½ cup [125 ml] white wine (or water with a splash of red wine or apple cider vinegar)

continued

Line a baking sheet with a rack or paper towels.

In a food processor, blend the soaked peas, onion, garlic, pickle spears, herbs, spices, and salt into a coarse but even paste.

Heat 1 in [2.5 cm] of neutral oil in a medium frying pan over medium-high heat. Scoop ¼ cup [34 g] of the paste into the hot oil and then flatten into a pancake by pressing with the back of a spoon. Repeat to fill the pan. Brown one side, about 4 minutes, and then flip and brown the other. Let drain on the prepared baking sheet. Repeat with any uncooked mixture.

Whisk together the yogurt, balsamic vinegar, and smoked salt.

Discard the oil from the frying pan (be careful, as it is probably still hot), wipe clean, and heat a glug of neutral oil over high heat. Add the greens with a pinch of salt and toss to coat in the hot oil. Push the greens to the sides to make a little nest. Crack the egg into the center of the nest, then season with salt and pepper.

Add the white wine (it will spit and sputter) and cover with a lid to steam the egg with the evaporating wine.

When the egg is cooked to your liking, scoop the greens and nested egg, place on top of a fritter, drizzle with the smoked yogurt, and serve.

Note: If the fritters are made well in advance (or pulled from the freezer), they can be reheated by toasting in either a dry frying pan or a hot oven.

variations

w/ratatouille + basil

Top the warm fritter with ½ cup [125 ml] of Ratatouille (page 57) and several tears of basil over the top. Adding some cheese like fresh mozzarella or goat cheese here would be *chef's kiss*.

w/spinach salad + bacon vinaigrette

Cut the already fried fritters into strips or cubes and recrisp in a frying pan or hot oven. Dress 3 oz [85 g] of spinach per person with ¼ cup [60 ml] of Bacon Vinaigrette (page 35) and several grinds of black pepper. Add the fritter croutons and serve.

w/red cabbage + ras el hanout apricot almond rig

Top the warm fritters with red cabbage, cut thinly as you would for coleslaw and dressed with several spoonfuls of Ras el Hanout Apricot Almond Rig (page 49) or the Lemon Parsley Mojo (page 48) or Mojo de Ajo (page 48) or Giardiniera (page 53)—you get the idea.

SOUP

What is modern midwestern food? This soup sort of sums it up. It's what your grandma might have made, but hopefully a bit brighter in flavor, smoother in texture, and no politeness needed.

split pea soup w/balsamic vinegar

The addition of balsamic vinegar comes straight from my friend Meg Fish's table. She ladled up big bowls of soup topped with four or five drips of the tangy, sweet liquid, and I've never gone back.

Olive oil

1 cup [225 g] thinly sliced onion

4 garlic cloves, minced

4 anchovy fillets

Salt

1 cup [250 ml] white wine or hard cider

2 cups [400 g] split peas, green or yellow

1 Yukon gold potato (about 8 oz [225 g]), peeled and cut into chunks

2 carrots (about 4 oz [120 g]), cut into chunks

2 oz [60 ml] sour cream per person

1 Tbsp balsamic vinegar per person

1 tsp Chili Oil (page 39) per person

1 Tbsp Lemon Parsley Mojo (page 48) per person

In a medium soup pot, heat a glug of oil over medium heat. Add the onion, garlic, and anchovies and a big pinch of salt and sweat until soft, about 7 minutes.

Add the wine and simmer until reduced by half. Add the split peas, potato, carrots, and 8 cups [2 L] of water and bring to a boil. Lower to a simmer and cook until the peas and vegetables are tender, about 25 minutes. Either leave loose and chunky or blend with an immersion blender to make the soup smooth. Adjust the seasoning as desired.

To serve, dish the soup into individual bowls and top each with a dollop of sour cream, a splash of balsamic vinegar, a spoonful of chili oil, and a swirl of lemon parsley mojo.

MARINATED

The Spanish technique, escabeche, submerges a just-cooked ingredient in an acidic dressing, pulling the flavor into the center as it cools. This is one of my favorite techniques when building grain salads because the rich, sometimes-heavy grains feel light and bright. I like to pair the marinated legume with an equal amount of grain for bulk and then a bunch of fresh vegetables for crunch and color. Because you can marinate with just about any dressing or relish, combine with any other cooked (or sprouted grain), and finish with any veg or herbs you have on hand, this is an endlessly riff-able Flavor Formula.

1.

START WITH 1 CUP [200 G] SPLIT PEAS, BOILED UNTIL JUST TENDER, ABOUT 10 MINUTES, THEN DRAIN

2.

DRESS THE WARM PEAS WITH ABOUT ½ CUP [125 ML] OF VINAIGRETTE OR DRESSING TO MARINATE

See pages 34 to 38 for inspiration.

3.

ADD 1 CUP [200 G] COOKED GRAINS TO THE MARINATING PEAS

See part 3, beginning on page 197, for inspiration.

4.

ADD A VEGETABLE OR GREEN (AS MUCH OR AS LITTLE AS YOU WANT)

5.

FINISH WITH A FEW EXTRA SPOONFULS OF THE DRESSING AND A HANDFUL OF CHOPPED HERBS OVER THE TOP

6.

YUM!

Note: These salads store well when dressed and so are good candidates for work lunches, picnics, and potlucks.

grains

I once worked at a bakery. After changing the type of flour used, we were forced to sort out some frustrations with how the bread was turning out. I remember saying, "Haven't humans been making bread since the dawn of time?" My quick-witted coworker said, "Doesn't mean it was good bread." Which led to the most productive conversation about what constitutes good food I've ever sat in on. The general consensus was consistency of product, long-lasting and balanced flavor, and executability regardless of temperature, humidity, and production volume. In short, we wanted to make loaves that looked and tasted the same day in and day out.

In a lot of ways, the grain growing is not so different from our goals with that bread. Slowly, wild grains collected from wild plants were farmed and domesticated; farmers cultivated prized characteristics like flavor, reliable germination, and overall heartiness in a specific growing region. Nowadays, alongside industrial agriculture, which prizes volume and consistency, there are more and more farmers growing larger varieties of grains, from heritage, open-pollinated corn to landrace wheats. A growth in regional grain economies supports jobs for seed cleaners and millers, who can then get more of these ingredients to our tables outside of the massive grocery store distribution networks, as we saw during the COVID-19 pandemic. The availability of local products meant that a slew of home cooks and bakers were turned on to fresh flours and regionally specific grains.

The following chapters deal mostly in grains that are widely available. My hope is that as you, dear reader, grow comfortable with barley in general, you might seek out an heirloom black barley and try that the next time. I believe comfort begets confidence, and confidence begets courage. When someone says to me, "I know I need to eat more whole grain, but I don't know where to start," my advice is just start—get comfortable with whatever grain feels the most familiar, and make your favorite thing. Then make that favorite thing with a new grain and explore the similarities and differences. And when all else fails and you feel like you should be eating even more whole grains, there's a recipe to turn any grain into a fritter on page 369, because even the most intimidating (or sanctimonious) ingredient can't be taken too seriously after it is deep fried.

barley

I'd like to take just a moment to acknowledge an obvious but easily overlooked fact. Every single ingredient highlighted in this book is a seed.

It is natural to forget the inherent magic each one, so small and unassuming, contains. A seed has, within itself, everything the plant needs to grow again. From a dried, hard kernel, life springs forth. A tiny grain, protected by rigid bran, tumbles along until softened by warmth and water, and then, needing nothing else at all, regrows to try again—tender and green, craning toward the sun.

We take those life-giving components and eat them. Extracting the nutrients, we propel our own lives forward.

I could go on, but this is not some sentimental, self-reflective manifesto. It's just a quick but important reminder that seeds are cool, and they literally give us life.

NOTES

BOTANICAL NAME: *Hordeum vulgare*

PLACE OF ORIGIN: Fertile Crescent

TOP GLOBAL PRODUCERS: Russia, Canada, Australia, Ukraine, and Turkey

GLUTEN FREE: No

PROTEIN CONTENT: 12.5 percent

TO SOAK OR NOT TO SOAK (THAT IS ALWAYS THE QUESTION): Soaking will decrease the cooking time by half. Pearled barley cooks quickly enough that it isn't necessary, but soaking will help draw out starch, allowing the grains to "fluff" more at the end of cooking.

BASIC WATER:GRAIN RATIO FOR STEWING: 3:1

AVERAGE BOILING TIME: 35 minutes for pearled; 45 for hulled

YIELD RATIO AFTER COOKING: 1:3

SIGNS OF DONENESS: Grains will have puffed and be tender without collapsing.

BARLEY

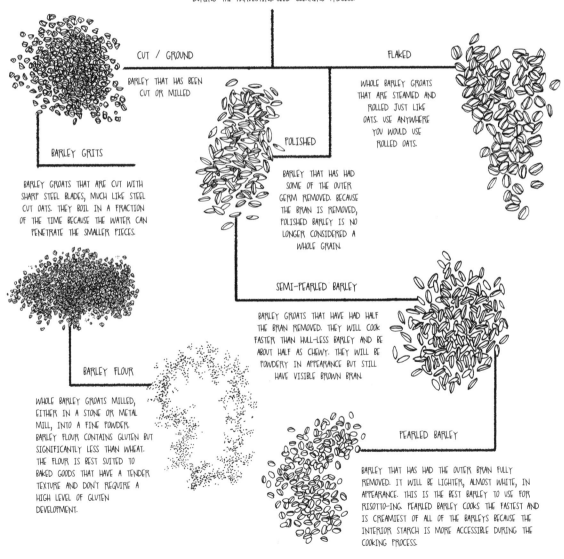

BARLEY GROATS THAT HAVE HAD THE INEDIBLE, SPIKY HULLS REMOVED. HULL-LESS BARLEY VARIETIES HAVE BEEN BRED TO HAVE LOOSE HULLS THAT USUALLY FALL OFF DURING THE HARVESTING/SEED CLEANING PROCESS.

CUT / GROUND

BARLEY THAT HAS BEEN CUT OR MILLED

FLAKED

WHOLE BARLEY GROATS THAT ARE STEAMED AND ROLLED JUST LIKE OATS. USE ANYWHERE YOU WOULD USE ROLLED OATS.

POLISHED

BARLEY THAT HAS HAD SOME OF THE OUTER GERM REMOVED. BECAUSE THE BRAN IS REMOVED, POLISHED BARLEY IS NO LONGER CONSIDERED A WHOLE GRAIN.

BARLEY GRITS

BARLEY GROATS THAT ARE CUT WITH SHARP STEEL BLADES, MUCH LIKE STEEL CUT OATS. THEY BOIL IN A FRACTION OF THE TIME BECAUSE THE WATER CAN PENETRATE THE SMALLER PIECES.

SEMI-PEARLED BARLEY

BARLEY GROATS THAT HAVE HAD HALF THE BRAN REMOVED. THEY WILL COOK FASTER THAN HULL-LESS BARLEY AND BE ABOUT HALF AS CHEWY. THEY WILL BE POWDERY IN APPEARANCE BUT STILL HAVE VISIBLE BROWN BRAN.

BARLEY FLOUR

WHOLE BARLEY GROATS MILLED, EITHER IN A STONE OR METAL MILL, INTO A FINE POWDER. BARLEY FLOUR CONTAINS GLUTEN BUT SIGNIFICANTLY LESS THAN WHEAT. THE FLOUR IS BEST SUITED TO BAKED GOODS THAT HAVE A TENDER TEXTURE AND DON'T REQUIRE A HIGH LEVEL OF GLUTEN DEVELOPMENT.

PEARLED BARLEY

BARLEY THAT HAS HAD THE OUTER BRAN FULLY REMOVED. IT WILL BE LIGHTER, ALMOST WHITE, IN APPEARANCE. THIS IS THE BEST BARLEY TO USE FOR RISOTTO-ING. PEARLED BARLEY COOKS THE FASTEST AND IS CREAMIEST OF ALL OF THE BARLEYS BECAUSE THE INTERIOR STARCH IS MORE ACCESSIBLE DURING THE COOKING PROCESS.

CARL WAGNER

Carl Wagner is a farmer and seed cleaner in Niles, Michigan. He and his family grow row crops and manage dairy cattle on 1,500 acres in southwest Michigan. In addition, he and his wife, Mary, run C3 Seeds, a seed-cleaning business that processes grains and seed stock for other growers. I wanted to talk with Mr. Wagner because seed cleaning is one of those invisible jobs that is integral to both grain farming and to using that grain for human consumption. I didn't even know it was a thing until a couple of years ago, so I figured others probably don't either. He chatted with me before work and dinner one evening in April 2020.

Abra Berens: Tell me about the history of your farm and how you came to farm.

Carl Wagner: I was raised on a dairy farm in Niles. We transitioned to row crops growing from 100 to 1,500 acres.

AB: So, if you grew up on a farm, how did you transition to seed cleaning?

CW: I graduated from Michigan State University with a degree in crop and soil agronomic sciences and have always been interested in the finer points of farming—how it is an art and a science. I am passionate about looking at the old ways of farming but with a constant eye toward innovation. In some ways, that's how seed cleaning came into it—wanting to diversify, add value, and make my own way on the farm. There is such demand for quality seed products and services, so it seemed like a good way to expand what we and other growers in the area need.

In 2013, I got into growing malting barley to sell to brewers. There was no seed grown in the state, so I started to grow it to plant myself and to sell to other growers looking to diversify into small grain, usually from corn and soy.

[I would take] all the grain to the grain association for custom cleaning. Then I found a seed cleaner who was retiring, so I bought his equipment and started up. Then I applied for a Michigan Department of Agriculture and Rural Development (MDARD) value-added grant and got it, which helped me expand the business.

Now I'm growing seed stock to sell and processing grain. I guess we're all always chasing the value added, and for me, the connection to the end user. I like to know where all this work is going. For example, you know I clean the rye Wes grows for Granor Farm that gets distilled by Journeyman in Three Oaks, Michigan. I know Wesley. and I know Matt McClain, the lead distiller, *and* I can go and buy a bottle of whiskey. That is really fulfilling—more so than just shipping something off on a truck.

AB: Can you explain, in very basic terms, what seed cleaning is?

CW: It is the process of taking harvested grain and ridding it of contaminants like stray weed seeds or broken or diseased seeds. There is also a difference in how you clean for seed that will be sold to a grower versus for food grade. The process isn't different, it is just how hard you clean it—quantity or quality. There is always going to be a bit of contamination, so how much can be handled? For example, all seeds are cleaned of chaff and weed seed, but how many broken or diseased kernels can the end user tolerate? A little bit is fine for planting stock. None is allowed in distilling or for milling into flour. You're always going to lose some good with the bad—that's the art to making the cut. The farmer generally wants quantity; the distiller or miller wants quality.

AB: So how do you do it?

CW: The first step in seed cleaning happens in the field with the combine [the tractor that harvests the grain]. The combine separates chaff and unthreshed heads. In what comes to me, the main contaminants are remaining chaff, weed seeds, insects, stones, sometimes the last seeds of the previous harvest if the combine or wagon wasn't cleaned out before the new grain was harvested.

Then the grains go through the debearder or dehuller, which breaks off the beards on any of the long-awned grains like barley. That leaves kernel exposed. Next is the fanning mill, which does the heavy lifting of the cleaning. After the seed goes over the fanning mill it's about 80 percent clean.

AB: What does a fanning mill look like and how does it work?

CW: It's a machine with a big hopper on top where you put the uncleaned grain. It sort of shuffles the grain down through different screens with smaller and smaller holes while a fan blows the chaff and debris off. After the fanning mill, the grain goes to the gravity table, which separates the seeds by their density. It's a bit like those air hockey tables where the air blows up the side—the seeds sort of float. Anything that is too light, which usually means some sort of disease or cracking, flies off to one side, and the more desired heavy grains pass to the other side.

Then the cleaned grain is sent to the packing line, where we mostly pack it in fifty-pound bags.

AB: How is barley pearled? Most of the barley I see in the grocery store is either pearled or semi-pearled, unless I'm getting some heirloom black barleys, which I've never bought in an unpolished state.

CW: We don't pearl barley—most of the barley we [process] is malting barley for brewers.

AB: What's the difference?

CW: There are specific varieties of barley intended for malting—higher protein barleys are better for food (animal or human), and lower protein is better for malting. Some can do both, but for brewers of any sort of scale they need the malt to be consistent to keep the beers consistent, so they tend to use malting barley instead of feed barley.

AB: How hard would it be for you to take on pearling or polishing food-grade barley?

CW: I've looked at the machine for it, and it wouldn't be so hard, but, like everything, there has to be a market for it to justify the expense. If we were to turn away from corn and soy in this region and lean into the small grains, there might be more reason to do that next level of processing. Until then, there's no real reason to do it besides that it would be cool.

AB: So what is the trajectory for your year?

CW: Time is moving differently for all of us right now, that's for sure. My year mostly goes in rhythm with the grain harvest. Pretty quiet until July, when barley, wheat, and rye are harvested. August is the busiest time—lots of cleaning and processing. Then in early October, doing barley and wheat seed prep for growers who are planting in the fall for harvest in the spring. After that, I'm just cleaning seed that is in bin storage. That's just on the cleaning side—the farm side is different.

AB: Understood. What do you wish nonfarmers knew about your work?

CW: Not even sure that they are aware of the process, so simply knowing that this is part of buying a bag of flour or a bottle of whiskey. In some ways, knowing that we exist is enough.

I also wish that consumers saw the downside of consolidation—the instability and insecurity of that. Both my dad and brother are dairymen; there are lots of issues in our system, but it is hard to have people see shortage on the shelf and surplus on the farm and not have any sense as to why. To be fair, too rarely do we do that awareness raising in the ag community either. It's often just one foot in front of the other. There is work we can do on the policy side to make a system that supports more sustainable businesses.

AB: What are the top three hurdles you face as a grower and processor?

CW: Economics—sadly always at the forefront. Looking at cash flow versus investment, and so on.

Getting financing as a start-up and young grower. I was fairly lucky, but it was not as easy as it should be. This is a big hurdle for younger growers—finding an institution that wants to put skin in the game and work with you. Size doesn't make a business more solvent, but that's not our current model.

Building the sustainability. I want to have a farm and business that will last into the next generation. To do that, the business needs to have economic, emotional, and environmental sustainability.

AB: What are the top three successes from the past year?

CW: You know one of the successes is that I enjoy the lifestyle. I have the opportunity to work outside, to be dependent on nature, and I work with family.

The variability of it is a good challenge—always changing and problem solving. Sometimes it gets to be too much, but by and by that's the fun part.

The biggest thing is creating something outside of just taking the grain to an elevator—seeing your product become something. That keeps a fire under me.

AB: OK, now the tough one. What's your favorite way to eat your barley?

CW: In a tall, frosty pint glass! [*laughs*] My wife, Mary, just reminded me that we bake a lot of bread. Beer, bread, and dairy—all my favorite food groups! Ha! I'm just kidding—we eat a lot of vegetables too.

AB: Hey, I'm with you! A balanced diet is certainly balanced out by beer, bread, and cheese!

A WEEK'S WORTH OF BARLEY WITHOUT ANY BOREDOM

When boiled, barley sort of unfurls (or uncurls?) to become one of those pleasing-to-the-eye, pleasing-to-the-tongue shapes, with a little dent or notch in each pearl. Like short, round pasta shapes, the form of cooked barley is practically perfect for holding a piquant dressing. But it also lends itself to a variety of other methods . . .

day one – boil 2 cups [260 g] dry barley for 6 cups [1.2 kg] of cooked

Bring a medium pot of salted water to a boil and then pour in the barley, stirring to keep it from clumping at the bottom of the pot. Boil the barley until tender (35 minutes for pearled, 45 for hulled) and drain.

day two

barley salad w/cauliflower, smoked whitefish, marinated mushrooms + arugula

1 cup [200 g] cooked barley	4 oz [120 g] cauliflower, shaved into thin vertical cross pieces, leaving the core intact	½ cup [125 ml] Pickle Liquid Dressing (page 37)
7 oz [200 g] Marinated Mushrooms (page 56)		Salt and freshly ground black pepper
	2 oz [60 g] arugula	
	2 oz [60 g] smoked whitefish, picked	

In a medium bowl, combine all the ingredients and toss to evenly coat with the dressing. Serve at room temperature; if dressing well in advance, leave out the arugula and add it just before serving.

day three

barley cakes underneath lamb chops w/roasted carrots + ras el hanout apricot almond rig

1 cup [200 g] cooked barley	1 lb [450 g] carrots, roasted	4 oz [120 g] spinach
2 eggs	2 or 3 lamb chops (about 5 oz [150 g] per person)	1 cup [150 g] Ras el Hanout Apricot Almond Rig (page 49)
Salt	Freshly ground black pepper	
Olive oil		

In a food processor, pulse together the barley, eggs, ¼ cup [60 ml] of water, and a couple of pinches of salt to make a thick batter. Heat a couple of glugs of olive oil in a large frying pan over medium-high heat. Spoon the batter into the hot oil like you are making pancakes and brown the bottoms evenly, 2 to 3 minutes, lowering the heat if necessary. Flip and brown the other side, adding more oil as needed. Transfer the cakes to a baking sheet and hold in a warm oven (or if making ahead, refrigerate, then rewarm in the oven just before serving).

Preheat the oven to 400°F [200°C] and roast the carrots on a baking sheet until tender inside and caramelized on the outside, about 30 minutes.

Season the lamb chops liberally with salt and pepper and grill or pan fry until medium-rare.

To serve, place a barley cake (or two, depending on the size) on a plate. Top the cake with the lamb chops and carrots. Dress the spinach with the apricot rig and a pinch of salt and place the salad on top of the whole thing.

continued

day four

barley breakfast porridge w/spiced milk, dried cherries + nuts

2 cups [500 ml] Spiced Milk (page 44)	½ cup [80 g] dried cherries	1 cup [130 g] nuts (pecans, walnuts, almonds)
1 cup [200 g] cooked barley		

In a saucepan, heat the spiced milk, cooked barley, and dried cherries until slightly thickened and warm throughout. Spoon into serving bowls and top each with a handful of nuts.

day five

crisped barley over roasted broccolini w/goat cheese vinaigrette

½ cup [125 ml] olive oil	2 bunches (2 lb [900 g]) broccolini, washed and stems trimmed	½ cup [125 ml] Goat Cheese Vinaigrette (page 36)
1 cup [200 g] boiled barley		
Salt	1 head radicchio (about 5 oz [150 g]) , cut into wide ribbons	

In a large frying pan, heat the olive oil over medium-high heat until it begins to shimmer, about 1 minute. Line a plate with paper towels. If the cooked barley is very wet, blot the excess moisture. Fry until golden and crisp, about 4 minutes. Remove the pan from the heat and use a slotted spoon to lift the crisped barley from the pan, leaving the oil behind. Drain the barley on the paper towel–lined plate. As it cools, season with a sprinkle of salt.

Return the pan with its oil to the burner and heat over high heat. Add the broccolini and pan fry with a pinch of salt until bright green and slightly charred, about 5 minutes. Transfer the broccolini to a serving platter.

In the same pan over high heat, pan fry the radicchio until lightly browned, about 4 minutes. Add the radicchio to the platter. Spoon the vinaigrette over the whole thing, top with the crisped barley, and serve.

day six

barley soup w/parsnips, chard + lemon parsley mojo

Olive oil

2 onions (about 1 lb [450 g]), thinly sliced

6 garlic cloves, minced

Salt

1 cup [250 ml] white wine or hard cider

3 lb [1.35 kg] parsnips, peeled (if the skin is thick) and cut into chunks

3 qt [3 L] chicken stock or water (or a mix)

2 cups [400 g] cooked barley

2 bunches (about 1 lb [450 g]) chard, cut into ribbons

½ cup [125 ml] Lemon Parsley Mojo (page 48)

In a soup pot, heat a couple of glugs of olive oil over medium heat. Add the onions and garlic with a couple of big pinches of salt and sweat until tender, about 7 minutes.

Add the wine and cook until reduced by half. Add the parsnips and stock. Bring to a boil, lower to a simmer, and cook until the parsnips are mostly tender, about 20 minutes.

Add the barley and cook until the parsnips are fully tender, about 20 minutes.

To serve, portion the chard ribbons among the serving bowls, ladle the hot soup over the chard to let it wilt gently, and top with a heaping spoonful of the mojo.

BOILED

Like all grains, barley can be boiled just like pasta or toasted in the oven and steamed to a similar result. The more of the hull that has been removed, the faster the cooking time. Cooked barley also freezes well; then you have it on hand for a very fast dinner. Boil an extra 2 cups [260 g] to use during a busy week.

roasted parsnips + endive w/mornay sauce + barley

Mornay is a classic, made by enriching a basic milk sauce with cheese. It holds well if you want to make it in advance—simply rewarm over low heat. It is a great thing to have on hand when you need to make a quick meal feel rich and decadent. If you are limiting gluten, you can substitute the Mushroom Cream Sauce (page 44), which relies on reducing the cream as opposed to thickening the cream with a roux.

4 lb [1.8 kg] parsnips, peeled and cut into 2 in [5 cm] long pieces of the same width

Olive oil

Salt and freshly ground black pepper

½ cup [65 g] dry barley

1 recipe Mornay Sauce (page 43)

2 heads (about 2 oz [60 g]) Belgian or curly endive or radicchio, cut into wide petals

15 sprigs parsley, roughly chopped

Preheat the oven to 400°F [200°C]. In a large bowl, toss the parsnips with a couple of glugs of olive oil and pinches of salt and pepper. Transfer to a baking sheet and roast until tender on the inside and caramelized on the outside, about 40 minutes.

continued

Bring a medium pot of salted water to a boil and then pour in the barley, stirring to keep it from clumping at the bottom of the pot. Boil the barley until tender (35 minutes for pearled, 45 for hulled) and drain.

In a medium saucepan, warm the Mornay sauce.

Dress the endive, parsley, and cooked parsnips with a glug of olive oil and a pinch of salt.

To serve, pool Mornay sauce onto each plate, add a couple of spoonfuls of the cooked barley, top with the parsnip-endive salad, and drizzle a bit more Mornay sauce over the top.

variations

w/roasted squash, gingered apples + spinach w/mustard vinaigrette

2 acorn or delicata squash (about 3 lb [1.35 kg], cut into 2 in [5 cm] thick wedges or half-moons	1 cup [150 g] Gingered Apples (page 54) Olive oil Salt and freshly ground black pepper	1 cup [200 g] cooked barley 4 oz [120 g] spinach, torn into pieces ½ cup [125 ml] Mustard Vinaigrette (page 36)

Preheat the oven to 400°F [200°C]. Toss the squash and apples in a big glug of olive oil, a couple of pinches of salt, and several grinds of black pepper. Spread on a baking sheet and roast until the squash and apples are tender, about 25 minutes.

Combine the barley, spinach, and vinaigrette. Add the roasted squash and apples to the barley salad, toss to combine, and adjust the seasoning as desired.

Serve warm or at room temperature.

w/grilled ramps, marinated mushrooms + gribiche

12 ramps, cleaned

Olive oil

Salt

1½ cups [300 g] cooked barley

½ cup [150 g] Marinated Mushrooms (page 56)

½ cup [125 g] Gribiche (page 47)

Heat a grill. Lightly coat the ramps with olive oil and a pinch of salt. Grill over medium heat until the bulbs are tender and the greens slightly charred.

Combine the barley and marinated mushrooms and toss to mix.

To serve, spoon the barley salad onto a serving platter or plates. Top with the grilled ramps and garnish with the gribiche.

barley-stuffed bell peppers w/anchovies + giardiniera

2 cups [400 g] cooked barley

10 anchovy fillets, roughly chopped

¾ cup [180 g] Cherry Tomato Conserva (page 52)

6 garlic cloves, minced

Olive oil

Salt

2 red, orange, or yellow bell peppers (about 12 oz [340 g]), cut in half and seeds removed

10 sprigs parsley, roughly chopped

1 cup [125 g] Giardiniera (page 53)

Preheat the oven 375°F [190°C]. Combine the barley, anchovies, tomato conserva, and garlic with a couple glugs of olive oil and a pinch of salt.

Fill the peppers with the barley mixture and place in an ovenproof baking dish. Bake until the peppers are soft and the filling is heated through, about 25 minutes.

To serve, combine the chopped parsley and giardiniera, then spoon over the peppers.

RISOTTO-ED

The difference between making something risotto style versus simply boiling or stewing it is the addition of hot water or stock, a ladleful at a time, and stirring constantly. The combined agitation of the stirring with the slow addition of liquid coaxes more starch from the grain, yielding a thickened, creamy sauce at the end. Plus, the 20 minutes or so of standing over the stove stirring gives you a good amount of time to think of any flavor combinations you want to add to the finished dish. Note that "barley-sotto" is best made with pearled barley, as the hull has been removed, speeding the cooking time and making the starch more accessible, for a creamier risotto. Save your heirloom black barley for boiling, which gives it more (inactive) cooking time to tenderize fully.

barley, risotto-ed

This is a base recipe for plain barley risotto. Serve it on its own as a side dish or with the following flavor variations as the main event.

Olive oil or butter

4 sprigs thyme or rosemary (optional)

1 onion (about 8 oz [225 g]), thinly sliced

6 garlic cloves, minced

½ tsp salt

1½ cups [300 g] pearled barley

1 cup [250 ml] white wine or hard cider

6 to 8 cups [1.5 to 2 L] water or stock, brought to a boil and kept hot

In a medium pot, heat a glug of olive oil over medium heat. Fry the thyme (if using) until the leaves stop popping and are fragrant, about 30 seconds. Remove from the pot and reserve for later.

Add the onion, garlic, and salt to the pot and sweat until tender, about 7 minutes. Add the barley and briefly toast, about 2 minutes. Add the white wine and start the stirring.

When the wine is completely absorbed, add a ladleful of the hot water and continue stirring. When that liquid is mostly absorbed, add the next ladleful.

Continue adding ladlefuls of liquid until the barley has swelled and is tender to the bite, about 20 minutes.

When the barley is tender but not falling apart, remove from the heat and dish into serving bowls. Top with the fried herb leaves and serve immediately.

variations

w/peas, chard + mushroom cream sauce

Cut 1 bunch of chard (2 to 3 leaves per person) into ribbons. With your final ladleful of hot cooking liquid, add 8 oz [225 g] of fresh or frozen peas to the risotto and continue stirring. To serve, dish the barley-sotto into serving bowls, top with the chard ribbons, and finish with a generous ladleful of Mushroom Cream Sauce (page 44), which will gently wilt the chard.

w/gingered apples, goat cheese + arugula

After dishing the barley-sotto into bowls, top with a couple of spoonfuls of Gingered Apples (page 54) and dot goat cheese all over. Dress the arugula with a glug of olive oil and a pinch of salt, then heap the salad on top of the risotto.

w/peperonata + creamed mozzarella

When the barley-sotto is finished cooking, dish into serving bowls and top with ½ cup [125 ml] of Peperonata (page 56) per person and several chunks of Creamed Mozzarella (page 43). Garnish with some chopped parsley or torn basil.

continued

w/squash purée + garnished w/shaved pears, rosemary lemon chili mojo + blue cheese

Before you make the risotto, cut a winter squash of any variety in half and roast, cut-side down, at 350°F [180°C], until it collapses when pushed with a prodding finger (protected with a mitt or pot holder). Allow it to cool enough to handle, then scoop the flesh out of the squash and put in a food processor. Blend the flesh with several glugs of olive oil and pinches of salt until smooth. Cook the barley-sotto and when it is tender, add 2 cups [500 ml] of squash purée to the risotto and stir to coat. Dish into serving bowls and top with thinly sliced pear, ½ pear per person. Drizzle 2 Tbsp Rosemary Lemon Chili Mojo (page 50) over each bowl, finish with several crumbles of blue cheese, and serve.

FLOUR

Barley flour can be used as a direct swap for all-purpose flour in any recipe, but know that the finished dish won't rise in the same way. Expect a slightly denser, chewier dish, but the change in texture is more than offset with the lovely warm, brown, nutty flavor. I know we all need another word besides nutty, but I haven't come up with it yet—toasty, cozy, perfect?

barley pancakes

I admit, it is a bit fiddly to separate the eggs and beat the whites separately, but because barley flour has less gluten than traditional all-purpose flour, it needs a little helping hand to get extra loft. Additionally, allowing the batter to rest for 10 minutes before adding the egg whites gives the gluten that *is* in the barley flour a chance to develop, giving the pancakes the best chance they have to hold their structure when cooking.

2 cups [250 g] barley flour	1 tsp salt	2 Tbsp sugar
2 tsp baking powder	2 cups [500 ml] whole milk or buttermilk	2 Tbsp butter, melted, plus more for cooking
1 tsp baking soda	4 large eggs, separated	

Preheat the oven to 200°F [95°C] and set a rack in a baking sheet to keep the pancakes warm after cooking.

Combine the barley flour, baking powder, baking soda, and salt until evenly distributed. Combine the milk and egg yolks, then whisk into the dry ingredients. Add the melted butter and whisk to incorporate. Let rest for 10 minutes.

Beat the egg whites until foamy, about 2 minutes. Spoon in the sugar and continue beating until stiff, another 5 minutes.

Add about a quarter of the beaten egg whites to the batter and stir in until completely incorporated—this lightens the batter and preps it to blend more easily with the rest of the whites. Add the rest of the egg whites and fold until just combined, with no streaks of white visible.

Heat a large frying pan with butter over medium-low heat. You may need to spread the pancakes with the back of a spoon. Pan fry until the first side is golden brown and the bubbles that come through hold their shape after they pop. Flip and griddle the other side. Transfer to the rack in the warm oven. Serve with copious amounts of salted butter, maple syrup, and jam or honey.

barley thumbprint cookies

I'd never really gotten into thumbprint cookies until my former coworker Lauren Bushnell left me a package of her barley thumbprint cookies. I can't remember what I did to receive the gift, but I remember thinking, *That's nice of her. Maybe Erik will like them.* I absentmindedly tossed them into my bag and headed home. Then the bus was late, it was raining, and I was grouchy. When the bus finally arrived and I got a seat, I popped a cookie into my mouth and was stopped in my tracks (thankfully the bus kept going). It was a little chewy, not too sweet, and much more flavorful than any regular jammy cookie I'd had before. "It's the barley flour," Lauren said casually as I fawned over her the next time I passed her in the kitchen.

1 cup [225 g] butter, softened

⅓ cup [65 g] granulated sugar

⅓ cup [70 g] brown sugar

2 cups [250 g] barley flour

½ tsp salt

Jam, flavor of your choosing—though I like the red fruits (cherry, raspberry, plum)

In a stand mixer, cream the butter and sugars together at medium speed until light and fluffy, about 6 minutes—take it further than you normally would, because this is the only way to add lightness to the finished cookie. Scrape down the sides of the bowl.

Combine the flour and salt. With the paddle attachment, gently work in the flour mixture until there are no more buttery streaks—it is harder to overwork these cookies because of the lower gluten in the flour, but it is still possible, so be tender.

Wrap and chill the dough for 30 minutes to firm up and protect the structure of the dough.

Preheat the oven to 325°F [165°C].

Scoop and roll the dough into 1 in [2.5 cm] balls and place 2 in [5 cm] apart on an ungreased or parchment-lined baking sheet.

Push your thumb into the center of each ball and spoon about 1 tsp of jam in the cookie's belly button. Bake until golden brown and slightly crispy on the edges, 12 to 15 minutes.

barley doughnuts soaked in marigold syrup

Soaking fried dough in heavy syrup comes up in all sorts of cultures, from Persian *bamieh* to Lebanese *awamat*. Tangerine marigold is one of my favorite summer flavors and makes a very lovely syrup for everything from cocktails to soaking these barley doughnuts. The doughnuts didn't suffer when I gave them a dip in maple syrup because I couldn't be bothered to make a simple syrup—you always have options.

FOR THE DOUGHNUTS

½ tsp sugar

1½ tsp active dry yeast

¼ tsp salt

3 cups [375 g] barley flour

Neutral oil, for frying

FOR THE SYRUP

1 cup [200 g] sugar

10 marigold stems (flowers removed and reserved for garnish) or 1 tsp orange-flower water or ¼ cup [60 ml] orange juice

Salt

To make the doughnuts: Combine the sugar, yeast, and 2½ cups [625 ml] warm water. Let sit for 10 minutes or until foamy.

Combine the salt and barley flour. Whisk in the water-yeast mixture and stir to form a slightly sticky dough. Cover and allow to double in size, 60 to 90 minutes.

To make the syrup: Combine the sugar and ½ cup [125 ml] of water and bring to a boil to dissolve the sugar. Remove from the heat, add the marigold stems, and allow to steep for 10 to 20 minutes. Strain the syrup and discard the marigold stems.

In a deep pot, heat 3 in [7.5 cm] of neutral oil to 375°F [190°C]. Spoon in 2 in [5 cm] wide balls of dough, enough to fill the surface area of the oil but not overcrowd the pan (in my pot, that is 8 or so at a time). Fry until golden brown and puffed, about 2 minutes. Flip the balls and brown the other side.

Lift from the oil and transfer to the syrup. Push the doughnuts down to fully submerge, then lift from the syrup and transfer to a serving platter. Sprinkle the doughnuts with a pinch of salt and the reserved marigold flowers and eat within the day.

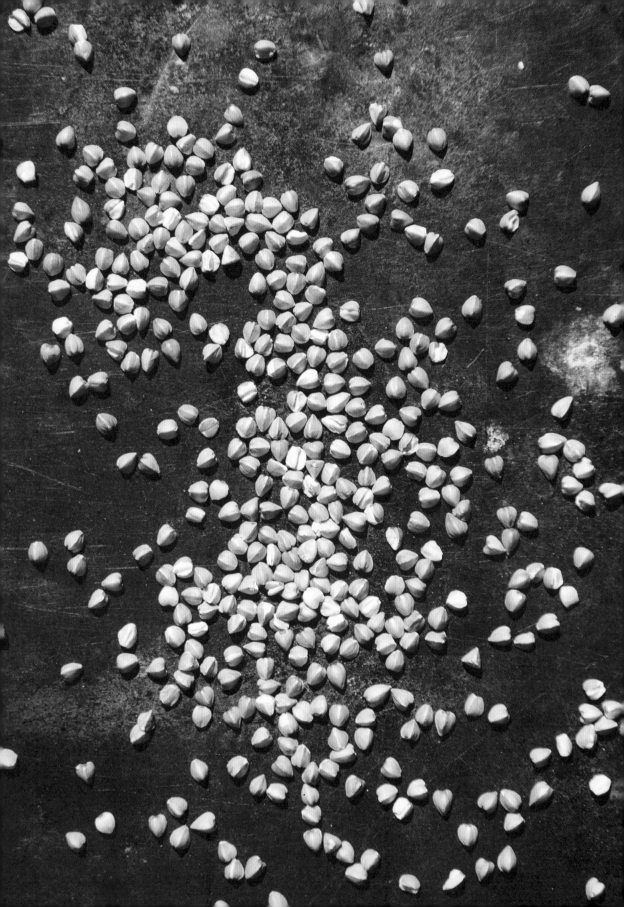

buckwheat

I often create characters out of ingredients, ascribing little personalities to each one, which presumably, though subconsciously, affects how I cook with them. Such attributes can be assigned due to their physical traits (long and tall celery playing Julia Child), their place of origin (flageolet beans conversing with a Parisienne accent and often smoking a cigarette), or simply how they are used in my kitchen (olive oil always speaking in heavy, rounded tones, matching my glugs).

Buckwheat is no exception—a wizened woman wearing a babushka wearied from having to claw sustenance from ungenerous soil. The little grains with their geometric edges spoke to me of poverty and what could be grown during short summers between long winters. The characteristic "earthy" flavor was a polite way of implying they were unrefined compared to the genteel wheat.

I'm not alone in my bias against buckwheat. Most people I asked in my (very unscientific) study associated it with the leaden breads of back-to-the-land, homesteader culture or the morning slog of hippie, all-shades-of-brown granola when all that was craved was the unending rainbow of sugary cereals. The kicker: Most respondents could not remember the last time they ate buckwheat.

Buckwheat is becoming an ever more important part of crop rotation and product for grain growers. Buckwheat is a green manure—a quick decomposing cover crop that adds nutrients back into the soil. Buckwheat production decreased dramatically in the twentieth century, but, until that point, buckwheat was used in rotation to build soil health and fertility. When, with the introduction of synthetic fertilizers, the productivity of other staple grains increased, the need for buckwheat as a rotator decreased.

Buckwheat is also used as a natural herbicide and erosion preventer. It grows quickly, outpacing most weeds. Once it reaches maturity, it can be cut and left as downed "green carpet," which both suppresses the weeds it outpaced and decomposes over the winter, adding organic matter when tilled back into the spring soil.

Because of buckwheat's shorter growing season, only 10 to 12 weeks from seed to harvest, it is an incredibly flexible grain for growers. It can be planted after an early crop is harvested—filling the gap before a winter crop needs to be planted. It can also go in late, which is a savior if spring rains keep fields flooded past the date other crops need to be planted.

For many growers, buckwheat isn't a viable option because the market doesn't seek out the grain. If they can't sell the crop and its benefits don't economically outweigh synthetic inputs, there is little incentive to add buckwheat back into the mix. However, increased interest in ancient grains and the rise of gluten-free needs has translated to an uptick in buckwheat production. The more of us who come to appreciate buckwheat, whether for health or convenience, the more demand there is for the pseudocereal, making it a viable option to more and more growers who face a changing climate and desire to limit synthetic agricultural inputs.

In short, buckwheat is basically perfect in every way; she just suffers from a bad reputation. She cooks up lightning quick—boiled tender in under 20 minutes. She's gluten free—not a wheat after all. She grows in almost all parts of the world and is a valuable piece of the crop rotation puzzle. Get to know her and come to love her.

NOTES

BOTANICAL NAME: *Fagopyrum esculentum*

PLACE OF ORIGIN: Southeast Asia

TOP GLOBAL PRODUCERS: Russia, China, Ukraine, and France

GLUTEN FREE: Yes

PROTEIN CONTENT: 13 percent

TO SOAK OR NOT TO SOAK (THAT IS ALWAYS THE QUESTION):
No need. Buckwheat cooks very quickly unsoaked.

BASIC WATER:GRAIN RATIO FOR STEWING: 2:1

AVERAGE BOILING TIME: 12 to 15 minutes

YIELD RATIO AFTER COOKING: 1:3

SIGNS OF DONENESS: The grains will be puffy and tender to the bite.

NOTES: Despite the name, it is not a wheat. Buckwheat is in the same family as rhubarb and sorrel.

Buckwheat has a tough, dark hull on the outside. If left intact, it adds grittiness (and a dark color) to buckwheat flour and increases cooking times of the whole grain dramatically.

If buckwheat (grain or flour) has been hulled, it is often light or slightly greenish in color.

Buckwheat flour oxidizes quickly, so store it in the fridge or freezer. The more it oxidizes, the "earthier" the flavor.

BOILED

Buckwheat cooks very quickly in boiling water, in about 15 minutes or so, whether it is toasted or raw. Raw buckwheat is greener in color and has a grassier flavor. Toasted buckwheat, a.k.a. kasha, is much darker in color and nuttier in flavor. Like all boiled grains in this book, simply bring a pot of salted water to a boil, toss the grains in, stir to keep them from sitting at the bottom of the pot, and drain when tender. Know, too, that several shakes of Tajín over the whole thing is a fine substitution for the flavored oil.

seared chicken thighs w/buckwheat, smashed cucumbers + tajín oil

The angular mouthfeel of the buckwheat plays well with the crunch of the cucumber and against the crisp of the chicken thigh. Serve the buckwheat warm or chilled, depending on your preference. If you aren't eating meat, the salad is a great lunch on its own or pairs well with an egg or fried tofu.

1 cup [250 g] buckwheat groats, toasted or not

Olive oil

2 medium cucumbers (about 1 lb [450 g] total), washed

¼ cup [60 ml] Tajín Oil (page 40)

Salt and freshly ground black pepper

¾ cup [180 ml] plain yogurt, Greek or traditional

1 lemon (about 1½ oz [45 ml]), zest and juice

10 sprigs parsley, roughly chopped

Any additional herbs you want, roughly chopped (mint, tarragon, thyme, cilantro)

Pinch of chili flakes (optional)

4 to 6 chicken thighs

Bring a large pot of salted water to a rolling boil over high heat. Toss in the buckwheat groats and give the pot a stir. Return to a boil, lower to a simmer, and cook the grains until tender, 8 to 15 minutes.

continued

Drain the groats, toss with a glug of Tajín oil, and set aside.

Trim the ends of the cucumbers and place on a cutting board. Using the widest knife (or frying pan) you have, press down on the cucumbers until their skin cracks and they break into irregular pieces. Dress the cucumbers with the Tajín oil and a pinch of salt.

Combine the yogurt with the lemon zest and juice, chopped herbs, chili flakes (if using), a pinch of salt, and two big glugs of olive oil. Set aside.

Blot the chicken skin dry and season with salt and pepper.

Heat a large frying pan over high heat until the pan is starting to smoke. Add a glug or two of oil, lower the heat to medium, and fry the thighs, skin-side down, until golden brown, 5 to 7 minutes. Flip the chicken and sauté until cooked through, 5 to 7 minutes more.

To serve, dish the buckwheat onto serving plates. Top with the chicken thighs and then the dressed cucumbers. Garnish with a thick spoonful of the herbed yogurt.

variations

salmon w/roasted squash + ras al hanout apricot almond rig

Neutral oil	2 cups [400 g] boiled or sprouted buckwheat	1 cup [225 g] Ras el Hanout Apricot Almond Rig (page 49)
1 side of salmon or four 5 oz [150 g] fillets	1 to 2 delicata or acorn squash, cut into wedges or half-moons and roasted until tender	
Salt and pepper		

Heat a large frying pan over medium-high heat. Add a glug of oil. Season the salmon liberally with salt and then sear it, skin-side down, until golden and crispy, 4 to 5 minutes. Flip and cook until medium or medium rare, 2 to 3 minutes more.

To serve, spoon the cooked buckwheat onto a plate or serving platter, pile up the roasted squash next to the buckwheat, place the fish skin-side up, and spoon the apricot almond rig all over.

w/poached egg, kale + lemon tahini dressing

5 kale leaves, cut into ribbons	½ cup [100 g] cooked or sprouted buckwheat	1 egg, poached or soft-boiled
Salt	¼ cup [60 g] Lemon Tahini Dressing (page 36)	

Sprinkle the kale with salt and massage until the leaves are tender and dark green.

Combine the kale with the buckwheat and tahini dressing and toss to distribute evenly. Taste the salad and adjust the seasoning as desired.

Top with the egg and eat while the egg is warm.

w/raw asparagus, radishes + brown butter vinaigrette

½ cup [100 g] cooked or sprouted buckwheat	3 radishes, any variety, shaved into thin rounds	5 sprigs parsley, roughly chopped (optional)
4 spears asparagus, shaved into ribbons	¼ cup [60 g] Brown Butter Vinaigrette (page 35)	Salt and freshly ground black pepper

Combine the buckwheat, asparagus, radishes, vinaigrette, and parsley (if using) and toss to coat evenly. Season with salt and pepper. Serve sooner rather than later because the salt will wilt the asparagus and radishes.

SPROUTED

Buckwheat sprouts the same way as other grains—soak for a bit, cover loosely, and rinse a couple times a day until you see the little tails—but because it is a bit thicker of a grain, it can take up to three days to get the tails. I soak them in warmer water than most to jump-start the process. Heads up: Toasted buckwheat (a.k.a. kasha) will not sprout. The toasting process disallows the germination that occurs when soaking and rinsing.

buckwheat w/dried cherries + hazelnuts over warm parsnip purée

This grain salad adds a good deal of crunch and tang to the decadently rich (but mercifully simple) parsnip purée. I like it with a side salad or with some greens chucked right on top. The parsnip purée holds in the fridge for about a week and freezes very well if making a big batch.

1 cup [250 g] untoasted buckwheat groats

1 onion, thinly sliced

Salt and freshly ground black pepper

½ cup [125 ml] white wine or hard cider

3 lb [1.35 kg] parsnips, peeled and cut into chunks

2 cups [500 ml] heavy cream

½ cup [80 g] dried cherries

1 shallot, minced

¼ cup [60 ml] balsamic vinegar

½ cup [65 g] hazelnuts, toasted and smashed

1 sprig rosemary, finely chopped

½ cup [125 ml] olive oil, plus more as needed

A generous handful of arugula, watercress, or other tender greens (optional)

Soak the buckwheat groats in warm water for 15 minutes. Drain, rinse, and transfer to a bowl or storage container, cover with a tea towel, and let sit until you see the tails start to form (rinsing the groats a couple of times a day to remoisten and wash away any gelatinous goo on the outside of the groats), 2 to 3 days.

continued

In a medium saucepan, heat a glug of olive oil over medium-low heat. Add the onion and ½ tsp of salt and sweat until soft. Add the wine and reduce until almost dry. Add the parsnips and cream and bring to a simmer. Cover the pot halfway with a lid and let simmer until the parsnips are tender, about 15 minutes.

Using a food processor or an immersion blender, purée the mixture until very smooth. Adjust the seasoning as desired.

Soak the cherries and shallot in the balsamic vinegar and a pinch of salt for 10 minutes. Combine the cherry mixture with the hazelnuts, rosemary, olive oil, a couple pinches of salt, and several grinds of black pepper.

Just before serving, combine the sprouted buckwheat with the hazelnut rig. Dish the purée into serving bowls and top with the buckwheat-cherry mixture and a handful of greens, if using.

variations

w/a soft egg, shredded carrot, kale + pickle liquid dressing

Grate a carrot on the largest tooth of a box grater. Cut a few leaves of kale into ribbons, sprinkle with salt, and massage until tender. Combine ½ cup [125 g] of sprouted (or boiled) buckwheat with the carrot, kale, and a ¼ cup [60 ml] of Pickle Liquid Dressing (page 37), adding a pinch or two of salt and black pepper. Top with a softly cooked egg and serve.

w/radishes, parsley + mushroom cream sauce

Shave a couple of radishes into thin rounds. Roughly chop a few sprigs of parsley. Combine the radishes and parsley with ½ cup [125 g] of sprouted (or boiled) buckwheat and a pinch of salt. Top with ½ cup [125 ml] of Mushroom Cream Sauce (page 44) and serve warm.

w/tomatoes, shaved summer squash, basil + parmesan

Take a handful of cherry tomatoes or one large tomato and cut into bite-size chunks. Shave half a summer squash into thin ribbons. Tear 2 basil leaves and shave 10 or so ribbons of Parmesan. Combine all the ingredients plus ½ cup [125 g] of sprouted (or boiled) buckwheat with a hefty glug of olive oil and a couple pinches of salt and toss together, adjusting the seasoning as desired. Serve as a light lunch salad or alongside any sort of grilled protein for a bigger meal.

FRIED

Maybe the best reason to boil (or sprout) more buckwheat than needed is to crisp up the extra and add those crunchy groats to just about anything. Two things to note: One, pat or air-dry the groats so that when they hit the hot oil they don't spit and spatter unnecessarily; two, you can have too much of a good thing—an entire salad of crisped buckwheat is a bit like eating gravel, so keep the buckwheat crispies to an accent on a larger salad.

roasted sweet potatoes w/fried buckwheat + harissa

Harissa can be made in large batches and kept in the fridge and at the ready for months on end. It can also be replaced here with a standard chili oil, or by simply roasting the sweet potatoes with chili flakes, if you are short on time.

2 to 4 sweet potatoes (about 3 lb [1.35 kg])

½ cup [125 ml] neutral oil, for frying, plus more as needed

Salt

½ cup [125 g] cooked or sprouted buckwheat, air-dried or blotted dry

Harissa (page 47)

Cilantro or parsley, chopped (optional)

Preheat the oven to 400°F [200°C].

Cut the sweet potato into large wedges, toss with a couple glugs of neutral oil and a couple pinches of salt, and roast until caramelized and tender, 25 to 35 minutes, depending on the thickness of the potato.

continued

In a medium frying pan, heat the neutral oil over medium-high heat until shimmering. Add the buckwheat and fry until golden brown and crunchy. Remove from the heat and add a few pinches of salt.

To serve, place the sweet potato wedges on a serving platter or plates, spoon the harissa over the top liberally (depending on your spice preference), and scatter the crisped buckwheat all over. Top with a handful of roughly chopped herbs, if desired. Serve warm or at room temperature.

variations

w/roasted asparagus + marinated mushrooms

Roast a bunch of asparagus spears (I usually allow almost ½ lb [225 g] per person, but we eat a lot of asparagus) after tossing the spears in a glug or two of olive oil and several pinches of salt. When the asparagus is done, spoon a bunch of the Marinated Mushrooms (page 56) over the asparagus and top with several sprinklings of crispy buckwheat.

w/tomatoes, ricotta + rosemary lemon chili mojo

Take several tomatoes of different colors and shapes and cut into thick slabs. Arrange on a large serving platter and sprinkle with salt. Dot spoonfulls of ricotta all over. Scatter crisped buckwheat over the top. Spoon Rosemary Lemon Chili Mojo (page 50) over the whole thing and serve.

w/red cabbage, cilantro, a poached egg + tajín oil

Shave a quarter head of red cabbage into thin ribbons. Chop up a bunch of cilantro and toss the cabbage and cilantro with about a ¼ cup [60 ml] of Tajín Oil (page 40). Season with salt. Top with a softly cooked egg (either poached or soft boiled), scatter a bunch of crisped buckwheat over the top, and eat while the egg is still warm.

FLOUR

Buckwheat can be ground into flour either with the dark hull or without. The differences between the two are primarily the color and texture. Buckwheat flour that includes the hull is much darker and will always cook up to a dark gray or brown. Buckwheat flour that is light in color has had the hull removed. As it ages, it will oxidize and turn more yellow. So, if you are buying pre-ground buckwheat flour, look for dark brown or bright white and either use it up quickly or store it in the freezer to prevent oxidization.

buckwheat crepes

Brittany, France, is the traditional home of buckwheat crepes. The thin pancakes make good use of the texture of gluten-free flour. The slightly nutty flavor of the buckwheat plays well with both sweet and savory fillings and especially well with the salty butter of the region.

The real "trick" of making crepes is getting the right heat on the pan. When you ladle in the batter and swirl it around, you want to hear a gentle sizzle but not have so much heat that it browns the pancakes. Luckily, this recipe makes about 20 small crepes or 10 pan-size crepes, so you'll have time to practice (which makes perfect). Additionally, the finished pancakes freeze very well and so are good contenders for pulling from the freezer as a pinch hitter when you need a fast dinner. Finally, a couple of notes: Don't be put off by the amount of butter in the recipe; it keeps these from sticking to the pan. This batter is considerably thinner than pancake batter; that's what allows for the easy spread as you swirl the pan. Have your ingredients at room temperature.

1 cup [155 g] buckwheat flour

¾ cup [180 ml] whole milk

3 large eggs

¼ cup [55 g] butter, melted

¼ tsp salt

continued

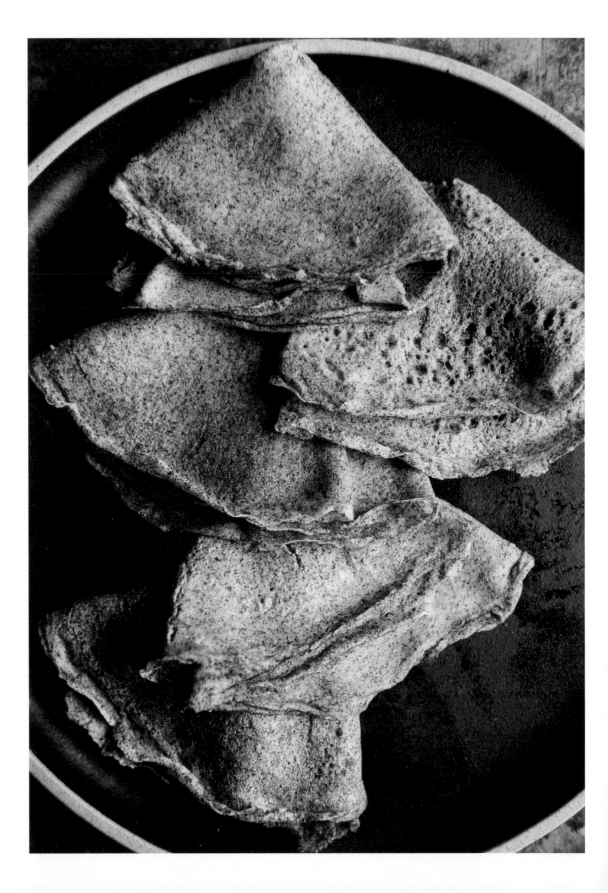

In a medium bowl, combine the flour, 1 cup [250 ml] of water, the milk, eggs, butter, and salt and whisk until free of lumps. Or blend with an immersion blender until smooth.

Heat an 8 inch [20 cm] frying pan (or two if you are up for it) over medium heat. Ladle about ¼ cup [60 g] of batter into the center of the frying pan, lift the pan, and swirl it to spread the batter evenly over the surface. Return the pan to the heat and allow the crepe to cook through, 2 to 3 minutes.

When the top of the crepe looks dry, use a small spatula or butter knife to lift the edge of the crepe and flip it over (you can also skip the flip, allowing it to get fully dry, but you'll be more likely to get some browning on the pan side of the crepe).

Allow the crepe to finish cooking, about 30 seconds, and then slide it from the pan onto a rack or tray to cool.

To fill the crepes, either place the filling on one side of the crepe and flip it in half to serve (like a diner omelet), schmear the filling all over and fold the crepe into quarters, place the filling on one edge and roll the crepe like a tube, or place the filling in the center and fold up the edges of the crepe to make an open-faced square. I like to fill the crepes and then either place them in a baking dish and warm them in the oven before serving or pan fry the folded crepes to create golden brown crunchy edges.

variations

w/cherry tomato conserva + ricotta

Spoon about 2 Tbsp of ricotta into the center of the cooked crepe. Top with a spoonful of Cherry Tomato Conserva (page 52) and fold up the edges of the circle to make an open-faced square. Warm in the oven (or pan fry for a crispy bottom) and just before serving, top with a couple of torn basil leaves or roughly chopped parsley leaves.

continued

w/mascarpone + berries

Whip some mascarpone with a splash of cream and a couple drips of honey. Spoon into the center of the crepe and fold or roll up to make a tidy rectangular package. Transfer to the oven to warm. Remove from the oven and top with a handful of fresh berries or a couple spoonfuls of jam and serve.

w/fried egg + sautéed kale

Soften some sliced onion in butter with a pinch of salt. Add several handfuls of kale cut into ribbons and cook until bright green. Add a splash of white wine or hard cider and let it evaporate completely. Spoon the kale into the center of the crepe and fold up the edges. Transfer to the oven to warm. Fry an egg and top the crepe with the fried egg to serve.

w/ratatouille + gruyère

Fill the crepe with Ratatouille (page 57) and top with a handful of grated Gruyère or other melty cheese. Transfer to the oven to melt the cheese and then serve.

w/goat cheese, shaved brussels sprouts + hazelnut rig

Fill the crepe with a hefty spoonful of goat cheese and fold up the crepe. Transfer to an oven to warm or pan fry. Shave a few Brussels sprouts (3 to 4 per person) thinly and dress with a glug of olive oil, a pinch of salt, and a grind of black pepper. To serve, top the crepe with the Brussels sprouts and spoon some Hazelnut Rig (page 47) over the top.

corn

Jim Harrison once wrote an essay detailing a conversation he had with his mother about the semantics between polenta and cornmeal mush. They are the same thing—ground cornmeal that is slowly cooked to a porridge consistency—but it was the name that changed.

"Do you want a bowl of cornmeal mush?"

"It is called polenta now."

"Mush has always been fine by me."

I respect his mother's sentiment. She didn't need the Italians to validate a dish that she had been cooking and eating happily for years. I also understand wanting to feel like what we eat in our homes mirrors the food traditions of others. Sometimes we adopt, sometimes we draw parallels, sometimes we can't be bothered.

Words matter, maybe least of all on menus, but even there they represent our culture and how we choose to showcase it. I don't like it when menus substitute words like aioli for mayonnaise because people don't like mayo but are fine with aioli (which is technically a very garlicy mayo made with a portion of olive oil worked in; see recipe on page 38). I don't like it when menus add fancily redundant descriptors like "hen's egg" when no rooster has ever threatened to encroach on the hen's sphere of influence. I don't like the tendency to skew menus to Italian or French words simply because it sounds sophisticated. I am proud of midwestern food traditions and the simplicity of calling a spade a spade.

But then there was the time that I put *Turkey Neck Sauce over Cornmeal Mush* on a menu. It was a nod to Harrison and the pinnacle of my #sorrynotsorry phase. Several other cooks read the menu and paused there, not saying a thing. Then it was my husband who finally broke it to me: "I don't think that 'neck' and 'mush' are doing you any favors here."

He was right. I begrudgingly changed the menu item to read *Turkey Collar and Tomato Sauce over Corn Porridge.* Compromise never feels like a total win, but it is certainly something to strive for. In the end, all of this is just a little story to encourage you to eat a warm bowl full of cooked cornmeal. You decide what to call it.

NOTES

BOTANICAL NAME: *Zea mays*

PLACE OF ORIGIN: Mexico

TOP GLOBAL PRODUCERS: United States, China, and Brazil

GLUTEN FREE: Yes

PROTEIN CONTENT: 8 to 15 percent, depending on variety

TO SOAK OR NOT TO SOAK (THAT IS ALWAYS THE QUESTION): No need because it is ground. Soaking hominy will decrease cooking time by half.

BASIC WATER:GRAIN RATIO: 4:1

AVERAGE BOILING TIME: When added to boiling water just after turning off the heat, 1 hour of passive cooking

YIELD RATIO AFTER COOKING: 1:1.5

SIGNS OF DONENESS: The cornmeal will have absorbed all of the liquid and will be tender, not grainy when tasted.

CORN

FIELD CORN

NOT A TECHNICAL CATEGORY OF CORN BUT A TERM USED COLLOQUIALLY TO INDICATE THAT WHEN YOU SEE BIG FIELDS OF CORN, IT'S NOT SWEET CORN. WHEN YOU SEE BIG FIELDS OF CORN, THAT'S FIELD CORN. SWEET CORN IS OFTEN GROWN IN SMALLER PATCHES AND HAND-HARVESTED DURING THE MILK STAGE, WHEREAS MOST FIELD CORN IS ALLOWED TO DRY ON THE COB IN THE FIELD AND THEN HARVESTED MECHANICALLY.

POPCORN

SPECIFIC VARIETIES OF CORN THAT MAINTAIN A BIT OF MOISTURE IN THE CENTER OF THE DRIED KERNELS THAT, WHEN HEATED, CONVERTS TO STEAM AND "POPS" THE KERNEL. IT IS POSSIBLE TO POP OTHER VARIETIES OF CORN, BUT WITH A LOWER SUCCESS RATE. IT IS ALSO POSSIBLE TO GRIND POPCORN AND USE IT LIKE OTHER CORNS.

SWEET CORN

HIGH SUGAR AND MOISTURE CONTENT, SO EAT IT FRESH OR PRESERVE BY FREEZING, PICKLING, OR DRYING.

DENT CORN

LOW SUGAR, HIGH STARCH CORN WITH A DIMPLE OR DENT IN THE MIDDLE OF EACH KERNEL THAT FORMS AS IT DRIES OUT. CAN ALSO BE FERMENTED INTO ANIMAL SILAGE OR USED FOR ETHANOL PRODUCTION. OFTEN, THE CORN IS GROWN AND PROCESSED DIFFERENTLY BASED ON THE END GOAL OF THE KERNELS.

FLINT CORN

APTLY NAMED BECAUSE THE OUTSIDE OF EACH KERNEL DRIES TO BE HARD AS FLINT.

CORN FLOUR

CORN WITH THE HIGHEST STARCH CONTENT, USUALLY DRIED AND GROUND INTO CORNSTARCH FOR BAKING AND THICKENING SAUCES.

GROUND CORN

COARSE: POLENTA (THE HARD SHELLS LEND TO THE DISTINCT POLENTA TEXTURE)

HOMINY

FLINT CORN THAT HAS GONE THROUGH NIXTAMALIZATION—TREATED WITH AN ALKALI—TO CHANGE THE STRUCTURE OF THE CORN, WHICH ADDS DIETARY CALCIUM AND MAKES THE NATURALLY OCCURRING NIACIN EASILY DIGESTIBLE.

GROUND

COARSE: HOMINY GRITS
FINE: MASA IS CORNMEAL MADE FROM GROUND HOMINY THAT IS USED TO MAKE TORTILLAS AND TAMALES.

BOILED

For the longest time, cooking polenta or grits was my least favorite kitchen task. Inevitably throughout the process I was burned by molten hot porridge spitting from the pan. Said porridge, flung from the pot, would adhere to the kitchen wall (sometimes the ceiling). More often than I like to admit, the bottom of the pot would scorch, rendering the whole process futile.

To avoid all this, I devised a way to cook corn porridge with very minimal active heat, minimizing the potential for burning ourselves or the grits. Bring a pot of salted water four times the volume of grits you want to cook to a rolling boil, whisk in the ground corn, turn off the heat, and let the hot water hydrate the grits over the course of an hour or so. It worked perfectly and continues to be my preferred method to this day.

corn porridge w/mushroom cream sauce + spinach

I generally don't add milk or cheese to corn porridge for two reasons. One, I like to keep the porridge tasting mostly of corn and find that excess cream dulls the sweet corniness. Two, the dairy increases the likelihood that I will burn the porridge even if I keep it over low heat. But corn and cream really love each other, so any sort of creamy sauce is right at home spooned on top of a big bowl of jiggly grits.

2 cups [320 g] ground cornmeal	6 oz [180 g] fresh spinach, torn if the leaves are large or unruly	1 recipe Mushroom Cream Sauce (page 44)

continued

In a large stockpot, bring 8 cups [2 L] of salted water to a rolling boil. Whisk briskly to make a whirlpool, then add the cornmeal, whisking until evenly distributed and not clumping. Cover the pot, remove from the heat, and let the cornmeal continue to cook and hydrate in the pot, about 1 hour.

Check the porridge and cook longer if you'd like it thicker. When done, keep over low heat to keep warm until ready to serve.

To serve, dish the corn porridge into individual bowls and top each with a big pile of fresh spinach and a hefty ladleful of mushroom sauce.

variations

w/fresh tomato, marinated eggplant + arugula

Make the corn porridge as in the base recipe. Cut up 1 medium tomato or a handful of cherry tomatoes per person into large chunks. Toss the tomatoes with the Marinated Eggplant (page 54) and a pinch of salt if desired. Dress a handful of arugula per person with a glug of olive oil and a pinch of salt and pepper. Spoon the corn porridge into a bowl. Top with the tomato eggplant mixture and finish with a handful of the arugula.

w/pork sunday gravy + massaged kale

I love using corn porridge in place of pasta or mashed potatoes to catch the juices of a rich, meaty sauce. Use any sort of pork ragu or Sunday gravy or Bolognese sauce you like. For the massaged kale, allow half a bunch of kale per person. Strip the leaves from the stems and cut into ribbons. Sprinkle with a bit of salt and then rub the ribbons between your hands until they are dark green and tender. To serve, spoon the porridge into serving bowls and top each with about ½ cup [125 g] of sauce and a portion of the greens.

w/sautéed greens + a fried egg

In a hot pan, heat a glug of neutral oil, then add several big hand-fuls of greens like kale, mustard, chard, or any of the chicories and a pinch of salt and chili flakes. When the greens are about half wilted, add a couple of glugs of white wine to soften the rest of the way. Then fry an egg. Top a bowl of porridge with the greens and the fried egg.

I usually serve this in individual portions, sautéing the greens in one pan and frying the eggs in another. If you want to serve it as a platter—say, for brunch—I recommend sautéing the greens in a large enough pan that you can then transfer them to a bowl, transfer the corn porridge to the pan, top with the greens, and crack the eggs (1 per person) over the top and bake in a hot oven to cook the eggs.

what to do with leftover grits (or porridge, polenta—whatever you call it)

grit dumplings + braised greens

Olive oil

1 small onion (about 4 oz [120 g]), thinly sliced

3 garlic cloves, chopped or minced

Salt

10 leaves kale, collards, or mustard greens, stemmed and cut into ribbons

2 cups [500 ml] stock or water

1 cup [200 g] cooked grits

1 egg

½ cup [60 g] all-purpose flour

½ tsp baking powder

Parmesan, for garnish (optional)

Heat a glug of olive oil in a frying pan over low heat. Sweat the onion and garlic with a big pinch of salt. Add the greens and braise with the stock until the leaves are dark green and tender, about 7 minutes.

Mix the leftover cooked grits with the egg, flour, baking powder, and a pinch of salt. Scoop into golf ball– or matzo ball–size lumps. Poach by floating in a pot of lightly simmering water until cooked through, about 4 minutes. To serve, dish the dumplings and greens into serving bowls and garnish with grated Parmesan (if using).

crispy grit cakes w/tomato, ricotta + herb salad

Line a baking sheet with parchment paper or plastic wrap. Spread the leftover grits across the sheet, pressing down in an even layer about 1 in [2.5 cm] thick, and chill overnight. When ready to fry, turn the slab out onto a cutting board and cut into 3 in [7.5 cm] squares. Heat a big glug of neutral oil over medium heat and pan fry the grit cakes until golden brown and warm all the way through. Serve with diced large tomato or halved cherry tomatoes, dots of Citrus Ricotta (page 43), and a handful of picked or chopped herbs on top. (I also like plain ricotta and any herby mojo if you have it on hand.)

gritcinis w/giardiniera mayo

1 cup [200 g] cooked grits, cooled	2 oz [60 g] Cheddar cheese	¼ cup [60 g] Giardiniera (page 53)
1 egg, beaten	4 oz [120 g] bread crumbs or panko	¼ cup [60 g] Basic Mayo (page 37)

Combine the grits and egg into an even dough that holds its shape, adding more beaten egg to bind if needed. Scoop the grits into golf ball–size rounds. Cube the Cheddar cheese and stuff the center of each gritcini with a cube. Roll the stuffed gritcini in bread crumbs and then freeze until solid to set the shape, 1 hour to overnight.

Deep-fry or bake the gritcini until golden brown and warm through-out. Blend the giardiniera and the mayo to make a thick relish the texture of tartar sauce. Serve the gritcinis with a dollop of the mayo on top or on the side.

FLOUR

Cornmeal may be the most quintessential North American ingredient. Corn was domesticated by Native Americans around 5000 BCE. Ground more finely than for polenta or grits, cornmeal makes crumbly, delicate bread and can be used in place of wheat for hoecakes. Different colored types of corn yield flours ranging from deep blue to white to almost pink from the red flecks from the outside hull. As with all ground grains, look for a local (preferably stone) mill and buy flour with the germ still intact. It is more volatile but also more flavorful.

all-corn cornbread w/jalapeños, peaches + ricotta

I've got a few Andrews in my life, and several of them influenced this recipe. I got the cornbread recipe from my friend Andrew Brix and use it as a regular staple for meals with guests who eat gluten free. The jalapeño peaches come from one of my first food teachers, Andrew Wilhelm, in our time together at Zingerman's Deli. Andrew Harris (along with Wes Rieth) grows the heirloom corn at Granor Farm that is now my go-to cornmeal. Thanks, Andrews.

3 cups [480 g] cornmeal

6 Tbsp [90 g] butter or lard or chicken fat

½ tsp salt, plus a pinch

1 Tbsp baking powder

1 egg, lightly beaten

2 medium peaches (about 12 oz [340 g]), sliced into wedges

1 jalapeño, sliced into very thin rings, seeds removed if you like it milder

1 Tbsp sugar

¼ tsp vanilla paste or extract

6 oz [180 g] ricotta

Preheat the oven to 450°F [230°C]. Put a medium ovenproof frying pan in the oven to preheat.

continued

Put half of the cornmeal (1½ cups [240 g]) into a heatproof bowl.

In a saucepan, add the butter and the ½ tsp of salt to 2 cups [500 ml] of water and bring to a boil.

Pour the boiling water mixture into the bowl of cornmeal. Whisk together and let stand for 1 minute.

Add the remaining cornmeal and the baking powder and egg to the cornmeal batter and whisk together.

Remove the frying pan from the oven and pour in the batter. Bake for about 30 minutes until the bread has a golden crust on top and a knife comes out clean when inserted in the center. Turn out onto a cooling rack.

Combine the peaches, jalapeños, sugar, vanilla, and the pinch of salt and let sit for 10 minutes to macerate.

To serve, cut the cornbread into wedges, dollop with the ricotta, and top with a hefty spoonful of the peach mixture.

variations

w/tomato, kale + goat cheese vinaigrette

Cut 2 large tomatoes into large chunks. Cut 10 or so stemmed kale leaves into ribbons. Combine the tomatoes and kale with several spoonfuls of Goat Cheese Vinaigrette (page 36) and toss to coat. Adjust the seasoning. Serve the salad with a large wedge of cornbread on the side or underneath.

w/poached or fried egg, mushroom cream sauce + tender greens

Cut the cornbread into wedges and place each wedge in a medium serving bowl. To serve, spoon warm Mushroom Cream Sauce (page 44) (about ½ cup [125 ml] per person) over the wedge and top with a poached or fried egg. Take a handful of tender greens (like spinach or arugula or whatever you have on hand) and top the cornbread with the greens.

w/peperonata + herb salad

Top the cornbread with about ½ cup [125 ml] of Peperonata (page 56) per person and a large helping of picked herbs (like parsley, cilantro, mint, arugula, or basil) and serve as an appetizer.

spoon pudding w/pork chops + cabbage salad

Spoon bread or spoon pudding has the same basic ingredients as cornbread. Increasing the amount of liquid (water and milk) and the amount of fat (milk and butter) and lowering the baking temperature yields a more soufflé-like texture that must be "spooned" out of the baking dish, unlike a sliceable cornbread. Spoon bread can be made on its own and served as a side or can be studded with other ingredients throughout the seasons.

FOR THE SPOON PUDDING

¾ cup [120 g] cornmeal

1 tsp salt

4 Tbsp [60 g] butter, melted

2 eggs, beaten

1 cup [250 ml] milk

2 tsp baking powder

FOR THE SALAD

½ head (about 1 lb [450 g]) red cabbage, shaved into thin ribbons

¼ cup [60 ml] olive oil

10 sprigs parsley, roughly chopped

1 lemon (about 1½ oz [45 ml]), zest and juice

½ tsp chili flakes

½ tsp paprika

Salt

4 pork chops, seasoned with salt and pepper and grilled

To make the spoon pudding: Preheat the oven to 350°F [180°C]. Grease an ovenproof baking dish or frying pan that can hold about 2 qt [2 L] total volume.

Combine the cornmeal, salt, 1 cup [250 ml] of boiling water, and the melted butter and whisk out any lumps. Combine the eggs, milk, and baking powder and add to the cornmeal batter. Pour into the prepared baking dish and bake until the edges of the spoon bread are just set and lightly browned, 30 to 40 minutes.

To make the salad: Combine the cabbage with the olive oil, chopped parsley, lemon zest and juice, chili flakes, paprika, and a couple pinches of salt. Toss to combine and adjust the seasoning as desired.

Serve the spoon bread alongside the grilled pork chops and cabbage salad.

hoecakes w/fresh mozzarella, tomato + soybeans

In *The Story of Corn*, Betty Fussell writes that colonial settlers saw cornmeal batter as "the sad paste of despair," bemoaning the lack of more refined wheat batters. One time, I had friends over and what I thought was chickpea flour for socca turned out to be cornmeal. I had already mixed equal parts of the flour and water, and it did look exactly like a sad paste. Not quite despairing, I took inspiration from my friend and Lexington, Kentucky–based chef, Ouita Michael, and fried up the batter. It yielded delightfully crispy, craggy cakes that paired perfectly with our succotash. Note: If your cornmeal is very fine, you can probably skip the wait for the cornmeal to hydrate.

1 cup [160 g] cornmeal

½ tsp salt

¼ cup [60 ml] olive oil, plus more for frying

1 ball (8 oz [225 g]) fresh mozzarella, torn into rough chunks

1 cup [180 g] green soybeans, blanched or left raw

1 lb [450 g] cherry tomatoes, cut into quarters

5 leaves basil, mint, cilantro, and/or parsley, roughly chopped or torn

Salt and freshly ground black pepper

Preheat the oven to 200°F [95°C] to keep the cooked hoecakes warm.

Whisk together the cornmeal, 1 cup [250 ml] of boiling water, and the salt. Let stand for 5 to 10 minutes to hydrate the cornmeal.

You'll fry the cakes in batches, just like pancakes. Heat a large frying pan over medium-high heat. Add ½ cup [125 ml] or so of olive oil (I know—it takes more than you might think). Pour the batter into the hot olive oil, making cakes about 6 in [15 cm] across. Turn down the heat to medium-low. Allow the batter to set on the edges and start to look dry in the center. Flip and brown the other side. Transfer the hoecakes to a baking sheet and hold in the warm oven.

continued

Combine the mozzarella, soybeans, tomatoes, herbs, ¼ cup [60 ml] of olive oil, and a couple pinches of salt and grinds of black pepper.

Remove the cakes from the oven and serve piled high with the tomato-soybean salad.

variations

w/gingered apples + manchego

Top the hoecakes with a spoonful of Gingered Apples (page 54) and shavings of Manchego.

w/giardiniera

Serve the hoecakes topped with Giardiniera (page 53) sprinkled over each cake. Maybe add some greens or shaved vegetables such as radish, cauliflower, Brussels sprouts, or cabbage.

w/fresh tomatoes + citrus ricotta

Serve the hoecakes with a schmear of Citrus Ricotta (page 43) and some halved cherry tomatoes.

HOMINY

Hominy is field corn that has gone through nixtamalization—soaking in an alkali solution, like water with lye, lime, and pot or wood ash. The solution softens the kernel's skin, puffs up the corn to almost double the size, and makes the corn more nutritious because the niacin it contains can now be easily absorbed by the body. After this process, the hominy is either dried or canned. Like beans, hominy can be used straight from the can or rehydrated from dried and cooked—simply boil with water and season with salt after the grains are tender. Coarsely ground hominy is often used for grits; finely ground is masa, used to make tortillas, tamales, and such.

For this recipe, seek out country ribs—they are cut from the blade end of the pork shoulder, which makes them rich and meaty. If you can't find country ribs, you can substitute spare, but cook more per person. If you're cooking for a big group, a whole pork shoulder can be cooked the same way as the ribs—rubbed with spices and slow roasted at a low temperature until falling-apart tender, which will take much longer than the smaller rib pieces.

paprika-honey country ribs w/hominy + lemon parsley mojo

8 country pork ribs (about 4 lb [1.8 kg])

¼ cup [15 g] Smoky Spicy Mix (page 41)

¼ cup [75 g] honey

2 cups [360 g] cooked or canned hominy

1 lb [450 g] red cabbage, shaved thinly

1 recipe Lemon Parsley Mojo (page 48)

Salt

continued

Rub the ribs all over with the spice mixture and, if possible, let cure for at least 4 hours.

Preheat the oven to 300°F [150°C]. Put the pork in a roasting pan, uncovered, and slow roast until the meat is tender when pulled with a fork, about 45 minutes. The outside will have a deeply colored, crispy crust.

When the pork is tender, remove from the oven and drizzle with the honey.

Turn on the broiler to high and char the ribs under the broiler to create a slightly burnt crust, about 3 minutes.

Combine the hominy, red cabbage, and half the mojo with a pinch of salt.

To serve, place the hominy salad on a serving platter, top with the pork, and spoon the remaining mojo over the top.

variations

w/black beans, summer squash, basil + mojo de ajo

2 medium summer squash, shaved thinly	½ cup [100 g] Mojo de Ajo (page 48)	1 cup [180 g] cooked or canned hominy, warmed
10 basil leaves, roughly torn	Salt	1 cup [280 g] basic black beans (page 95), warmed

Combine the summer squash with the torn basil, mojo, and a pinch of salt. Adjust the seasoning as desired.

To serve, spoon the hominy and black beans into a serving dish and top with the squash salad.

continued

w/peperonata + arugula

2 cups [360 g] cooked or canned hominy	1 cup [240 g] Peperonata (page 56)	Olive oil
		Salt
	4 oz [120 g] arugula	

Warm the hominy and the peperonata.

Dress the arugula with a glug of olive oil and a pinch of salt.

Spoon the hominy into a serving bowl, top with the peperonata, and garnish with the arugula salad (adding a poached or soft-boiled egg would be very nice here too).

w/seared chicken thighs, radish salad + smoked yogurt

4 to 6 chicken thighs (2½ lb [1.2 kg] total)	½ cup [125 ml] chicken stock or water	½ cup [125 ml] Smoked Yogurt (page 45)
Salt	5 radishes, shaved thinly or cut into matchsticks	5 sprigs parsley, chopped (optional)
2 cups [360 g] cooked or canned hominy		

Preheat the oven to 400°F [200°C]. Heat a medium frying pan over medium-high heat. Sprinkle the chicken thighs liberally with salt. Pan fry the thighs skin-side down until golden brown, 5 to 7 minutes. Remove the thighs from the pan.

Add the hominy and stock and bring to a boil.

Place the chicken thighs, skin-side up, on top of the hominy. Transfer the frying pan to the oven and roast until the chicken thighs are cooked through, about 12 minutes.

Combine the radishes and the yogurt (and add that handful of chopped parsley, if using).

To serve, place a portion of the hominy and a thigh on each dinner plate and top with the radish salad.

POPCORN

Popcorn pops because a tiny bit of moisture is held in the kernels. When heated, that water evaporates, causing steam. As it expands and forces its way out, the kernel explodes. Homemade popcorn is not only fast, easy, and way cheaper than any other option but also the only way to control the exact amount of butter, cheese, salt, and so on that goes on your corn.

ck special pop

Named for our dear friend Colin Kerr, who perfected the art of popcorn well before the rest of us. The only change that I've made is to use the very hot pan from popping the corn to melt the butter and soften some garlic.

½ cup [100 g] popcorn kernels

Neutral oil

4 oz [120 g] butter

2 garlic cloves, minced

Salt and freshly ground black pepper

Parmesan or Cheddar for grating

In a large stockpot, combine 2 or 3 popcorn kernels and a couple glugs of neutral oil over medium-high heat. Cover with a lid. When the kernels pop, add the rest of the popcorn, replace the lid, and shake the pan to evenly coat and distribute the kernels in the pot.

Lower the heat to medium-low and let the corn cook, shaking the pot every 30 seconds or so. Cook until the popping has subsided.

Pour the popped popcorn into a bowl and wipe out the pot with a dry towel.

continued

Add the butter to the hot pot (off the burner) to melt. When melted, add the garlic and a pinch of salt. Let the garlic soften, about 1 minute.

Meanwhile, sprinkle the popcorn with salt, several grinds of black pepper, and several gratings of cheese.

When the garlic is soft, add the melted butter to the popcorn and toss to coat evenly.

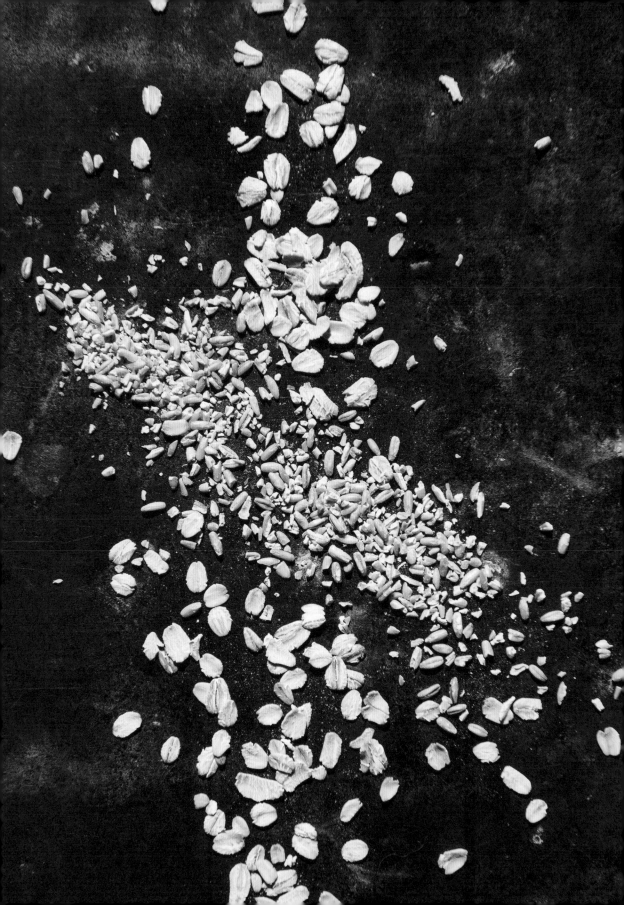

oats

In every farmer interview for this book, I've asked, "What do you wish nonfarmers knew about farming?" My friend and colleague Wesley Rieth responded, as he usually does, in an extremely thoughtful way, and at just that moment, my voice memo app stopped working (and I wasn't taking handwritten notes). I emailed him to ask if he could repeat his thoughts. He sent me this:

So, what do I wish nonfarmers knew? That there is no such thing as an agnostic farmer. Each farmer possesses some deep-seated belief, however repressed or expressed it might be, that their work is inseparable from an inherent purpose far greater than their own self. "Belief" seems like the proper term here because farming instills in us a certain type of illogical, unreasonable, and by most accounts unwise hope that each growing season holds the intoxicating promise of growing and cultivating and harvesting like we never have before. This is why farming, as an occupation, and all the things that go with it—farm policy, farm owner-ship, farm economics, farm health, and so on—are so very complex. A farmer does not just carry on their shoulders the burden of a physically demanding job; each carries with them the history, the dreams, the connections, the family, the obligations, the vision, and the knowledge that they have been given from those before them. My own suspicion is that human will alone is not strong enough to carry this burden through years of unprofitability, debt, consolidation, physical and emotional pain, and untimely death; it is only with the addition of belief that farmers are able to remain ready, even hopeful, for the years that lie ahead of them.

It is this idea of belief and being tied to something larger than oneself that has been the unspoken underpinning of so many of these conversations. To work to feed people, to work to be a good steward of the land and the land downstream, to follow, expand, and pass on the traditions of this work.

This seems no more relevant than when talking about oats. In 1950, Iowa farmers planted 6.6 million acres of oats; in 2020 it was 120,000 acres. Production has shrunk so much that Iowa-based Quaker Oats now imports the grain from Canada. Oats were often grown as feed for the horses, hogs, and chickens that were part of a diversified farm. Oats, grown in conjunction with red and white clover, acted as fertilizer and weed suppressant. Tractors replaced horses. Hogs and chickens were consolidated into their own mass-produced farms. Synthetic fertilizers and herbicides replaced crop rotation. Corn and soy were supported via agricultural research and farm policy, and oats faded from the scene.

Enter oat milk. Forget for a moment the hubbub about whether or not it should be called milk; it is no secret that the market is expanding rapidly. To make oat milk, one needs oats. Oats were an important part of the crop rotation, especially on dairy farms, which are now the fastest folding sector of American agriculture. There is a very thin timeframe between production and consumption for dairy. The margins are tiny, and most dairymen see the best way to ensure profitability is through increased scale—adding more head of cattle to the operation and earning through volume because the prices are low.

The Swedish nondairy, dairy company Hälsa has been actively seeking oats from American dairy farmers to provide them an additional revenue stream to keep them in business. This isn't altruistic. Dairy farmers are some of the last growers to give up growing oats because it feeds their cows, so they still have the relevant knowledge and equipment to grow oats in a volume needed for a multinational corporation.

I'm not expert enough to say whether or not oat milk will change the way that American grain growers farm, but it feels exciting that it might. I agree with Wes: every grower I know sees their work in terms of their own lives but also a greater good that pushes forward innovation toward a future we can't always see but that we hope the next generation will. Who knows? Maybe it's oat milk that will keep herdsmen farming.

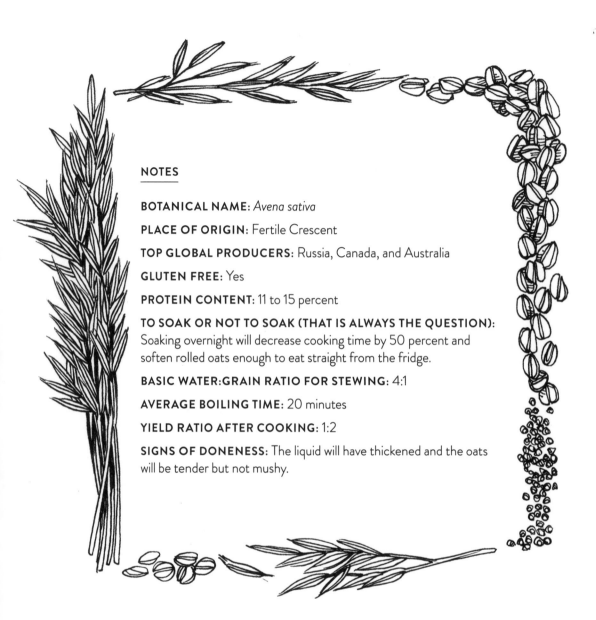

NOTES

BOTANICAL NAME: *Avena sativa*

PLACE OF ORIGIN: Fertile Crescent

TOP GLOBAL PRODUCERS: Russia, Canada, and Australia

GLUTEN FREE: Yes

PROTEIN CONTENT: 11 to 15 percent

TO SOAK OR NOT TO SOAK (THAT IS ALWAYS THE QUESTION): Soaking overnight will decrease cooking time by 50 percent and soften rolled oats enough to eat straight from the fridge.

BASIC WATER:GRAIN RATIO FOR STEWING: 4:1

AVERAGE BOILING TIME: 20 minutes

YIELD RATIO AFTER COOKING: 1:2

SIGNS OF DONENESS: The liquid will have thickened and the oats will be tender but not mushy.

OATS

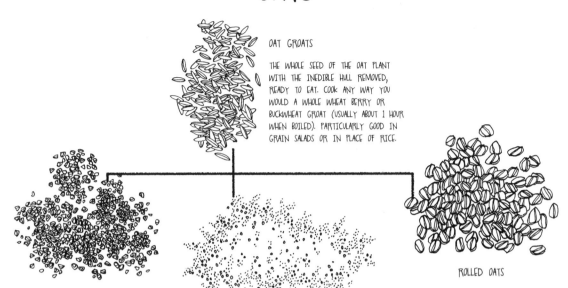

OAT GROATS

THE WHOLE SEED OF THE OAT PLANT WITH THE INEDIBLE HULL REMOVED, READY TO EAT. COOK ANY WAY YOU WOULD A WHOLE WHEAT BERRY OR BUCKWHEAT GROAT (USUALLY ABOUT 1 HOUR WHEN BOILED). PARTICULARLY GOOD IN GRAIN SALADS OR IN PLACE OF RICE.

STEEL CUT (A.K.A. IRISH) OATS

WHOLE OAT GROATS ARE CUT INTO A FEW PIECES WITH SHARP METAL BLADES. COOKING TIME IS DECREASED TO ABOUT 25 MINUTES BECAUSE THE PIECES ARE SMALLER. THE COOKING LIQUID WILL ALSO BECOME CREAMIER BECAUSE THE STARCH WILL COMBINE WITH THE COOKING LIQUID MORE EASILY.

STONE GROUND (A.K.A. SCOTTISH) OATS

WHOLE OAT GROATS GROUND ON A STONE MILL BUT LEFT VERY COARSE. COOKING TIME IS 10 TO 15 MINUTES BECAUSE THE PIECES ARE SMALLER THAN STEEL CUT. THE TEXTURE IS ALSO CREAMIER BECAUSE THE STARCH IS EVEN MORE ACCESSIBLE FROM THE MILLING.

ROLLED OATS

WHOLE OAT GROATS ARE SOFTENED BY STEAMING AND THEN FLATTENING THEM THROUGH A ROLLER MILL. STEAMING STABILIZES THE HEALTHY OILS, MAKING THE OATS SHELF STABLE WITHOUT REFRIGERATION WHILE MAINTAINING THEIR HEALTH BENEFITS.

OLD-FASHIONED ROLLED OATS

COOKING TIME IS SIMILAR TO STONE GROUND OATS. THE STEAMING PARTIALLY COOKS THE OATS AND THE ROLLING INCREASES THE SURFACE AREA WHILE DECREASING THE DENSITY, MEANING THE WATER CAN PENETRATE AND COOK THE ENTIRE FLAKE MORE QUICKLY.

FLOUR

OATS GROUND INTO A FINE POWDER VIA A MILL, BLENDER, OR FOOD PROCESSOR. USED IN BAKING AND AS A GOOD COATING FOR PANFRIED FOODS.

QUICK COOKING OATS

SAME AS "OLD-FASHIONED" OATS BUT STEAMED FOR LONGER AND ROLLED THINNER TO DECREASE THE COOKING TIME EVEN FURTHER. USUALLY CAN BE FULLY COOKED IN UNDER 5 MINUTES.

INSTANT OATS

STEAMED UNTIL FULLY COOKED, ROLLED EVEN THINNER THAN QUICK COOKING OATS, THEN DEHYDRATED TO MAKE SHELF STABLE. OFTEN HAVE A CREAMIER TEXTURE THAN QUICK COOKING OATS. CAN BE PREPARED BY SIMPLY POURING BOILING WATER OVER THE OATS AND LETTING THEM REHYDRATE.

PORRIDGE

Oats have a very annoying tendency to boil over despite my best efforts. Erik once had them boil over on him while he was stirring (and looking at his phone simultaneously). I've tried all the old wives' remedies and have found the only thing that works is to use a saucepan that is slightly larger than you think you need so that there is enough volume in the pot for the oats to boil up and not go over the edge.

cut oatmeal w/brown sugar, heavy cream + salt

My best friend Tim Mazurek always has a bottle of Drambuie on hand. "For the oatmeal!" he insists. Adding a shot of the honeyed and slightly spicy whiskey brings complexity to a morning's bowl of porridge on its own or with any number of toppings. Oats' slightly savory nature also plays well with salty garnishes.

1 cup [200 g] steel-cut or ground oats	2 oz [60 ml] Drambuie or other whiskey or brandy	½ cup [125 ml] heavy cream
	Coarse salt	Brown sugar

In a medium saucepan (a bit larger than you might think), dry toast the oats over medium heat until lightly browned, stirring now and then, about 1 minute. Add the whiskey and let cook off completely.

Add 4 cups [1 L] of water with a pinch of salt and bring to a boil. Lower to a simmer and cook until the water is absorbed and the oats are tender, about 30 minutes (half as long if soaked overnight).

Transfer to serving bowls and top with a hearty splash of cream, a sprinkle of brown sugar, and a large pinch of crunchy salt.

continued

variations

w/fruit compote + sour cream

Replace the cream/brown sugar/salt topping with a hefty scoop of Fruit Compote (page 53) and an equal size scoop of sour cream and serve.

w/a basted egg, sautéed kale + cheddar

2 oz [60 g] (per person) Cheddar, grated	4 leaves (per person) kale, washed and cut into ribbons	Salt and freshly ground black pepper
Neutral oil		¼ tsp chili flakes
		1 egg (per person)

Add the Cheddar to the prepared oatmeal and stir to melt. In a frying pan, heat a glug of neutral oil over high heat until almost smoking. Sauté the kale with a pinch of salt and the chili flakes until wilted. Lower the heat to medium and make a little nest with the kale. Crack the egg into the kale nest and season with salt and pepper. Place a lid on the frying pan to steam baste the egg, then transfer the kale/egg nest on top of the oatmeal and serve.

w/roasted mushrooms, cherry tomato conserva + fresh spinach

2 oz [60 g] (per person) mushrooms, pan roasted until tender and caramelized	¼ cup [60 g]) (per person) Cherry Tomato Conserva (page 52)	Olive oil
		Salt and freshly ground black pepper
	1 oz [30 g] (per person) spinach	

Dish up the oatmeal and top with the roasted mushrooms and tomato conserva. Dress the spinach with a glug of olive oil, a pinch of salt, and a grind of black pepper. Top the whole thing with the spinach and serve.

PAN FRIED

I remember being a young cook and taking the leftover polenta home from work—pressing it diligently into a baking sheet and then cutting into squares to pan fry. Proudly announcing, upon serving the crispy-edged squares to my dinner guests, "This was going to be thrown out." That self-satisfaction continues to this day when I come up with another way to repurpose leftovers. And with that, I present oatmeal gnocchi. Essentially the same as polenta cakes or panisse, but with oatmeal.

crispy gnoatcchi w/cherry tomatoes, creamed mozzarella + mint almond relish

Just about any food will hold its shape and get crunchy on the outside if fried in enough oil, but an extra coating of dry flour on the outside helps the process along. If you don't want to take the time to blitz up some oat flour, feel free to skip or substitute wheat flour or finely ground cornmeal.

2 cups [400 g] cooked steel- or stone-cut oats, pressed into a greased container and chilled until firm

½ cup [50 g] rolled oats, pulsed in a food processor to make a coarse flour, or ½ cup [60 g] all-purpose flour

Neutral oil, for frying

Salt and freshly ground black pepper

1 lb [450 g] cherry tomatoes, halved, or 2 cups [480 g] Cherry Tomato Conserva (page 52)

1 recipe Mint Almond Relish (page 48)

Two 6 oz [180 g] balls fresh mozzarella, torn into irregular chunks

½ cup [125 ml] heavy cream or sour cream

continued

Preheat the oven to 200°F [95°C]. Line a plate or baking sheet with paper towels. Flip the sheet of gnoatcchi onto a cutting board and cut into 4 rectangles or square logs. Dredge the cut gnoatcchi logs in the oat flour and set on the paper towels.

In a large frying pan, add ¼ in [6 mm] of oil and heat over medium heat until it begins to shimmer, about 1 minute.

Working in batches, gently slide the dredged gnoatcchi logs into the hot oil and fry until the fried side is golden brown, 3 to 4 minutes. Flip the logs and fry the other side until equally golden, another 2 to 3 minutes. Lift the logs from the oil, season with a sprinkle of salt, return to the paper towels, and place in the oven to keep warm.

Just before serving, add the cherry tomatoes to the almond relish and toss gently.

Combine the mozzarella with the cream and a pinch of salt and a grind of black pepper.

To serve, place the gnoatcchi logs on a serving platter or individual plates, nestle a couple of pieces of the creamed mozzarella next to the logs, and top with the almond relish.

variations

poached salmon w/gnoatcchi, arugula + hazelnut rig

Prepare the oat gnocchi as in the basic recipe.

To poach the salmon, cut up an onion or two and some slices of lemon or herbs if you have them. Lay the aromatics in the bottom of a pan that will fit the salmon fillets snugly. Place the salmon skin-side down and add enough water to just cover the fish. Heat over medium heat just until you see the first bubbles of the water coming to a boil. Then turn off the heat, leave uncovered, and let the fish finish poaching until it tests anywhere from medium to fully cooked. Lift the fish from the poaching liquid (and slip the skin off if you like).

To serve, dress a handful of arugula with a glug of olive oil and a pinch of salt. Place a crispy gnoatcchi on the plate and top with the fish, the arugula, and a few spoonfuls of Hazelnut Rig (page 47).

w/peas, mushrooms, greens + buttermilk

Prepare the gnoatcchi the same way but double the portion per person.

In a large frying pan, roast 1 lb [450 g] of any type of mushrooms (cut any way you prefer) in plenty of olive oil until golden brown and crispy. Add 1 cup [200 g] of frozen or fresh peas and ½ cup [125 ml] of white wine and cook until the peas are bright green, about 4 minutes. Season with salt.

To serve, place the gnoatcchi on a serving platter or plate. Spoon the mushroom and pea mixture over the top. Dress tender lettuce leaves with a couple of glugs of buttermilk and pinches of salt and black pepper.

w/tuna mayo, carrot salad + giardiniera

Prepare the gnoatcchi the same way. Shave a couple of carrots (ideally of different colors) into ribbons with a vegetable peeler. Dress the carrots with a healthy glug of olive oil, ½ cup [100 g] Giardiniera (page 53), and a pinch of salt.

To serve, dollop the gnoatcchi with the Tuna Mayo (page 38) and top with the carrot salad.

BAKED

My favorite dishes are everyday ingredients rejiggered with unexpected flavors, textures, or temperatures. Baked oats may be the most illustrative example of that love. Granola—nothing new there. Salty, spiced granola layered with fresh vegetables and decadent cheese—mundane no more. See the Flavor Formula on page 294 for inspiration.

savory granola

For brunch, I found myself growing very tired of yogurt and granola, so I started topping all sorts of dishes with granola. This recipe doubles easily and stores well. It can also be made with any spice mixture (like the ones on pages 39–42) and lots of other seeds (like flax, chia, sesame). This can also be made in a 350°F [180°C] oven by tossing all the ingredients together and baking until the oats are golden brown, about 10 minutes.

¼ cup [60 ml] olive oil

1 tsp smoked paprika

½ tsp ground coriander seed

½ tsp ground fennel seed

½ tsp nigella seed (optional)

1 cup [100 g] rolled oats

1 tsp honey

½ tsp Za'atar (page 42, optional)

¼ tsp salt

5 sprigs thyme, leaves picked (optional)

Up to 1 cup [120 g] any additional seeds or nuts you want to add

In a medium frying pan, heat the olive oil over medium heat. Add the paprika and the coriander, fennel, and nigella seeds (if using) and fry in the oil to bloom, about 30 seconds.

Add the oats, toss in the spiced oil, and sauté, stirring occasionally, over medium heat until toasty and fragrant, about 3 minutes.

Add the honey, za'atar, salt, and thyme leaves (if using) and toss to coat. Cook for another 2 minutes. Remove from the heat, add any additional seeds or nuts, toss to combine, and let cool.

Once cool, store in an airtight container at room temperature but out of direct sunlight (which will warm the jar and soften the oats) for up to 2 weeks.

mollie's granola

Mollie Hayward is the food-styling force behind every picture in both *Ruffage* and now *Grist*. When she arrived at my house for the very first *Ruffage* photo shoot, she had a jar of granola in hand for snacking. I thought, *I have yet to find a granola I actually want to eat.* When we broke for an afternoon coffee and quick bite, I ate one handful of her granola and then another and then another. It is perfectly sweet while walking the salty line, so it pairs well with savory food too. This is now the only fruit granola I make at home, at work, for gifts, and beyond. Mollie was willing to share it with you all, word for word (and of course made the photo of it beautiful). Note: Ovens vary, so to be on the safe side, start checking your granola for doneness at 15 minutes.

2 cups [200 g] rolled oats

1 cup [120 g] sliced nuts or seeds (I usually use pepitas)

¾ cup [90 g] sunflower seeds (I usually use salted and roasted because it's what I have, but it's fine with any kind)

¼ cup [60 ml] canola oil

½ cup [150 g] honey

Pinch of salt

1 cup [120 g] dried fruit (I love cranberries or cherries, something with some tartness)

Preheat the oven to 300°F [150°C]. In a large bowl, combine the oats, nuts, sunflower seeds, canola oil, honey, and salt. Spread the mixture on a half sheet tray (sometimes I use a silicone mat and sometimes I don't; it works both ways, so now I generally don't bother). Bake, stirring occasionally, until the honey is deeply caramelized, the whole mess is golden, and the granola stops sticking to a wooden spoon, 20 to 30 minutes, checking after 15 minutes.

Remove from the oven, stir in the fruit, and let it sit for a little while before you start scraping it up if you want big chunks. Cool completely before storing in an airtight container for up to 2 weeks.

how to build a myriad of granola-topped dishes

1.	2.	3.
START WITH PRODUCE	**ADD A FAT**	**ADD ANOTHER POP OF FLAVOR**
Roasted parsnips	Citrus Ricotta (page 43)	Arugula leaves (peppery)
Melon wedges	Creamed Mozzarella (page 43)	Shaved ham or prosciutto
Spinach	Poached egg	Anchovy Vinaigrette (page 35)
Grilled green beans	Herbed Yogurt (page 45)	Marinated Summer Squash (page 56)
Ratatouille (page 57)	Za'atar Chili Oil (page 40)	Herb salad
Cucumber planks	Feta slabs	Olive Rig (page 49)
Roasted winter squash wedges	Goat Cheese Vinaigrette (page 36)	Pickled Dried Cherries (page 57)
Roasted carrots	Sage Fried Brown Butter (page 50)	Hazelnut Rig (page 47)

4.

TO SERVE

Lay the parsnips on a serving platter, dot with the ricotta, dress the arugula with a glug of olive oil, and scatter the granola on top.

Lay the melon wedges on a platter, spoon the creamed mozzarella on top, tuck in the shaved ham, and sprinkle with granola.

Dress the spinach with the anchovy vinaigrette, top with the egg, and finish with a big handful of granola.

Toss the green beans and marinated summer squash together, spoon the herbed yogurt all over, and garnish with granola.

Dish up the ratatouille, spoon the spice oil on top, and garnish with a fluff of herb salad and handful of savory granola.

Lay the cucumber and feta on a platter, spoon the olive rig all over, and garnish with savory granola.

Toss the roasted winter squash, goat cheese vinaigrette, and pickled cherries together and garnish with granola.

Lay the carrots on a platter, spoon the hazelnut rig on top, and garnish with crunched-up fried sage leaves and granola.

FLOUR

Making oat flour is truly as simple as blitzing up some oats in either a blender or food processor until it's, well, the texture of flour. Rolled oats grind faster than steel-cut or stone-ground, but either will work. If you want to make the flour coating more pronounced, blend them more coarsely. Happily, any other flour will substitute if need be.

oatmeal-encrusted perch w/tomato, cucumber + feta salad

I tried and tried to make this work without the addition of the egg, but alas, it just sticks better if you dredge the fish in egg and then press into the oat flour. If you are avoiding egg, I had decent results whipping the aquafaba from canned chickpeas instead, though the crust often slipped off the fish a bit.

½ cup [125 ml] neutral oil, plus more for frying

1 tsp smoked paprika

1 tsp cumin seed

½ tsp chili flakes (optional)

1 cup [100 g] oats (rolled, stone-ground, or steel-cut)

Salt

1 lb [450 g] perch fillet

2 eggs, whisked

1 lb [450 g] cherry or slicing tomatoes, halved or cut into chunks

2 medium cucumbers (1 lb [450 g]), half-peeled and cut into ¾ in [2 cm] thick wedges

4 oz [120 g] feta, crumbled

1 shallot or small onion (about 2 oz [60 g]), minced

10 sprigs parsley, roughly chopped

Heat ¼ cup [60 ml] of the neutral oil in a small saucepan over medium-high heat until it shimmers. Add the paprika, cumin seed, and chili flakes (if using) and allow to bloom in the hot oil until fragrant, about 1 minute.

Remove from the heat and add the remaining ¼ cup [60 ml] of neutral oil to cool the mixture. Let steep for 10 minutes.

In a blender or food processor, blitz the oats to a fine powder, then transfer to a bowl or small baking sheet. Add a pinch or two of salt to the flour.

In a large frying pan, heat about ½ in [12 mm] of neutral oil over medium-high heat until it shimmers. Set a rack over a tray or line a baking sheet with paper towels to drain the fried fish.

Dip the fish fillets in the whisked egg and then in the oat flour. Shallow fry the fish until the oats are golden, 4 to 5 minutes, then flip and fry the other side. Repeat in batches until all the fish is fried, transferring to the prepared draining tray.

Combine the tomatoes, cucumbers, feta, shallot, and parsley with several spoonfuls of the spiced oil and a couple of pinches of salt. Toss to combine and adjust the seasoning as desired.

To serve, transfer the fish to a serving platter or plates, top with the tomato salad, and add another spoonful of the spiced oil as desired.

continued

variations

chicken breasts w/peas + mushroom cream sauce

4 skinless, boneless chicken breasts (about 2 lb [900 g])	Neutral oil, for frying	Salt
	½ cup [125 ml] white wine	1 lemon (about 1½ oz [45 ml]), zest and juice
2 eggs, whisked	1 onion (about 8 oz [225 g]), thinly sliced	
1 cup [100 g] oat flour	1 lb [450 g] shelled peas	1½ cups [375 ml] Mushroom Cream Sauce (page 44)

Lay the chicken breasts between two layers of plastic wrap and pound to an even thickness, about ¼ in [6 mm]. Preheat the oven to 200°F [95°C]. Dip the chicken breasts in the egg mixture and then the oat flour.

Heat ½ in [12 mm] of oil in a large frying pan over medium heat until shimmering. Fry the chicken breasts until golden brown on both sides and cooked through, 2 to 4 minutes. Remove from the pan and hold in the warm oven until ready to serve.

Add the white wine to the frying pan to deglaze. Add the onions and peas with a big pinch of salt and cook until the onions are soft and the peas are bright green, about 4 minutes. Add the lemon zest and juice and the mushroom sauce. Allow to warm fully and adjust the seasoning as desired. To serve, top the chicken breasts with the pea-laden mushroom sauce.

eggplant w/peperonata + lemon caper mayo

1 to 2 medium eggplant (about 2 lb [900 g]), cut into rounds or long planks	½ cup [125 ml] Basic Mayo (page 37)	2 cups [500 ml] Peperonata (page 56), warmed
	1 cup [100 g] oat flour	¼ cup [60 ml] Lemon Caper Mayo (page 37)

Slather the cut sides of the eggplant with the mayonnaise, then press them into the oat flour to coat. Pan fry or bake until the eggplant is cooked through and an inviting shade of brown.

continued

To serve, place the eggplant on serving plates, top each with a healthy scoop of peperonata, and garnish with the lemon caper mayo.

pork cutlets w/parsnip purée, arugula + hazelnut rig

1 onion (about 8 oz [225 g]), thinly sliced	3 lb [1.35 kg] parsnips, peeled and cut into chunks	2 eggs, whisked
Salt		1 cup [100 g] oat flour
Butter	1 cup [250 ml] heavy cream	Olive oil
½ cup [125 ml] white wine		2 oz [60 g] arugula
	4 pork cutlets (about 2 lb [900 g]), pounded to even thickness	½ cup [125 ml] Hazelnut Rig (page 47)

In a medium pot, sweat the onions with a pinch of salt in a knob of butter over medium heat. Add the white wine and cook until almost dry. Add the parsnips and toss to coat.

Add the cream and cover with a cartouche (parchment paper lid), turn down the heat to low, and simmer until tender, 20 minutes.

Transfer to a food processor and process to a very smooth purée. Adjust the seasoning as desired and set aside.

Dip the pork cutlets in the eggs, then the oat flour. Pan fry until cooked through and enticingly brown and crisp on the outside, about 4 minutes.

Dress the arugula with a glug of olive oil and a pinch of salt. To serve, spoon the parsnip purée onto a platter or individual plates, top with a pork cutlet, top with the arugula, then spoon the hazelnut rig over the whole thing.

MILK

Oat milk has truly changed my afternoon routine. I used to drink coffee with a heart-stopping amount of half-and-half in it. Now I froth up a bit of oat milk every afternoon for my 3 p.m. decaf coffee.

The oil in the recipe helps the oat milk hold a froth. Feel free to omit as you see fit. I used to soak the oats for 10 minutes before blending, but it makes the whole thing a bit slimier. I also no longer strain the oat milk. I don't mind the flecks of oat, and it makes me feel very self-righteous to have gotten even more fiber into a cup of coffee while avoiding any food waste.

oat milk base recipe

½ cup [50 g] rolled oats   2 Tbsp [30 ml] neutral oil

Whiz together the oats and oil with 2 cups [500 ml] of water in a blender until very smooth.

That's literally it. You can strain it if you want, but I don't bother.

It will separate, so shaky shaky before you pour it.

Store in the fridge for up to a week or until it goes sour, which is very unpleasant, so you'll know when it's happened.

rice family

Ages and ages ago, I sat in on a cooking class my friend Rose Hollander taught. Demonstrating a handful of recipes that were integral to her time in Singapore, she also gave this informational tidbit that has always stuck with me—in many parts of Asia, the traditional greeting translates to "Have you eaten rice today?" Imagine a comestible so much a part of a culture that it opens every conversation. Imagine an ingredient so important that it travels from its place of origin, in this case the Chinese Yangtze River Basin, to the Indian subcontinent to the Italian Po River Valley and then on to the Americas.

　　Maybe it's because I grew up in more of a potato family— we grew potatoes, we didn't grow rice. I never really thought about rice that much until, when interviewing Rachel Roche for this chapter, I asked if and how she eats the rice she grows in the Louisiana bayou. She responded, "Well, I'm Cajun," implying that her cultural identity is, in part, signified by rice as her daily sustenance. Something so consistent, it could even be a greeting.

rice, basmati and jasmine

It was rice that started it all. In cooking school, I spent a lot of time trying to memorize the different water-to-grain ratios for cooking rice. How much for pilaf, how much for steamed, how much for long grain, how much for short? I could never remember. I never bought a rice cooker. I rarely cooked rice.

Then, years later, my friend and fellow cook, Allison Scott, said, "Oh, I never bother with that anymore and just cook it like pasta. I don't rinse it either because it is cooking in such an abundance of water that the extra starch is rarely an issue."

Lightning bolt. Never went back. Now I cook rice all the time.

It was Christina Chaey who made lightning strike twice. She said, "Cook any grain in copious amounts of salted water for good results." Different ingredient, same technique—that makes sense in my brain. I continued down that path, and here we are, four hundred-some odd pages later.

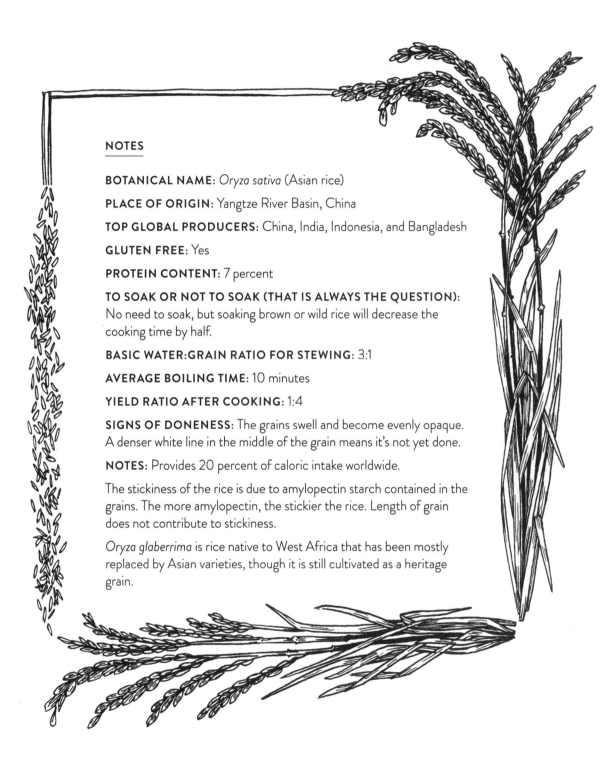

NOTES

BOTANICAL NAME: *Oryza sativa* (Asian rice)

PLACE OF ORIGIN: Yangtze River Basin, China

TOP GLOBAL PRODUCERS: China, India, Indonesia, and Bangladesh

GLUTEN FREE: Yes

PROTEIN CONTENT: 7 percent

TO SOAK OR NOT TO SOAK (THAT IS ALWAYS THE QUESTION): No need to soak, but soaking brown or wild rice will decrease the cooking time by half.

BASIC WATER:GRAIN RATIO FOR STEWING: 3:1

AVERAGE BOILING TIME: 10 minutes

YIELD RATIO AFTER COOKING: 1:4

SIGNS OF DONENESS: The grains swell and become evenly opaque. A denser white line in the middle of the grain means it's not yet done.

NOTES: Provides 20 percent of caloric intake worldwide.

The stickiness of the rice is due to amylopectin starch contained in the grains. The more amylopectin, the stickier the rice. Length of grain does not contribute to stickiness.

Oryza glaberrima is rice native to West Africa that has been mostly replaced by Asian varieties, though it is still cultivated as a heritage grain.

RICE

RICE IS THE SEED FROM AQUATIC GRASSES. ANY VARIETY CAN BE RED/BLACK, BROWN, OR WHITE. THE RED OR BLACK HAVE THE EXTERIOR HULL STILL IN PLACE. BROWN RICE HAS THE HULL REMOVED BUT THE BRAN STILL INTACT. WHITE HAS HAD THE BRAN REMOVED, EXPOSING THE INTERIOR STARCH.

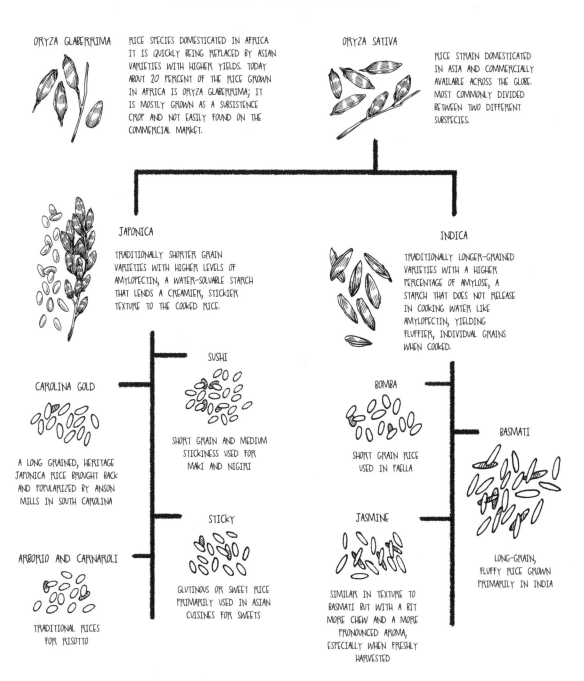

ORYZA GLABERRIMA

RICE SPECIES DOMESTICATED IN AFRICA. IT IS QUICKLY BEING REPLACED BY ASIAN VARIETIES WITH HIGHER YIELDS. TODAY ABOUT 20 PERCENT OF THE RICE GROWN IN AFRICA IS ORYZA GLABERRIMA; IT IS MOSTLY GROWN AS A SUBSISTENCE CROP AND NOT EASILY FOUND ON THE COMMERCIAL MARKET.

ORYZA SATIVA

RICE STRAIN DOMESTICATED IN ASIA AND COMMERCIALLY AVAILABLE ACROSS THE GLOBE. MOST COMMONLY DIVIDED BETWEEN TWO DIFFERENT SUBSPECIES.

JAPONICA

TRADITIONALLY SHORTER GRAIN VARIETIES WITH HIGHER LEVELS OF AMYLOPECTIN, A WATER-SOLUABLE STARCH THAT LENDS A CREAMIER, STICKIER TEXTURE TO THE COOKED RICE.

INDICA

TRADITIONALLY LONGER-GRAINED VARIETIES WITH A HIGHER PERCENTAGE OF AMYLOSE, A STARCH THAT DOES NOT RELEASE IN COOKING WATER LIKE AMYLOPECTIN, YIELDING FLUFFIER, INDIVIDUAL GRAINS WHEN COOKED.

SUSHI

SHORT GRAIN AND MEDIUM STICKINESS USED FOR MAKI AND NIGIRI

CAROLINA GOLD

A LONG GRAINED, HERITAGE JAPONICA RICE BROUGHT BACK AND POPULARIZED BY ANSON MILLS IN SOUTH CAROLINA

BOMBA

SHORT GRAIN RICE USED IN PAELLA

BASMATI

LONG-GRAIN, FLUFFY RICE GROWN PRIMARILY IN INDIA

STICKY

GLUTINOUS OR SWEET RICE PRIMARILY USED IN ASIAN CUISINES FOR SWEETS

ARBORIO AND CARNAROLI

TRADITIONAL RICES FOR RISOTTO

JASMINE

SIMILAR IN TEXTURE TO BASMATI BUT WITH A BIT MORE CHEW AND A MORE PRONOUNCED AROMA, ESPECIALLY WHEN FRESHLY HARVESTED

RACHEL ROCHE

Rachel Roche is a fourth-generation rice and crawfish farmer in Lake Arthur, Louisiana. Alongside her dad, she rotationally cultivates 300 acres every year on their 600-acre farm. The acreage left out of the rice production either lies fallow or is used for their growing crawfish operation. I didn't know anything about growing rice or farming in Louisiana and wanted to know how Rachel's day-in and day-out is similar to or different from that of growers in the Great Lakes region. Ms. Roche took the time to tell me about her farm (after working until sundown) in mid-March 2020.

Abra Berens: I'm born and raised in Michigan; rice is not a part of my agrarian culture. Can you walk me through a year in the life of a rice farmer?

Rachel Roche: It's spring now, which means we've been replowing fields that were prepped in the winter—getting fields ready to plant. Our last frost is usually mid-March. In a good year—meaning that fields are dry enough to get a tractor in and the weather is warm enough for germination—we'll start planting in mid-March and have everything drilled in by early April.

Rice growing depends on good water management. Our fields are connected by a network of irrigation ditches to flood and drain off the water throughout the season. In the spring, the rice needs water to germinate, so after planting, we flood the fields with just a bit of water.

When the flurry of planting ends, there's a bit of a slowdown as the rice takes root and starts to send up shoots. Then most of our job is managing the water levels of each field as well as weed and pest pressure on top of equipment maintenance.

Usually by late July and early August we'll start to drain the fields to get ready for harvest. At this point the rice plants are starting to turn from bright green to gold. Like everything in farming, it's about timing and weather. We need to keep water on the plants long enough for the rice to fully mature but not so long that the grains start to drop from the heads. Additionally, the fields need time to drain and dry so we can get cultivators in to cut the rice.

After cutting, the rice plants lie in rows on the field to dry; then a combine comes through to separate the grains from the plants. The grains are then transferred to the drying pits. Coming off the field, most grains of rice are at about 16 percent hydration. We need to dry them down to about 11 percent for proper storage and selling.

After the first cutting, we can flood the fields again and get a second crop. This comes from shoots of the already-cut plants and the whole process starts again, but faster, because we're not waiting on the plant to germinate and send up shoots. The plant is already there; it is just sending up secondary shoots.

In a good year, there will be a third crop from fallen rice grains that germinate while the fields are flooded for the second crop. This is all happening while we're physically shoveling the first crop rice from drying pit to storage bins, monitoring fields, fixing equipment, and sometimes sleeping and getting something to eat.

First frost is usually mid-November, after which we're working the fields again to prep them for spring before winter sets in. Dried-down rice is stored in the grain bins, and we're negotiating its sale. We work with an agricultural broker, in our case the Farm Bureau, so we sell to the broker and the broker sells it to the end user.

It's always a gamble when to sell, looking at prices commodity-wide, but then it can be six months before the rice is picked up. You can agree on a price, but we don't know what the actual dollar amount will be until the rice is graded at pickup.

AB: Are you paid any sort of down payment or retainer when you agree on a price?

RR: We don't get paid until the rice is picked up. We effectively get one paycheck a year. Ideally that paycheck covers the expenses of production and seed cost for the next year. Often money comes in after rice is already in the ground for the next season. Sometimes we're working to get last season's rice out of the bin to make room for this season's harvest.

AB: What are the biggest obstacles for you throughout the year?

RR: [*laughs*] What isn't? Mostly weather. We need the fields to be covered in water in a controlled manner. We've had four significant floods in the past three years. If that flooding happens when the plants are young, they can uproot. If it happens as we're trying to drain the fields, it delays harvest and causes downed plants, as their seed heads get heavier and heavier. If it storms in the days when the rice is cut and drying before we can cultivate the rice out of the field, that unleashes a whole host of problems.

AB: So you do hard, physical labor, often in the sweltering heat and humidity of a Louisiana summer, managing any number of variables out of your control, to get one paycheck, and you never know what that paycheck is going to be . . . why do this?

RR: Well, when you put it like that! [*laughs*] I like feeding people. It isn't like at a farmers' market where we are selling directly to people who go home and cook this food. But we grow food that feeds people. It's not biofuel or animal feed. Plus, I'm Cajun, so we eat a lot of rice!

AB: When you think to the future of your farm, what are you most excited about?

RR: I'm excited about finding more and more sustainable ways to grow. We know that climate change is real; we see the effects. I'm looking at finding ways to farm that have a positive impact on our environment. I don't know if I'll be able to. In a lot of ways, farming is an unnatural act. We grow a nonnative plant and are managing Mother Nature, who does what she wants, to produce high yields of rice that are consistent and uniform. That's not hunter-gathering. If we find that the cost of production outweighs the benefit, we'll quit. I just hope we never get to that point.

I'm also excited about growing the rice that I eat. I eat only Toro rice, but we don't grow Toro. It's a Louisiana rice, a long grain that cooks up fluffy and tender. The flavor is incredible. But I don't know anyone growing Toro rice.

AB: Where does your rice go?

RR: Last year, I think it was sold to the Mahatma rice company.

AB: What are the three things that you want nonfarmers to know about what you do?

RR: [**long pause**] I think people know that farming is hard work—not just physically, though that's true, but mentally. There's a lot of uncertainty: no two seasons are the same, we get paid once a year, etc. It takes an incredible amount of ingenuity and creativity to anticipate problems before they occur and find solutions to keep these plants alive. I think people think that farmers are kind of dumb. Like we can't figure out a better way to do it, so we just keep doing it the same way no matter the results.

AB: Yes. Modern American farmers are more Jeffersonian than people think. And it takes a tremendous amount of "institutional" knowledge to be a farmer.

RR: I also want people to know that we are still here. There is a huge amount of agricultural activity in this country—especially in places that get talked about as though they are destitute. Our closest neighbor is maybe a few miles away, but we're here and doing this work.

AB: OK, final question and hopefully it's the fun one: How do you cook rice?

RR: Ha! What don't we eat with rice? My favorite is rice and gravy—not a thick gravy like in other parts. You brown some meat and then add onions and cook that down, then some water or broth to make the gravy and have it with rice. Chicken gravy, like a fricassee (pronounced "fric-A-SAY") but not a real fricassee. Lightly flour the chicken and brown it, then add onion and stock to make the gravy.

*AB: But **how** do you cook the rice? Boil it, steam it, pilaf?*

RR: Honestly, we almost always use a rice cooker. It comes out perfect every time, and we make so much rice and are in and out of the house. It's a lot like the convenience of a slow cooker.

BOILED

Boiled rice may be the most straightforward recipe in this entire book, but it was a real revelation to me when fellow chef Allison Scott said she stopped cooking rice with a specific water-to-grain ratio but instead transitioned to treating it like pasta. Simply bring a big pot of heavily salted water to a boil, add rice, boil until tender, and drain. That led me to treating all grains and legumes the same way, and hence a cookbook is born.

boiled + buttered rice w/seared chicken thighs + green salad

When people say simple food is the best food, I think of this combination: a well-cooked chicken thigh, a bright green salad, and perfectly cooked buttery rice to tie it all together. That said, boiled rice is an excellent vehicle for presenting spices. This dish is made dramatically different by changing the rice with any of the flavor variations listed.

1 cup [200 g] rice, any nonsticky variety

3 oz [85 g] butter

4 to 6 chicken thighs (about 2½ lb [1.2 kg] total)

Salt and freshly ground black pepper

Neutral oil

4 oz [120 g] salad greens

1 lemon (about 1½ oz [45 ml]), zest and juice

¼ cup [60 ml] olive oil

Bring at least 8 cups [2 L] of salted water to a boil. Add the rice and stir to prevent any grains from sticking to the bottom. Turn down the heat to a high simmer and cook the rice until tender, 10 to 35 minutes, depending on the variety.

continued

Drain the cooked rice, reserving ¼ cup [60 ml] of the cooking water. Transfer the drained rice to a heatproof bowl. Add the cooking water and butter and toss to coat. Cover and hold in a warm place until ready to serve.

Blot the chicken skin dry and season liberally with salt and pepper.

In a large frying pan, heat a glug of neutral oil over medium heat. Sear the chicken until golden brown, about 7 minutes. When the skin is crispy and golden, flip the thighs. Turn down the heat to low and cook the chicken, uncovered, until it is cooked through, another 8 to 10 minutes.

Dress the salad greens with the lemon zest and juice, the olive oil, and a couple pinches of salt and grinds of black pepper.

To serve, fluff the rice and transfer to a platter or individual plates. Top with the chicken thighs and serve with the greens alongside or on salad plates.

variations

floral rice

Dress the just-boiled rice with ¼ cup [60 ml] of Chamomile Lemon Oil (page 39) and serve.

green rice

Blend 2 cups [50 g] of picked herbs (parsley, cilantro, mint, basil, chervil, chives, tarragon, lemon balm, and the like) into ¾ cup [180 ml] of olive oil and combine with just-boiled rice and a big pinch of salt.

marrakech rice

Add 1 Tbsp of Ras el Hanout (page 41) and 10 pitted and chopped dates to the cooking water and let steep for 5 minutes, then add to the rice. To serve, top with ¼ cup [60 ml] of Harissa (page 47).

mediterranean rice

Bloom 2 Tbsp of Mediterranean Spice Mix (page 41) in ¼ cup [60 ml] of olive oil and dress the rice.

orange rice

When the rice is done, replace the cooking water and butter with ½ cup [120 g] of Cherry Tomato Conserva (page 52), ¼ cup [55 g] of Paprika Cumin Oil (page 40), and 3 garlic cloves, minced.

saffron + cinnamon rice

Add 10 saffron threads, 3 star anise, and 1 tsp of cinnamon to 1 cup [250 ml] of reserved cooking water and let steep for 5 minutes, then pour over the rice, with the butter, and toss to coat.

spiced milk

When the rice is cooked, replace the cooking water and butter with 1 cup [250 ml] of Spiced Milk (page 44). Note: The rice will be saucier than traditional buttered rice, so consider serving in a dish with a lip to prevent spilling.

yellow rice

Bloom 2 Tbsp of Yellow "Curried" Spice Mix (page 41) in ¼ cup [60 ml] of oil and add to the warm boiled rice.

MARINATED

Now that we're cooking rice like pasta, we might as well use it like pasta to make satisfying, flavorful, veg-filled one-bowl dishes for the next day's lunch or a hearty midweek dinner.

rice salad w/marinated eggplant, tajín oil + broccolini

The marinated eggplant in this recipe can be made in much larger batches and held at the ready in the fridge for weeks on end. Same for the Tajín oil—meaning that if you already have these two pantry staples on hand, this meal requires only a quick pan fry of the broccolini to finish it off.

½ cup [125 ml] Tajín Oil (page 40)

2 cups [500 g] cooked rice

2 medium eggplants (about 2 lb [900 g])

Salt

Neutral oil

1 onion (about 8 oz [225 g]), thinly sliced

6 garlic cloves, minced

1 Tbsp capers, roughly chopped (optional)

¼ cup [60 ml] balsamic vinegar

¼ cup [60 ml] olive oil

2 bunches broccolini (about 2 lb [900 g])

Warm the Tajín oil in a medium frying pan, then pour the oil over the cooked rice and set aside.

Cut the eggplant into rounds or large chunks and put in a large bowl. Reheat the frying pan over medium-high heat. Toss the eggplant with a few pinches of salt and several glugs of neutral oil to coat. Pan fry until the eggplant is golden brown on the sides and cooked through, flipping as needed, about 7 minutes.

Turn down the heat to low. Add the onion, garlic, and capers (if using) and cook until soft, about 3 minutes.

continued

Transfer the mixture to a bowl. Immediately add the vinegar and olive oil and toss to combine and marinate.

Heat the frying pan one last time over medium-high heat with a couple glugs of neutral oil. Pan fry the broccolini with a pinch of salt until bright green and tender.

Combine the Tajín-spiced rice, the eggplant mixture (include all the marinating liquid), and the fried broccolini. Adjust the seasoning as desired and serve.

variations

w/marinated mushrooms, peas + baby kale

Toss 1 cup [250 g] of cooked rice with ½ cup [100 g] of Marinated Mushrooms (page 56), 1 cup [250 g] of blanched peas, and 2 oz [60 g] of baby kale. Dress with a couple of glugs of olive oil and pinches of salt. Adjust the seasoning as desired.

w/cucumbers, summer squash + lemon parsley mojo

Cut 1 medium cucumber and 1 medium summer squash into half-moons. Toss 1 cup [250 g] of cooked rice with the vegetables, ½ cup [125 ml] of Lemon Parsley Mojo (page 48), and a couple of pinches of salt and grinds of black pepper. Adjust the seasoning as desired.

w/roasted roots + brown butter vinaigrette

Cut 2 lb [900 g] of various roots (parsnips, carrots, beets, potatoes, celery root, or sweet potato) into chunks or 2 in [5 cm] long sticks and toss with olive oil and a couple of pinches of salt. Arrange on a baking sheet and roast at 400°F [200°C] until golden brown and cooked through, about 40 minutes. Remove from the oven and immediately toss with 2 cups [500 g] of cooked rice and ½ cup [125 ml] of Brown Butter Vinaigrette (page 35).

CRISPED

These crisped rice patties are somewhere between risotto al salto—a pan-fried cake made with leftover risotto—and the crisped rice bowl from Ria Barbosa at Sqirl LA. The egg binds the rice into clusters, but if you are avoiding eggs you will certainly have good (if crumbly) results by simply pan frying the rice on its own. The key is the textural difference between the crunchy exterior and the starchy interior. Note: Freshly cooked rice doesn't fry up as quickly as drier rice that's a few days old.

crisped rice w/carrots, chickpeas + mojo de ajo

At home, I like this dish as one big weird salad sort of thing. In a restaurant, I would keep the rice as a medium-size pancake, with the carrot, chickpea, and spinach salad delicately piled on top for aesthetics.

2 lb [900 g] carrots, cut into chunks or 2 in [5 cm] long sticks

Salt

Olive oil

1 cup [240 g] cooked or canned chickpeas

2 cups [500 g] cooked rice

1 egg, beaten

Neutral oil

2 oz [60 g] fresh spinach

1 recipe Mojo de Ajo (page 48)

Preheat the oven heat to 400°F [200°C]. Toss the carrots with a pinch of salt and a couple of glugs of olive oil. Arrange on a baking sheet and roast until tender and caramelized, about 40 minutes.

Add the chickpeas to the carrot-filled baking sheet and return to the oven for an additional 5 minutes to warm.

continued

Combine the cooked rice and egg with a pinch of salt. In a medium frying pan, heat a couple of glugs of neutral oil over medium-high heat until it begins to shimmer, about 1 minute. Add the rice/egg mixture and pan fry until the outside is golden brown, 2 to 3 minutes. Flip the rice, breaking up any large pieces into little clusters, and fry the other side, 1 to 2 minutes.

To serve, toss the carrots, chickpeas, crisped rice clusters, and spinach together in a bowl and dress with the mojo to taste and a couple pinches of salt.

variations

w/cucumbers, scallions, cilantro + mojo de ajo

Make the crisped rice clusters as in the main recipe. Toss them with 1 or 2 cucumbers, cut into large wedges or chunks; 3 scallions, cut into thin rounds; 1 bunch of cilantro, roughly chopped; and ¼ cup [60 ml] of Mojo de Ajo (page 48). Adjust the seasoning by adding salt or more mojo as desired.

w/sweet potato wedges, goat cheese, olive rig + za'atar chili oil

Make the crisped rice clusters as in the main recipe. Cut 2 lb [900 g] of sweet potatoes into large wedges and roast in a 400°F [200°C] oven until deeply caramelized and cooked through, 25 to 35 minutes. Lay the sweet potato wedges on a serving platter. Scatter the clusters all over. Dot with 2 to 4 oz [60 to 120 g] of fresh goat cheese, and dollop ½ cup [120 g] of Olive Rig (page 49) all over. Spoon the Za'atar Chili Oil (page 40) liberally over the whole thing and scatter with a handful of chopped parsley (optional).

w/roasted asparagus + lemon parsley mojo

Oven or pan roast 1 lb [450 g] of asparagus, scatter the rice clusters over the top, and spoon ¼ to ½ cup [65 to 125 ml] of Lemon Parsley Mojo (page 48) all over it.

PORRIDGE

One winter I got the flu, twice. The second time around, I felt so weak and over it that all I could bring myself to eat was some version of this rice porridge. It is thicker than a traditional congee and is a great way to use up all the one-off random vegetable odds and ends in your fridge. The sweet version is one of my favorite super-homey breakfasts; if push comes to shove, it can double as a light dessert. Either of these versions is also great substituting 2 cups [500 ml] of Spiced Milk (page 44) for the 2 cups [500 ml] of the cooking liquid listed in the recipe.

savory rice porridge w/cheddar, chicken stock + greens

Note that this porridge can be made with water to keep it vegetarian/vegan friendly. It can also be made with almost any variety of rice, including wild rice, but doesn't work so well with risotto rice, as it gets very clumpy.

6 cups [1.5 L] chicken stock	2 oz [60 g] sharp Cheddar cheese	Chili Oil (page 39, optional)
Salt	2 bunches kale, chard, spinach, rapini, or escarole, or about 1 lb [450 g] greens, cut into ribbons	
½ cup [100 g] rice, most varieties		

Bring the chicken stock to a boil with a few pinches of salt. Add the rice and cook until the rice is fully tender, about 20 minutes. Remove from the heat. Grate the cheese into the rice to melt and thicken. Add the greens and stir to wilt.

To serve, spoon into individual bowls and drizzle chili oil over the top.

sweet rice porridge w/dried cherries + five spice

My grandfather loved this slightly sweet porridge for breakfast but used one stick of cinnamon instead of the Chinese five spice because the five spice was too spicy for his delicate palate. If you don't have dried cherries, I'm sorry. You can use raisins or dates instead. I like big, juicy California flame raisins and/or Medjool dates if you can get them. I sometimes gild the lily by sprinkling a handful of chopped almonds all over the top.

4 cups [1 L] milk

Salt

½ cup [100 g] rice, most varieties

2 Tbsp brown sugar

1 tsp Chinese five spice (or plain cinnamon)

Zest of 1 orange

½ cup [80 g] dried cherries

In a large saucepan, bring the milk, 2 cups [500 ml] of water, and a pinch of salt to the scalding point over medium-high heat.

Add the rice, brown sugar, and five spice. Turn down the heat to a simmer, cover, and cook until tender, stirring regularly to keep the rice from sticking or the pot from boiling over, about 20 minutes.

When the rice is tender, remove from the heat. Add the orange zest and cherries and let sit for 5 minutes to plump the cherries before serving.

MILK

Making rice milk is really as simple as blending softened rice with water to pull the starch from the grains and suspend in the water. Horchata, the traditional Mexican beverage, adds almonds, cinnamon, and brown sugar to sweeten.

horchata base recipe

½ cup [100 g] long-grain rice	½ cup [50 g] blanched almonds	2 Tbsp brown sugar
	2 cinnamon sticks	Salt

Combine the rice, almonds, and cinnamon in a frying pan and toast until fragrant, about 3 minutes.

Meanwhile, bring 4 cups [1 L] of water to a boil. Transfer the toasted rice mixture to a large bowl and pour the just-boiled water over the mixture. Add the brown sugar and a pinch of salt. Let steep for 2 hours or until the rice is soft.

Remove the cinnamon sticks and blend the mixture in a high-powered blender until smooth. Serve over ice.

continued

variations

horchata ice milk

Stir ½ cup [100 g] of sugar into 2 cups [500 ml] of horchata base until it dissolves. Churn the mixture in an ice cream machine until it's the texture of soft serve. Transfer to a freezer-safe container and freeze until firm, at least 4 hours.

horchata-poached chicken breasts

2 cups [500 ml] Horchata Base Recipe (page 327)	Salt	4 oz [120 g] fresh spinach
1 cup [250 ml] chicken stock or water	4 boneless, skinless chicken breasts	Chopped almonds, for garnish (optional)
	1 cup [200 g] cooked rice	

In a pot, bring the horchata and chicken stock to a simmer with several pinches of salt. Place the chicken breasts in the liquid and poach gently until the chicken is cooked through, 8 to 12 minutes. Remove the chicken from the cooking liquid.

Bring the liquid to a boil, then remove from the heat. Add the rice and spinach and allow the spinach to wilt.

Cut the chicken breasts into ¼ in [6 mm] thick slices.

Serve the brothy rice-spinach mixture with the sliced chicken breasts on top. Add a handful of chopped almonds (if using).

horchata bulgur porridge

1½ cups [375 ml] Horchata Base Recipe (page 327)	½ cup [100 g] bulgur	Zest of 1 orange
	6 oz [180 g] raspberries	Sugar

Combine the horchata and bulgur and soak overnight in the fridge.

Combine the raspberries, orange zest, and a couple pinches of sugar and let sit for 10 minutes to soften.

Dish the horchata-bulgur porridge into serving bowls and serve with the raspberries on top.

rice, risotto

There are kitchen tasks that are a litmus test for how stressed I am. If I'm on schedule, picking thyme leaves is an absolute joy; if I'm late, I want to murder someone, myself, and the entire thyme plant. Risotto used to be that way. It doesn't take long to make, but the work is entirely active. You have to stir the rice the entire time, multitasking not allowed. I used to crane around and try to reach another project, thinking I could scoop cookies or some other of the unending things that seem to always need to be done, getting frustrated along the way.

Finally, I just stopped—submitted to the fact that nothing else gets done except for the risotto. I took it as an opportunity to stand in one place (for once) and stir. Sure, my thoughts would roam, but my feet and attention stayed still. I found that I didn't resent the risotto after I just let her take over.

Now I make risotto in especially chaotic times. Not only because it requires very little planning beyond having risotto rice on hand and heating up some water—which, if everything is on fire, I probably haven't thought much about dinner—but also because risotto gives me the excuse to set all the rest of the world to the side and stir and stir and organize my thoughts.

NOTES

BOTANICAL NAME: *Oryza sativa*

PLACE OF ORIGIN: East Asia

TOP GLOBAL PRODUCERS: Italy

GLUTEN FREE: Yes

PROTEIN CONTENT: 4.4 percent

TO SOAK OR NOT TO SOAK (THAT IS ALWAYS THE QUESTION): No

BASIC WATER:GRAIN RATIO FOR STEWING: 4:1

AVERAGE BOILING TIME: Don't boil it!

YIELD RATIO AFTER COOKING: 1:4

SIGNS OF DONENESS: Risotto will be creamy and the grains will be tender but structurally intact.

6.

3.

2.

4.

8.

1.

5.

9.

RISOTTO

Risotto has a bit of a bad rep for taking forever. On the contrary, I have always found that it takes me about 19 minutes to cook a batch of risotto, making it a very fast dinner. That said, it is 19 minutes of active cooking—standing over the stove and stirring. The keys to a great risotto are (1) high-quality short-grain rice, (2) adding the hot liquid in small additions throughout the cooking process, and (3) constant stirring to coax the starch out of each grain. So pony up or grab a chair, but be prepared to stir for your quick dinner.

carte blanch risotto

This is a basic ratio and method for making risotto. You can add any number of flavors to the beginning or end to gussy it up, but even the plainest risotto is pretty great. Additionally, risotto scales up very easily, leaving you with leftovers to make arancini or risotto al salto.

8 cups [2 L] stock or water	1 onion (about 8 oz [225 g]), thinly sliced	1 cup [200 g] arborio or carnaroli rice
Olive oil or butter	Salt	1 cup [250 ml] white wine, red wine, or hard cider

In a large stockpot, covered, bring the stock to a boil. Lower the heat and keep the liquid hot.

In a large frying pan, warm a couple glugs of olive oil or knobs of butter over medium heat. Add the onion and a big pinch of salt and sweat until translucent and tender. Add the rice and briefly toast, about 2 minutes.

Add the wine and start the constant stirring. When the wine is fully absorbed, add a ladleful (about 1 cup [250 ml]) of the hot cooking liquid and continue stirring. When that liquid is fully absorbed, add another ladleful and stir until fully absorbed.

Continue adding ladlefuls of liquid and stirring constantly until the risotto is creamy and tender, about 20 minutes; you may not need all the liquid. Season with salt as desired.

variations (see photo, pages 332–333)

1. w/tomato + olive rig

At the end of cooking the risotto, stir in 1 to 2 cups [250 to 500 ml] of tomato sauce (either your favorite brand or Cherry Tomato Conserva, page 52). Transfer the risotto to a serving platter and spoon Olive Rig (page 49) all over. Finish with several gratings of Parmesan or Manchego if you're up for it.

2. w/squash, paprika chili oil + arugula

At the end of cooking the risotto, stir in 1 cup [250 ml] of puréed squash (roasted squash blended in a food processor with a bit of salt and olive oil until smooth). Transfer to a serving platter. Spoon Paprika Cumin Oil (page 40) over the whole thing and top with a handful of olive oil–dressed arugula.

3. w/leek + bacon

Replace the onion in the main risotto recipe with 2 leeks (cleaned and cut into thin half-moons) and cut 6 oz [180 g] of bacon or pancetta into thin strips. At the beginning of cooking, render the bacon or pancetta over low heat until the fat is released and it is starting to brown. Add the leeks and sweat until tender. Continue as directed in the main recipe. I also really like this risotto with a splash of cream at the end—more is more.

continued

4. w/swiss chard, parmesan + tarragon sunflower seed rig

Separate the stems from 1 bunch of Swiss chard; slice the stems and cut the leaves into thin ribbons. Add the sliced stems to the onion at the beginning of cooking the risotto. At the end of cooking, fold the sliced leaves into the risotto. Transfer to a serving platter and top with several gratings of Parmesan and a spoonful of the Tarragon Sunflower Seed Rig (page 50).

5. w/sweet peas + mint almond relish

At the end of cooking the risotto, add 2 cups [200 g] of fresh or frozen shelled peas to the risotto and let the heat of the risotto gently cook the peas—in about 2 minutes they will be bright green. Transfer to a serving dish and spoon the Mint Almond Relish (page 48) all over it.

6. w/beets + walnut aillade

At the end of cooking the risotto, stir 1 cup [250 ml] of beet purée (roasted beets blended in a food processor with salt and olive oil until smooth) into the risotto. Transfer to a serving platter and spoon the Walnut Aillade (page 50) all over it.

7. w/parsnips, blue cheese + pickled dried cherries

At the end of cooking the risotto, stir 2 cups [500 ml] of parsnip purée (boiled parsnips blended in a food processor with salt, olive oil, and cream until smooth) into the risotto. Transfer to a serving platter and crumble about 4 oz [120 g] of blue cheese all over it. Scatter the drained Pickled Dried Cherries (page 57) over the top and serve.

8. w/pumpkin, chili oil, pepitas + cocoa nibs

At the end of cooking the risotto, stir 1 to 2 cups [250 to 500 ml] of pumpkin purée (either homemade or canned) into the risotto. Transfer to a serving platter, drizzle several glugs of Chili Oil (page 39) over the risotto, and sprinkle with toasted pepitas and cocoa nibs.

9. w/wine, pears + goat cheese

At the beginning of cooking the risotto, reduce a bottle of red wine down to 1 cup [250 ml] of liquid and use that in place of the wine in the basic recipe. At the end of cooking, transfer the risotto to a serving platter and top with very thinly sliced pears, dots of goat cheese, and some chopped parsley.

two ideas for leftover risotto

arancini

Chill the leftover risotto overnight. Scoop it into balls using a cookie or ice cream scoop. If you have any extra cheese lying around, cut it into ¼ in [6 mm] cubes, press into the center of each ball, and then roll the ball to make it a compact sphere. Roll the rice balls in bread crumbs or panko and freeze. Deep-fry or bake (but deep-frying is the nicest) at 375°F [190°C] until the outside is golden brown and the spheres are warm throughout.

risotto al salto

Chill the leftover risotto overnight. Heat several glugs of neutral oil in a medium frying pan. When the oil is almost smoking hot, press the risotto into the pan and allow it to fry until the rice is golden brown and starting to crisp. Flip the rice pancake and cook the other side until golden. While the pancake is still warm, grate a hefty amount of Parmesan over it and serve warm or at room temperature, cut into wedges. I especially like it dipped into Romesco (page 49) or Herbed Yogurt (page 45).

rice, wild

Wild rice is top of mind when thinking about traditional foods of the Great Lakes region. Feeding into the freshwater basin are vast networks of inland lakes. These lakes are the wellspring for wild rice, which isn't technically a rice at all but an indigenous aquatic grass. Truly wild rice, as you'll read in the interview, is hand-harvested and unique to the season, the paddy in which it is grown, and the hands that take it from lake to table.

Historically, those hands belonged to members of the First Nations, Ojibwe in my region. Images of wild rice knocked into birch canoes and parched over large fires in traditional woven baskets not only are romantic but also represent a long-held revenue source for tribes. We all have to come to terms with the fact that we live on occupied land. Buying true wild rice from Indigenous harvesters is maybe the babiest of baby steps, but I hope that it is your first on a path toward celebrating Indigenous culture and foodways. I hope that celebration then leads to further support, emotional and monetary, so that voices like Hillel Echo-Hawk, Brit Reed, Kristina Stanley, and Sean Sherman continue to drive the conversation.

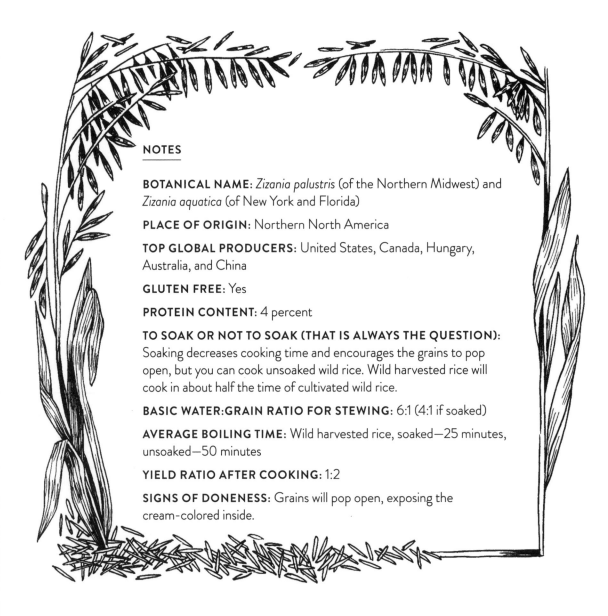

NOTES

BOTANICAL NAME: *Zizania palustris* (of the Northern Midwest) and *Zizania aquatica* (of New York and Florida)

PLACE OF ORIGIN: Northern North America

TOP GLOBAL PRODUCERS: United States, Canada, Hungary, Australia, and China

GLUTEN FREE: Yes

PROTEIN CONTENT: 4 percent

TO SOAK OR NOT TO SOAK (THAT IS ALWAYS THE QUESTION): Soaking decreases cooking time and encourages the grains to pop open, but you can cook unsoaked wild rice. Wild harvested rice will cook in about half the time of cultivated wild rice.

BASIC WATER:GRAIN RATIO FOR STEWING: 6:1 (4:1 if soaked)

AVERAGE BOILING TIME: Wild harvested rice, soaked—25 minutes, unsoaked—50 minutes

YIELD RATIO AFTER COOKING: 1:2

SIGNS OF DONENESS: Grains will pop open, exposing the cream-colored inside.

LARRY GATES

Larry Gates is a wild rice forager in Cass Lake, Minnesota. He produces wild rice for retail and restaurant customers. I was put in touch with him via my friend, chef and former Minnesotan Paul Berglund. I wanted to talk with Mr. Gates to learn more about the difference between commercial foraging and farming, as well as the current state of wild rice production. He spoke with me in early March 2020.

Abra Berens: Can you tell me about the life cycle of wild rice—how it grows, when it's harvested, and so on?

Larry Gates: Well, let's start with the harvest. Rice is usually ready to harvest mid-August to mid-September. It usually takes a few weeks going from paddy to paddy and then going back again for the second flush. The rice doesn't produce all at once, not like cultivated crops. So you go back out and keep collecting until there's no more—usually about a month or so.

The thing that has changed the most [about foraging wild rice] is how few people are out now to harvest. It used to be big community affairs, with families going out in the boats to knock rice. Now very few people are out at any given time. With that and circling back around, time just adds up. Two people are usually harvesting together; one person moves the canoe by pushing it with a pole. Paddles don't do much good because of the thicket of plants. The other person knocks the rice [from the flower heads] into the belly of the boat to collect it.

After the final pass for collecting, the unharvested seeds fall to the water and sink to the bottom. There they lie until the weather warms in the spring, when they germinate and send up shoots. Wild rice is a grass, much closer to wheat than to Asian rice varieties. These grains can stay in the soil underwater for upward of ten years, so if there is a bad crop one year, plants will still come up the next without our intervention. Unlike cultivated wild rice (or paddy rice, as we call it), these seeds are true to the wild rice from hundreds of years ago. There's some natural variation, but it is an ancestral crop.

The stalks come up around June and then you're just waiting. Hoping that storms don't come through and knock 'em back. Hoping that there's enough rain to keep off a drought. Hoping there's not too much rain to keep the fields from germinating in the first place.

AB: What's the difference between wild rice and paddy rice?

LG: The University [of Minnesota] started to cultivate wild rice to make it a more commercially viable crop in the early 1970s. Wild rice is a completely natural product, so it changes from year to year in quality, flavor, yield. When you cultivate something, you're taking out the variability and making it more consistent, which is better for the businesses that sell it on a larger scale. They want it all to come on at the same time, ripen at the same time, look the same, taste the same. Wild rice is subject to the whims of the weather and the location of the plants. It tastes different from paddy to paddy; it looks different. It has its own characteristics even within one harvest. We don't control it, which also means it's expensive, because it takes skill to hand-harvest, and the yields can vary so much.

So when folks like Uncle Ben's wanted to have wild rice on the shelf, they needed lower prices and a consistent product. The University set about to convert it to a more traditional row crop. Now that is displacing a lot of the natural rice fields, making it even harder to protect those wild spaces.

AB: So the cultivated or paddy rice is grown in the same places as where wild rice would grow? It isn't taking the place of, say, a corn or soybean field?

LG: That's right.

AB: Hmm. And is that why there are fewer people participating in the harvest of late?

LG: I don't know if it is a direct corollary, but you know, people used to be able to make a good living from ricing. Now it is more of a hobby for most folks.

AB: And how can people tell if they are buying paddy rice or true wild rice?

LG: Well [*laughs*] if it's cheap, it isn't wild rice. Honestly, that's the first thing. Secondly, look at it. Cultivated wild rice is jet black and uniform down the length of the grain. Wild rice is a flecked brown that is dull or matte. Cultivated rice is shiny. Also, someone told me once that you can tell cultivated rice by boiling it with a stone. When the stone is tender, the rice is just about done. Cultivated rice takes a lot longer to cook. And, well, I'm a Minnesotan, so I'm always going to say that Minnesota rice is the best, but if it says California on the label, it is probably cultivated.

AB: I'm from Michigan, and we have some wild rice producers up north, so let's just say Minnesota or Michigan! Now, what do you wish nonfarmers knew about your work?

LG: That what you buy matters. Wild is a special thing. It sustained life for hundreds of years. It is a regional delicacy. By buying from a small harvester or just by caring about what you're buying, you're saying that it is important and worth all of our time and tradition.

STEWED

As with all the grains in this book, you can add wild rice to a pot of boiling water, lower the heat, and simmer until the grains are tender. I find that the liquid after boiling is so flavorful that I don't want to lose it down the drain, so I tend to stew wild rice, adding more liquid along the way as needed and fortifying the flavor of the rice with its cooking liquid.

I generally account for about 6 cups [1.5 L] of liquid to stew 1 cup [200 g] of unsoaked wild rice and about 4 cups [1 L] of liquid if the rice has been soaked. Note: Any excess pot liquor can be stored in the fridge for up to a week or in the freezer indefinitely.

wild rice w/seared salmon, fennel + salted plum salad

The earthiness of the wild rice, the fatty richness of the salmon, and the crunch and tang of the lemon-soaked fennel with surprisingly briny salted plums—I love this dish. If plums are not in season, substitute prunes or dried apricots. The result won't be as juicy, but it will be no less flavorful.

Neutral oil

1 small onion (about 4 oz [120 g]), thinly sliced

2 garlic cloves, minced

½ tsp salt, plus more as needed

1 cup [250 ml] white wine or hard cider

1 cup [200 g] wild rice, soaked or unsoaked

6 cups [1.5 L] chicken stock or water (4 cups [1 L]) if the rice has been soaked)

1 lemon (about 1½ oz [45 ml]), zest and juice

5 to 7 sprigs parsley, roughly chopped

¼ cup [60 ml] olive oil

1 bulb fennel (about 8 oz [225 g])

4 tart plums (about 1 lb [450 g])

Four 4 oz [120 g] salmon fillets, skin on

continued

In a large pot, heat a glug of neutral oil over medium heat until it begins to shimmer, about 1 minute. Add the onions, garlic, and salt and sweat until the onions are soft but not browned, about 7 minutes. Add the wine and cook until fully evaporated.

Add the wild rice and toast briefly, about 2 minutes. Add the stock and bring to a boil. Lower the heat to a simmer and cook until the rice is tender—about 25 minutes if soaked, 50 minutes if unsoaked—adding more water along the way as needed to keep the rice moist as it cooks.

Meanwhile, combine the lemon zest and juice, parsley, olive oil, and a couple of pinches of salt. Shave the fennel into thin ribbons and dress it with the lemon dressing to keep the pieces from oxidizing.

Cut the plums into quarters or sixths, depending on the size, and transfer to a small bowl. Sprinkle the plums with a few pinches of salt and let sit for 10 minutes to allow the salt to pull some of the moisture from the plums, making a light brine.

In a large frying pan, heat a couple of glugs of neutral oil over high heat. Blot the skin of the salmon dry, then season liberally with salt. Sear the fish, skin-side down, until the skin is well seared and the fillets move easily when nudged with a spatula, 4 to 6 minutes. Flip the fish and lightly sear the other side to cook to medium rare, about 2 minutes. Remove from the heat and let rest.

Season the rice with salt as desired.

To serve, spoon some wild rice onto a serving platter or individual plates. Top with a portion of fish, skin-side up. Pile the fennel next to the fish and top the whole thing with a couple of spoonfuls of the salted plums and their brine.

variations

w/roasted radishes, turnips, spinach + bacon dressing

Neutral oil

6 salad turnips or 3 purple top turnips (about 1 lb [450 g]), leaves removed and roots halved

6 radishes (about 8 oz [225 g]), leaves removed and roots halved

2 cups [400 g] cooked wild rice

4 oz [120 g] spinach

½ cup [125 ml] Bacon Vinaigrette (page 35), warmed

Heat a couple of glugs of neutral oil in a large frying pan over high heat. Pan fry the turnips and radishes until they are golden brown on the cut side.

If the greens are nice, roughly chop them and add to the frying pan at the last minute.

In a large bowl, combine the wild rice, spinach, the roasted roots and their greens, and the bacon dressing and toss. Adjust the seasoning as desired and serve.

squash stuffed w/wild rice, parmesan, cherry tomato conserva + lemon parsley mojo

1 small onion (about 4 oz [120 g]), thinly sliced

1½ cups [350 g] cooked wild rice

1 cup [240 g] Cherry Tomato Conserva (page 52)

2 oz [60 g] Parmesan, grated

4 garlic cloves, minced

Olive oil

Salt

2 kabocha or acorn squash (about 2 lb [900 g]), cut in half and seeds scooped out

½ cup [125 ml] Lemon Parsley Mojo (page 48)

Preheat the oven to 375°F [190°C]. Combine the onion, wild rice, conserva, Parmesan, and garlic with a couple glugs of olive oil and pinches of salt.

continued

Fill the cavities of the squash halves with the rice mixture and place in an ovenproof dish.

Cover the dish with foil or a lid and bake until the squash is tender, about 30 minutes.

To serve, spoon the mojo over the top.

w/seared chicken thigh, celery root + lemon caper mayo

Neutral oil	2 cups [400 g] cooked wild rice	¾ cup [125 g] Lemon Caper Mayo (page 37)
4 chicken thighs (about 1½ lb [675 g])		
Salt	2 celery roots (about 1 lb [450 g]), grated or cut into matchsticks	

Heat a large frying pan with a big glug of neutral oil over medium heat. Pat the skin of the chicken thighs dry and season liberally with salt. Pan fry the chicken until the skin is golden brown, about 7 minutes. Flip the chicken and cook the other side, another 5 to 7 minutes.

Combine the cut celery root with the mayo to make a crunchy slaw.

To serve, portion the rice among four plates. Top with the chicken thighs and garnish with a hearty spoonful of the slaw.

SOUP

Cooking the wild rice in enough water to provide the broth for the soup ensures a thicker, heartier soup. You can substitute cooked wild rice for any of these recipes, but expect the soup to be a bit brothier.

chicken + wild rice soup w/kale + tomato paprika mayo

It sounds pretty terrible to float mayonnaise in a soup—at least that is what I thought when I read a recipe for French fish stew finished with rouille, a red pepper mayo traditional in Provence. Turns out it isn't gross, unless you don't like mayo, in which case consider turning your head when you scoop it into the soup bowl and give it a stir; within 30 seconds it will have melted, and the soup (and life) will be better.

Neutral oil

2 onions (about 1 lb [450 g]), thinly sliced

6 garlic cloves, minced

Salt and freshly ground black pepper

1 cup [250 ml] white wine or hard cider

1 lb [450 g] carrots, diced

1½ cups [300 g] wild rice, soaked or unsoaked

8 cups [2 L] chicken stock

2 boneless, skinless chicken breasts (about 1 lb [450 g]), sliced into strips

10 leaves any variety of kale, leaves stripped from the stems and cut into ribbons

¼ cup [60 g] Cherry Tomato Conserva (page 52) or 2 Tbsp tomato paste

1 recipe Tomato Paprika Mayo (page 38)

In a soup pot, heat a glug of neutral oil over medium heat. Add the onion and garlic with a big pinch of salt and a couple of grinds of black pepper and sweat until tender, about 7 minutes. Add the wine and cook until almost evaporated, about 3 minutes.

continued

Add the carrots and wild rice and stir to combine and briefly toast. Add the chicken stock and bring to a boil, then lower the heat to a simmer and cook until the rice is tender, about 25 minutes for soaked and 50 for unsoaked.

When the rice is tender, add the chicken breasts to the soup. Drop in one slice at a time—if you plunk the whole pile in together, sometimes the slices fuse back together as the proteins constrict. Poach until the chicken is cooked through, 5 minutes or so.

To serve, portion the kale into soup bowls and ladle the soup over the kale, allowing it to wilt gently. Combine the conserva and mayo in a small bowl and blend until smooth. Spoon a couple of dollops of the conserva mayo on top of each bowl.

variations

wild rice soup w/mushrooms, ramps + peas

10 ramps, bulbs and leaves separated, and both thinly sliced	1 lb [450 g] mushrooms, any variety, thinly sliced	8 cups [2 L] chicken stock or water
Butter or neutral oil	1 cup [250 ml] white wine	1 lb [450 g] peas
Salt and freshly ground black pepper	1½ cups [300 g] wild rice, soaked or unsoaked	¼ cup [60 ml] olive oil
		1 lemon (about 1½ oz [45 ml]), zest and juice

In a large pot, sweat the ramp bulbs in a knob of butter and a couple pinches of salt until soft, about 7 minutes. Add the mushrooms with a couple more pinches of salt and grinds of black pepper. Cook the mushrooms until they have released their moisture and started to brown, about 6 minutes. Add the wine and cook until reduced by half.

Add the rice and toast briefly, about 2 minutes, then add the stock and bring to a boil. Lower the heat to a simmer and cook until the rice is tender, about 45 minutes. Adjust the seasoning as desired.

continued

Just before serving, add the peas and let them cook until they are bright green, 3 to 4 minutes.

Combine the ramp leaves, olive oil, lemon zest and juice, and a couple of pinches of salt. Dish the soup into bowls and garnish with a hearty spoonful of the ramp leaf rig.

wild rice soup w/tomato, squash + walnut aillade

2 onions (about 1 lb [450 g]), thinly sliced	8 cups [2 L] chicken stock or water	1 cup [240 g] Cherry Tomato Conserva (page 52)
6 garlic cloves, minced	1 lb [450 g] winter squash, peeled and cubed	½ cup [125 g] Walnut Aillade (page 50)
Olive oil	1½ cups [300 g] wild rice, soaked or unsoaked	
Salt		

Sweat the onion and garlic in a soup pot with some olive oil and pinches of salt for about 7 minutes.

Add the stock, winter squash, wild rice, and tomato conserva. Bring to a boil, lower the heat to a simmer, and cook until the rice and squash are tender, about 35 minutes (the squash may break apart a bit, but that's OK). Adjust the seasoning.

To serve, dish the soup into bowls and top with a few spoonfuls of the walnut aillade.

wild rice, chard + corn soup w/poached egg

2 onions (about 1 lb [450 g]), thinly sliced

6 garlic cloves, minced

Olive oil

Salt

1 cup [250 ml] white wine

8 cups [2 L] chicken stock or water

1 lb [450 g] corn kernels

1½ cups [300 g] wild rice, soaked or unsoaked

10 leaves chard, cut into ribbons

1 egg per person

Sweat the onion and garlic in a soup pot with some olive oil and pinches of salt, about 7 minutes. Add the white wine and cook until reduced by half.

Add the stock, corn kernels, and wild rice with several pinches of salt. Bring to a boil, lower to a simmer, and cook until the rice is tender, about 35 minutes. Adjust the seasoning.

Just before serving, bring the soup to a simmer, add the chard, break the eggs into the soup, and let the eggs poach in the hot soup, 4 to 6 minutes.

To serve, dish out the soup, including one egg per person, into soup bowls, and sprinkle each egg with a bit of salt.

tiny seed grains

I feel like every year some new "superfood" grain bursts on the scene in the glossy magazines with the promise that a scoopful a day will make you lose weight and grow long lustrous tresses, and ensure general happiness. These grains are often imported, along with colonialist-inspired marketing of their production in far-flung places by mysterious people who hold the secret key to overcoming our day-to-day woes.

Inevitably, interest in those grains spike, so the prices spike too, often making it difficult for the growers and their communities to eat that food, because they simply can't afford it while still (hopefully) benefiting from the increased income from a new "hot" crop. We saw that with quinoa. True too with wild rice.

The problem is not with exploring ingredients from other areas; in fact, that is one of the true joys of a globalized world. The problem is in mass consumption with little regard for how the crops are produced, how they function within the society of origin, or for the folks who grow and depend on the ingredient as a daily diet staple.

Yewande Komolafe articulates this point with shimmering clarity in her essay "The Problems with Palm Oil Don't Start with My Recipes." She explains how red palm oil is critical to the food of Nigeria, her home country. Red palm oil is an unrefined foodstuff that is produced only on a small, sustainable scale. "Palm oil" is a horse of a different color. Komolafe explains that problematic palm oil has been refined, bleached, deodorized, and "processed on an industrial scale that goes beyond most traditional West African culinary practices."

In short, it is not the ingredient's fault; rather, too much of a good thing ends up being a bad thing. That bad thing is only intensified when an ingredient is decontextualized from its place of origin and production practices. Komolafe later crystalizes the issue: "Suggesting that West African cuisine reconsider an ingredient that corporations have come to produce and exploit is like arguing a fonio farmer in Senegal should not water her crops because somewhere else in the world water is sold in plastic bottles."

If we, as a society, are going to grapple with our own, unsustainable system of monoculture cropping, we must also recognize that creating demand for a single ingredient has similar effects in other farming systems across the world. In short, everything in moderation, even the most super of superfoods.

NOTES

AMARANTH

BOTANICAL NAME: *Amaranthus caudatus*

PLACE OF ORIGIN: Pre-Columbian Mexico

TOP GLOBAL PRODUCERS: China, Peru, Bolivia, and Mexico

GLUTEN FREE: Yes

PROTEIN CONTENT: 14 percent

TO SOAK OR NOT TO SOAK (THAT IS ALWAYS THE QUESTION): No

BASIC WATER:GRAIN RATIO FOR STEWING: 3:1

AVERAGE BOILING TIME: 20 minutes

YIELD RATIO AFTER COOKING: 1:3

SIGNS OF DONENESS: Grains will have puffed and become fluffy without collapsing.

FONIO

BOTANICAL NAME: *Digitaria exilis*

PLACE OF ORIGIN: West Africa

TOP GLOBAL PRODUCERS: Ethiopia

GLUTEN FREE: Yes

PROTEIN CONTENT: 10 percent

TO SOAK OR NOT TO SOAK (THAT IS ALWAYS THE QUESTION): No

BASIC WATER:GRAIN RATIO FOR STEWING: 3:1

AVERAGE BOILING TIME: 5 to 7 minutes

YIELD RATIO AFTER COOKING: 1:3

SIGNS OF DONENESS: Grains will have puffed and become fluffy without clumping.

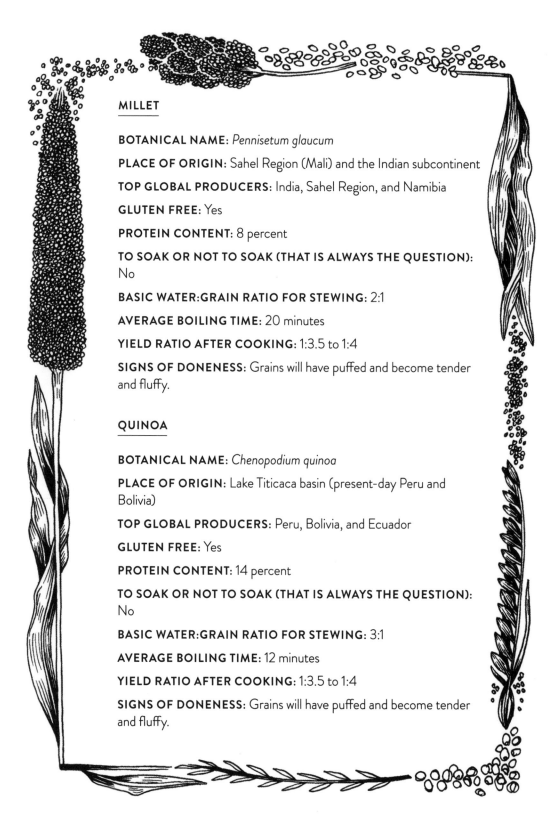

MILLET

BOTANICAL NAME: *Pennisetum glaucum*

PLACE OF ORIGIN: Sahel Region (Mali) and the Indian subcontinent

TOP GLOBAL PRODUCERS: India, Sahel Region, and Namibia

GLUTEN FREE: Yes

PROTEIN CONTENT: 8 percent

TO SOAK OR NOT TO SOAK (THAT IS ALWAYS THE QUESTION): No

BASIC WATER:GRAIN RATIO FOR STEWING: 2:1

AVERAGE BOILING TIME: 20 minutes

YIELD RATIO AFTER COOKING: 1:3.5 to 1:4

SIGNS OF DONENESS: Grains will have puffed and become tender and fluffy.

QUINOA

BOTANICAL NAME: *Chenopodium quinoa*

PLACE OF ORIGIN: Lake Titicaca basin (present-day Peru and Bolivia)

TOP GLOBAL PRODUCERS: Peru, Bolivia, and Ecuador

GLUTEN FREE: Yes

PROTEIN CONTENT: 14 percent

TO SOAK OR NOT TO SOAK (THAT IS ALWAYS THE QUESTION): No

BASIC WATER:GRAIN RATIO FOR STEWING: 3:1

AVERAGE BOILING TIME: 12 minutes

YIELD RATIO AFTER COOKING: 1:3.5 to 1:4

SIGNS OF DONENESS: Grains will have puffed and become tender and fluffy.

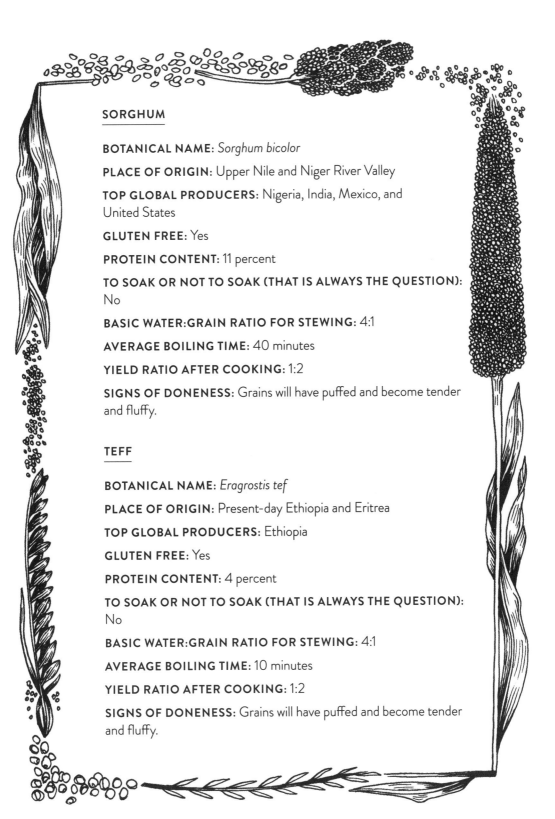

SORGHUM

BOTANICAL NAME: *Sorghum bicolor*

PLACE OF ORIGIN: Upper Nile and Niger River Valley

TOP GLOBAL PRODUCERS: Nigeria, India, Mexico, and United States

GLUTEN FREE: Yes

PROTEIN CONTENT: 11 percent

TO SOAK OR NOT TO SOAK (THAT IS ALWAYS THE QUESTION): No

BASIC WATER:GRAIN RATIO FOR STEWING: 4:1

AVERAGE BOILING TIME: 40 minutes

YIELD RATIO AFTER COOKING: 1:2

SIGNS OF DONENESS: Grains will have puffed and become tender and fluffy.

TEFF

BOTANICAL NAME: *Eragrostis tef*

PLACE OF ORIGIN: Present-day Ethiopia and Eritrea

TOP GLOBAL PRODUCERS: Ethiopia

GLUTEN FREE: Yes

PROTEIN CONTENT: 4 percent

TO SOAK OR NOT TO SOAK (THAT IS ALWAYS THE QUESTION): No

BASIC WATER:GRAIN RATIO FOR STEWING: 4:1

AVERAGE BOILING TIME: 10 minutes

YIELD RATIO AFTER COOKING: 1:2

SIGNS OF DONENESS: Grains will have puffed and become tender and fluffy.

BOILED

Each tiny grain boils in its own time. The Notes Boxes on previous pages list the tiny grains most used in my kitchen along with their average cooking times. When in doubt, consult the packaging the grains came in. Pro tip: If transferring the grains from the original packaging to a glass storage jar, write the cooking time and ratio of water to grain on painter's tape and stick it to the bottom of the jar for quick reference.

braised rabbit w/tiny grains, radishes + tarragon sunflower seed rig

Rabbit is one of the most sustainable animal proteins available. They have a low carbon footprint, they convert plants into protein efficiently, and they are, ahem, adept at procreation. Plus, rabbit is delicious. Farm-raised rabbit is very mild, juicy, and tender compared to her wild hare cousin. Try; don't scoff. Of course, if you don't have rabbit in your local market, really any protein will substitute; or leave it off entirely and you'll be no worse for ware (rabbit).

One 5 lb [2.25 kg] rabbit or whole chicken, back bones removed and left as two halves

Neutral oil

Salt and freshly ground pepper

2 onions (about 1 lb [450 g]), thinly sliced

10 sprigs thyme

2 Tbsp mustard (whole-grain or Dijon)

1 cup [250 ml] white wine

1 cup [250 ml] stock or water

1½ cups [300 g] tiny grains

4 oz [120 g] spinach, leaves torn if large

10 radishes (about 1½ lb [675 g]), cut into wedges

1 recipe Tarragon Sunflower Seed Rig (page 50)

Preheat the oven to 325°F [165°C]. Blot the rabbit dry with paper towels.

In a large frying pan, heat a glug of neutral oil over medium-high heat. Season the meat liberally with salt and pepper.

Sear the meat on one side until golden brown, about 7 minutes. Remove from the pan and reserve.

Add the onions and thyme to the pan with a big pinch of salt and black pepper. Sweat over medium heat until soft, about 5 minutes. Add the mustard and white wine to deglaze the pan. Cook, allowing the wine to reduce by half.

Add the stock and the meat (skin-side up if using chicken). Cover, place in the oven, and braise until the meat is tender when pulled with a fork, 30 to 40 minutes.

continued

Bring a large pot of salted water to a boil and boil the grains until tender—cooking time will vary depending on the grain you've chosen. Consult the Notes Boxes (pages 357–359) for an estimated time.

Drain and dress the grains with a glug of oil to keep from clumping.

When the meat is done, remove the lid and separate the meat into four even portions.

If using chicken, crisp the skin under a broiler before serving.

To serve, divvy the grains among plates or spread on a serving platter. Dress the spinach with a glug of olive oil and a pinch of salt, then pile next to the grains. Top with the meat and a few spoonfuls of the braising liquid. Dress the radishes with the tarragon sunflower seed rig and add alongside or on top of the whole lot.

variations

w/tomato, cucumber + parsley salad

Combine 1 lb [450 g] of cherry tomatoes (halved) or slicing tomatoes (cubed) with 1 lb [450 g] of cucumbers, half-peeled and cut into half-moons, and ½ cup [125 ml] of Lemon Parsley Mojo (page 48). Pile the salad over a nest of boiled tiny grains, about ½ cup [100 g] per person.

w/shaved cauliflower, roasted squash + spinach

Thinly slice ½ head (about 1 lb [450 g]) of cauliflower. Cut 2 delicata or acorn squash (about 2 lb [900 g]) into rounds or wedges, dress with neutral oil and salt, and roast in a hot oven until caramelized and tender. Combine the cauliflower and roasted squash with 4 oz [120 g] of baby spinach and 1½ cups [300 g] of boiled tiny grains. Dress with ¼ cup [60 ml] of Rosemary Lemon Chili Mojo (page 50) and serve.

w/roasted sweet potatoes, dates, kale + paprika cumin oil

Cut 3 lb [1.35 kg] of sweet potatoes into large rounds, dress with neutral oil and a big pinch of salt, and roast until tender and deeply caramelized. Slice 1 cup [65 g] of dates. Thinly slice 10 stemmed kale leaves and massage with a pinch of salt until tender. Dress the dates, kale, and 1 cup [200 g] of boiled grains with ¼ cup [60 ml] of Paprika Cumin Oil (page 40). Transfer the roasted sweet potatoes to a serving platter and top with the kale-date-grain salad.

MARINATED

In cooking school, we learned that a traditional dinner plate consists of a protein, a vegetable, and a starch. The implicit understanding is that the protein is the star and everything else is filler. In thinking about celebrating grains and how to incorporate more grains into each meal, I wanted to evolve their role to one more integral to the plot. Marinated grains soak up acidity and seasoning as they cool in a dressing. I like to incorporate these grains into any given dish, adding an unexpected punch of flavor and texture. While there are recipes that follow, I most often spoon marinated grains over a large platter of very simply roasted vegetables.

baby beets w/marinated sorghum + smoked yogurt

The best ideas often are not our own but filter through the influence of others. My sister, Sally, gave me a big jar of smoked salt as a gift, and I wondered how to best utilize it. I first made smoked yogurt when cooking from *Cooking for Good Times* by Paul Kahan and Perry Hendrix. In their restaurants, they smoke the yogurt, but at home, smoked salt or even liquid smoke do the job just fine. That was my gateway recipe, and I now use smoked salt in any number of dishes.

2 cups [400 g] sorghum or other tiny grains

10 to 15 small to medium beets (about 2 lb [900 g])

Neutral oil

Salt

1 recipe Sorghum Vinaigrette (page 37)

½ cup (4 oz [125 ml]) Smoked Yogurt (page 45)

10 sprigs dill, roughly chopped

continued

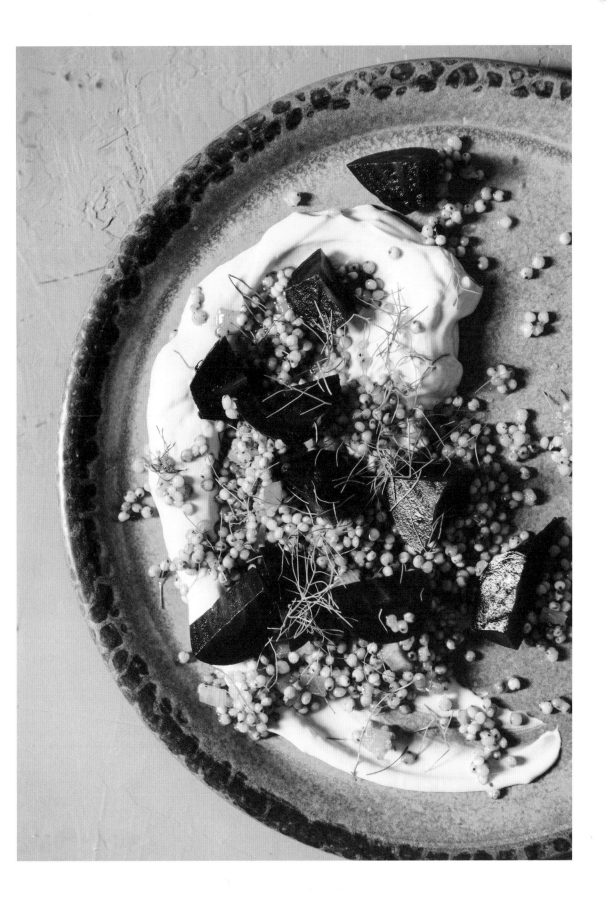

Preheat an oven to 350°F [180°C].

Boil the sorghum grains until tender, about 40 minutes.

While the sorghum cooks, toss the beets in a glug of neutral oil and a big pinch of salt. Transfer to a baking dish, add a splash of water, cover, and roast until tender, about 20 minutes depending on size.

When the grains are tender, drain well, then dress with the vinaigrette.

When the beets are tender, allow to cool for 5 to 10 minutes, rub off the skins, and cut into large wedges.

To serve, spoon the yogurt onto a large serving platter, lay the beets on top of the yogurt, top with several spoonfuls of the marinated sorghum, and scatter the dill all over.

variations

w/summer tomato slabs + arugula

Cut 1 large slicing tomato into thick slabs, top with cottage cheese or goat cheese (if you like), then a spoonful of marinated grains and a handful of arugula dressed in olive oil and a pinch of salt and black pepper.

w/fall root vegetables + celery + herb salad

Roast 1 lb [450 g] of root vegetables per person. Toss the roasted roots with ¼ cup [50 g] of marinated grains per person. Top with a salad of a couple of stalks of celery thinly sliced and dressed with a handful of picked herbs and olive oil or a spoonful of Lemon Parsley Mojo (page 48).

w/poached egg + bitter greens winter salad

Combine 1 cup [200 g] of marinated tiny grains with 5 oz [150 g] bitter greens (chicories, arugula, baby mustard greens, and so on). Top the salad with 1 poached egg per person and 2 spoonfuls of Rosemary Lemon Chili Mojo (page 50) (or any other dressing you like) and serve.

FRIED

I'm a big fan of "desert island" thinking, which is to say, if I woke up stranded on a desert island and suddenly found a bowl of cooked grains and wanted to make a fritter, what would be my starting point? There are lots of other things that would probably be of primary concern—water, shelter, how did I get to said island—but eventually I'd get around to the fritter. After puzzling and trying lots of iterations, the most foolproof way to make a fritter with any grain (or grated vegetable or anything really) is choux dough. Choux dough is the same puffy egg-based dough used for cream puffs, gougères, and eclairs. The technique is straightforward and takes only a couple of attempts to master. Then you'll have a dough that can bind anything you want to deep-fry—or try your hand at cream puffs, gougères, or eclairs.

any grain fritter base recipe

This is my go-to choux dough recipe. Without the grains, it makes great gougères or can be piped and baked into large buns for deliciously decadent sandwiches.

3 oz [85 g] butter

1½ tsp salt

1 cup [120 g] all-purpose flour

3 eggs

1 cup [200 g] any boiled grain

2 oz [60 g] hard cheese, grated (optional)

1 Tbsp chopped parsley (optional)

Neutral oil, for frying

In a medium saucepan, bring ¾ cup [180 ml] of water and the butter and salt to a boil. When the butter is melted and the water boiling, add the flour and stir, stir, stir over medium heat to make a ball of dough. Keep cooking until the flour smells a bit cooked and starts to stick to the bottom of the pan, about 2 minutes.

continued

Remove from the heat and transfer the ball to a stand mixer (or be prepared to beat it with a wooden spoon). Turn the mixer on to medium speed. Add 1 egg and let it fully incorporate into the dough. When fully mixed, add the next egg and repeat. When all 3 eggs are mixed in, the dough should be silky.

Add the grains, cheese, and parsley (if using) and beat until very evenly distributed. Allow the dough to cool, covered, for at least 30 minutes.

In a large pot, heat 4 in [10 cm] of neutral oil to 375°F [190°C]. Set a rack on a baking sheet or line a plate with paper towels.

When the oil is hot, scoop ping-pong-size balls of dough into the oil and fry until one side of the fritter is golden, about 4 minutes. Flip and fry the other side. Lift from the oil and drain on the rack or paper towels.

Fritters can be made ahead and then rewarmed and crisped in a 350°F [180°C] oven. The dough can also be made up to 2 days in advance and kept refrigerated.

Serve with any dipping sauce you like.

SPROUTED

This recipe is one part Ballymaloe Brown Yeast Loaf (the very first yeasted bread I made in cooking school) and one part Big Seedy Loaf, the sprouted grain bread from Nic Theisen of Farm Club in Traverse City, Michigan. The idea is to bind as many sprouted grains with as little bread dough as needed to hold it together, yielding a custardy, grain-dense loaf that holds together enough to be sliced and slathered with salted Irish butter or cream cheese and smoked salmon or roasted vegetables and fromage blanc from Leelanau Cheese Company or whatever you have on hand to make a snack. Note: The smallest grains—amaranth, teff, fonio—work just fine unsprouted. If you do sprout the tiniest grains, drain in cheesecloth and wring the water out. Also note: The recipe title sounds better with an Irish accent.

sprouted yeasted brown loaf

| Butter or non-stick cooking spray | 1 tsp active yeast | 1 lb [450 g] tiny grains, sprouted (see page 236) |
| 1 tsp honey | 1 lb [450 g] whole wheat flour | ½ tsp salt |

Grease two 5 by 8 in [13 by 20 cm] loaf pans.

Add the honey and yeast to 15 oz [425 ml] of tepid water and let bloom for 10 minutes or until foamy.

Combine the yeast mixture with the flour, sprouted grains, and salt.

Using your hand (shaped like a claw), bring the dough together so that everything is evenly distributed and there are no lumps of flour—it will be a loose, wet dough.

Divide the dough between the two loaf pans, cover with a damp tea towel, and let rise until almost doubled in volume, 1 to 2 hours.

Preheat the oven to 450°F [230°C]. Bake the loaves until golden brown, with an internal temperature of 200°F [95°C], 45 to 60 minutes. Unlike other breads, this doesn't sound hollow when tapped.

Remove from the oven and let cool in the pan for 10 minutes.

Turn out the loaf, loosening the sides with a knife if necessary, and let cool completely before slicing.

This loaf will store, uncovered, at room temperature, out of direct sunlight, for several days. It also freezes well. I regularly double the recipe, eat one loaf right away, and slice, wrap, and freeze the other loaves so I can pull out individual slices for morning toast.

wheat family

While researching this chapter, I sent my friend (who also happens to be a talented grain grower) the text—"HOW CAN SOMETHING SO SIMPLE BE SO COMPLICATED?!?!?!" This text shout of frustration came after several texts asking how this specific wheat is related to another and why it is called something else in Italian. Her response, "I'm not sure it is that simple. Wheat is very old. And the older something is, the more complex it tends to get." Words to live by.

Wheat is very old. Over the last 10,000 years of cultivation, numerous species of wheat have been developed through natural selection (wild crosses picked up by foragers) and artificial selection (by farmers throughout domestication). That diversity of species, combined with the fact that wheat is grown across much of the globe, has added layers of identification, naming, and usage to the daily staple. Here's how I think about wheat. I'm sure that a taxonomist would find flaws in this reasoning, but it works for me and I hope it clarifies something for you.

Einkorn is the founding grain of the wheat family. It has less gluten than common wheat, and the grains are very small, sometimes sold as *farro piccolo*. Domesticated einkorn crossed with a wild goat grass (*Aegilops triuncialis*), begetting emmer.

Emmer is the second-oldest ancestral wheat to be domesticated. Today, it is most commonly sold as farro (though farro is also the ethnobotanical term for einkorn and spelt—more on that on page 404). Stay with me . . .

Years of growing and selecting seed from emmer led to the development of **durum wheat**. Durum is the (modern day) second-most cultivated wheat species after common wheat. It is the hardest of the wheats (highest in protein) but not very elastic. This makes it better for things like pasta and less ideal for bread because it lacks the elasticity of other high-protein wheats.

Khorasan wheat is the daughter of durum, often called Pharaoh's wheat because of its large, king-like berry and regal chew. It is also sold as **kamut** in the United States. Why is it called different things? Who knows? I assume marketing.

Emmer also crossed with a different wild goat grass, begetting **spelt**. Spelt is (of course) also called dinkel wheat (because why not?!) and has been cultivated since 5000 BCE. After the evolution of common wheat, spelt fell out of favor, and was mostly grown as a relict crop in central Europe and northern Spain. Its production has upticked as it has grown favor in health and ancient-grain loving communities. Spelt is often described as having a nutty flavor and has less gluten than durum or high-protein common wheats.

Common wheat was developed through seed selection and quickly (over a few thousand years) became the favored (and most grown) wheat across the world—often displacing the production of other wheats, barley, and rye. But wait . . . there's more!

Common wheat didn't just stay the same from 100 BCE to today; it mutated and changed, and the seeds were saved and regrown, begetting numerous varieties of common wheat. Varieties like Lancaster Red, Fife, Marquis, Rouge de Bordeaux, and Turkey Red Grains, often referred to as heritage or heirloom wheats, were cultivated through open pollination and seed selection. Landrace, as a term, is used slightly differently. It is a technique for planting heritage grains in small trial plots and then selecting and saving seed from those grains that did the best, building a seed stock particular to that land or region. Since the Green Revolution of the 1950s, most farmers have been growing the hybridized and high-yielding wheats with the aid of chemical fertilizers, herbs, and fungicides, as well as controlled water supply.

This all brings us to today, where there are six additional categories under the common wheat umbrella, indicating:

1. Color: red or white
2. Protein content: hard or soft
3. Season of planting: spring or winter

Kernza is a registered trademark wheat developed by The Land Institute to be grown as a perennial wheat. The goal of perennial grain advocates is to minimize the erosion and soil compaction resulting from yearly tractor work while maximizing soil health through deep-rooted perennial plants that do not require the addition of synthetic herbicides or fertilizers. Kernza is not yet widely available but signals a potential shift (with all of its pros and cons) in how wheat could be grown in the future.

Oh, yeah. I almost forgot about rye. **Rye** is an old species within the wheat family related to barley. Rye is notoriously hearty; it grows well in poor soils and is resistant to drought. Today, it is primarily grown in eastern, central, and northern Europe for human consumption, animal fodder, and cover cropping. Rye has a lower gluten content than common wheat and often tastes spicier, with notes of pepper. I often blend it with wheat flour for stability.

In addition to species confusion, wheat is also sold as both **bulgur** and **freekeh**, which do not refer to a type of wheat so much as differences in post-harvest processing, affecting flavor and cooking (more on that on pages 396 and 426, respectively).

I can feel you growing impatient (maybe now you understand my shouting texts referenced at the start of all this). There are just a couple more vocab words regularly used and rarely defined. I blame the Italians (because these are all their terms).

Farina is coarsely ground wheat that is not durum. It is most often used to make porridge (think Cream of Wheat) or used on the underside of bread or pizza when baking.

Semolina is an Italian term for medium-ground durum wheat that is finer than farina (which, remember, is not durum wheat) but not as fine as 00.

00 or zero doppio is flour from any wheat (often durum) that is very finely ground. Traditionally, the Italian scale for flour goes from 2 (very coarse) to 00 (very fine). This flour is often sought after for pizza and pastas.

That's it. That's what I know. I find all of this interesting, but it shouldn't get in the way of cooking. You don't need to know where kamut falls in the wheat lineage to make a good salad with it. Just turn the page and move along.

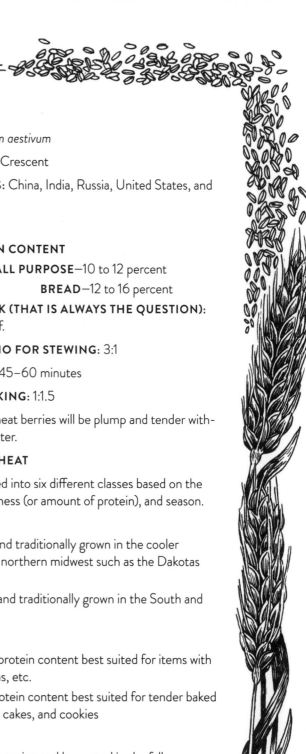

NOTES

BOTANICAL NAME: *Triticum aestivum*

PLACE OF ORIGIN: Fertile Crescent

TOP GLOBAL PRODUCERS: China, India, Russia, United States, and Canada (in that order)

GLUTEN FREE: No

AVERAGE FLOUR PROTEIN CONTENT

CAKE FLOUR—7 percent   **ALL PURPOSE**—10 to 12 percent

PASTRY FLOUR—9 percent   **BREAD**—12 to 16 percent

TO SOAK OR NOT TO SOAK (THAT IS ALWAYS THE QUESTION): Shortens cooking time in half.

BASIC WATER:GRAIN RATIO FOR STEWING: 3:1

AVERAGE BOILING TIME: 45–60 minutes

YIELD RATIO AFTER COOKING: 1:1.5

SIGNS OF DONENESS: Wheat berries will be plump and tender without any chalky line in the center.

CLASSES OF COMMON WHEAT

Common wheat is categorized into six different classes based on the characteristics of color, hardness (or amount of protein), and season.

COLOR:

> **RED**—Darker in color and traditionally grown in the cooler climates, especially the northern midwest such as the Dakotas and Montana

> **WHITE**—Paler in color and traditionally grown in the South and Pacific Northwest

HARDNESS:

> **HARD**—Higher gluten protein content best suited for items with structure: breads, pastas, etc.

> **SOFT**—Lower gluten protein content best suited for tender baked goods: scones, biscuits, cakes, and cookies

SEASON:

> **SPRING:** Planted in the spring and harvested in the fall

> **WINTER:** Planted in the fall, overwintered, and harvested in the spring

GRAIN'S ANATOMY

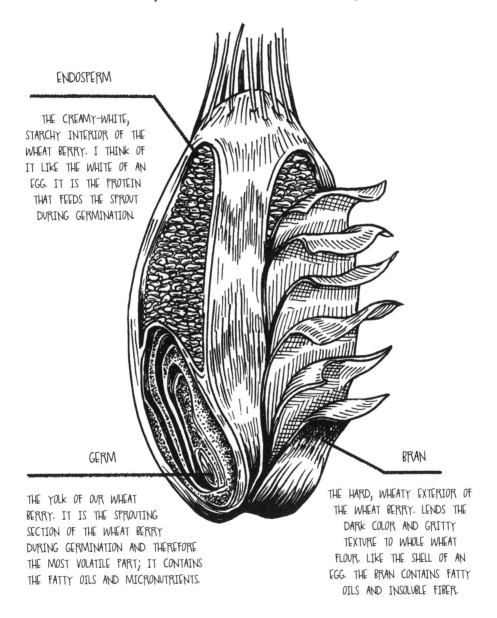

ENDOSPERM

THE CREAMY-WHITE, STARCHY INTERIOR OF THE WHEAT BERRY. I THINK OF IT LIKE THE WHITE OF AN EGG. IT IS THE PROTEIN THAT FEEDS THE SPROUT DURING GERMINATION.

GERM

THE YOLK OF OUR WHEAT BERRY. IT IS THE SPROUTING SECTION OF THE WHEAT BERRY DURING GERMINATION AND THEREFORE THE MOST VOLATILE PART; IT CONTAINS THE FATTY OILS AND MICRONUTRIENTS.

BRAN

THE HARD, WHEATY EXTERIOR OF THE WHEAT BERRY. LENDS THE DARK COLOR AND GRITTY TEXTURE TO WHOLE WHEAT FLOUR. LIKE THE SHELL OF AN EGG. THE BRAN CONTAINS FATTY OILS AND INSOLUBLE FIBER.

MEADOWLARK ORGANICS

Halee Wepking, her husband John, and Paul Bickford own and operate Meadowlark Organics in Ridgeway, Wisconsin. In addition to growing a wide variety of heritage wheats and beans, they mill flour in their stone mill. I wanted to talk with Ms. Wepking because Meadowlark Organics is one of a growing force of regional millers converting their crops to ingredients and creating alternative markets for flours, grains, and beans. She spoke on the phone with me in early June 2020 while waiting out the rain to get back into the fields.

Abra Berens: Tell me about the history of your farm and how you came to farm.

Halee Wepking: John and I met cooking at Prune in New York and decided that we wanted to leave New York City to move back to his family's farm in Lancaster, Wisconsin. We were working at a cafe and farming his family's 150 acres. There wasn't a clear path toward managing that land the way we wanted to with the rest of the family. I started looking for other jobs and found Paul's ad that said, "I am seeking a forward-thinking individual or couple to join my 950-acre farming operation. . . ethics and trust are a cornerstone of organic farming and are important to my operation. I want to share my forty years of farm experience with someone who is willing to improve my farm." We, naturally, gave a call.

It was sort of a perfect storm for why we became grain growers. We were inspired by what we had seen in New York City—heritage and heirloom staple crops (not just the fancy garnishes) starting to be really utilized in restaurants. We started working (and working well) with Paul and so suddenly had access to hundreds of acres of land. That meant we could grow at a scale that was profitable. Plus, Lonesome Stone Mill was only thirty-five minutes away, and we had enough grain to make milling viable. It was a complicated relationship with Lonesome Stone but instrumental to growing our business.

We were able to get a USDA grant and buy Lonesome Stone, so right now we are in the process of moving the mill to our farm. The benefits to taking over the milling for our region are broad. It makes it easier for us to sell directly to customers. We'll be able to mill for other growers, creating infrastructure for producers here— Meadowlark Community Mill. Plus, obviously any time you don't have to truck thousands of pounds of anything thirty-five minutes each way is a boon!

AB: What is the trajectory for an average year for you?

HW: It's funny; it's not even technically summer, but it feels like the end of summer already. It's early June now. We are playing the weather game—hoping for rain when we need it and not when the grain is flowering, because of disease spread. By middle of July we'll be harvesting and always hoping for a dry harvest because it eases a whole host of potential problems. After harvest we immediately switch to getting all that seed cleaned and then stored as whole grain to be milled when needed. There's a little bit of a break in early September, though we're always managing hay and corn after grain is harvested. Plus, we plant a lot of our small grain for the next season in the fall. October, we hand select seed for open-pollinated seed corn and then into combining dry and soybeans. Winter's supposed to be slow, but it's not—we always find ourselves going to so many conferences, financial planning, negotiating contracts, planning crop rotation, which is always evolving, so a lot of time to plot that out each year. Then we're back at it.

AB: Can you tell me a little bit about that crop rotation?

HW: We farm 750 acres, but it is 120 individual fields. We always have a plan B and C because rotation gets out of whack, especially last year when it was so wet. We couldn't get into fields and ended up planting a ton of buckwheat to salvage the calendar. That throws the order off.

The milling work is different. It is continuous activity but generally slows in the summer, because people bake less in the summer, and speeds up again when it gets cool.

AB: *How about an average day?*

HW: Well, no day ever looks the same!

We spend a good amount of time cleaning grain. The first step of engaging with regional grain economy is [securing] grain-cleaning equipment. John got up and was cleaning grain by 6 a.m. and now is driving the grain to Lonesome Stone. For efficiency's sake, we try to clean 4 tons in one lot to take 8,000 pounds per run to the mill. For now we manage a lot of logistics of moving grain back and forth, but all of this will change when the mill is across the driveway. It's so exciting for a ton of reasons—not least of all is all the time we'll get back.

My day is mostly spent talking with customers, working with the mill, packing and shipping orders.

On the growing side, we have a pretty diverse farm—hay, organic seed corn, planting beans. We never want to grow only grain. A lot of care needs to go into our land because this region, the Driftless Region, is very hilly and so highly erodible land. So that means a lot of rotation to limit tilling. For farm work there is normal cycle cultivation, planting, harvesting. There's always something going. On the milling side, the day is more flexible than for most growers because the work depends on volume of orders, not the growing calendar or the weather. We are working toward a weekly cycle where we know the capacity of the mill and we know what orders are coming in and so can get it all done. We exclusively mill to order right now, lacking storage capacity for milled flour at Lonesome Stone. Always a balance, because it is not shelf stable, but we also want to make the mill schedule efficient.

AB: *Tell me more about that—I think most people think of flour as super shelf stable.*

HW: Freshly milled flour is so alive! That's how it should be. Yes, by having the bran and the germ in the flour it will go rancid faster because of those oils, but for me it is really about how it smells and behaves. Freshly milled flour smells like milk powder to me, which I know sounds odd, but it is just such a different product than something that has been on a shelf for a long time (or can be on a shelf for a long time). I want to be careful to not say it is better, because then we get into people's expectations. It is truly just a different product.

AB: That reminds me of freshly roasted coffee. I remember the first time I ever took a coffee class at Zingerman's Deli in Ann Arbor, the way the grounds bloomed up versus the very old preground coffee was a real eye-opener for me.

HW: Yes, very similar. For a day in the life of the mill, it is all about trying to be as efficient as possible. Our mill is a 36-inch stone Meadows Mill. We do whole wheat and bolted flours—that's sifted to make more of a white flour by removing the bran. We organize the day so that we can do all of the bolted flours at one time. There's a lot of time spent cleaning between different batches, so we make sure to not go back and forth between types unnecessarily.

Milling corn requires adjusting the stone—always monitoring the quality of the flour. Always checking the ratio of extraction—weighing the flour and mids (the sifted-out particles), tightening the stones or loosening them up, sharpening the stones, and so on. Also checking the temperature of the flour after it is milled. You really don't want it to get too hot—say above 120°F. After it is milled it goes into 25- or 50-pound bags. We have an automated bagger now for the smaller, retail bagging. Stone milling is really a dying art, so there aren't a lot of resources or money put into research in terms of nutrition or storage of stone milled flour. There are a lot of feelings about it that it is superior, and it makes a lot of sense that it would be, but not a ton of data.

AB: My friends Heidi and Molly call that a "science feel"—like I really feel like this would be backed up by data.

HW: [*laughs*] Yes, totally. You know, thankfully there is a network of sharing of information—not unlike farming in the organic community—which helps give some grounding. That's what I love about this work; it is so dependent on community. We do not want to be the only ones doing this. We build seed cleaner, but that is to serve other people. Regional grain economy is so fun because it engages so many people in so many different places. We need those middle players (seed cleaners, millers, distribution) to get the product into the market. For the system to work, it needs to have all the parts of the system in place—cleaning, transportation, storage for raw and milled grain, and then the outlets for the end product.

AB: What do you wish nonfarmers knew about your work?

HW: Sometimes I wish people knew the real power they have as
consumers. I was vegan in college for a while as part of animal rights.
I realized that I had more power as a consumer to change the system
of how animals are raised by buying from people who raise them the
way I wanted. There is an environmental impact of everyone's buying
choices. We believe that farmers can help mitigate climate change—
to see us as part of the solution, an act of environmental activism. If
people choose to spend their dollars with farmers who support those
practices, it makes a huge difference.

AB: What are the top three hurdles you face as a grower?

HW: Weather—just like every other farmer.

Money—bank lenders are finally coming around, but they have
been really hesitant to lend to us for our alternative ideas. It's easier
to get money for more conventional ag. It is easier to build a manure
slurry than grain cleaning facility. Still waiting on the bank to hear if
they are going to give money to pay for the building that is currently
being put up. We're really grateful for the Food Financial Institute,
founded by Tara Johnson of Tara's Whey. They help people in agriculture who are starting food businesses get financing, because it is
really hard to convey our work.

Human capital—finding other motivated, ambitious, able bodies
who want to do the hard work. Paul used HB2 visas a lot in the
dairy industry. We're looking to build a smaller crew of year-round
work, which is also where diversification comes in. Instead of being
just seasonal, there is winter work in the shop, at the mill, and in grain
cleaning.

AB: What are the top three successes from the past year?

HW: Finding a miller—someone to help follow through with the plan.
Receiving a grant from the Wisconsin Department of Agriculture to
help with the mill transition. Hiring an additional farmer. It's all about
the people right now.

We see it as food that we're growing for our communities—there's
a sense of real accomplishment to feed others. And a lot of attention
is paid to resilience, especially about climate insecurity. I know we
are still the minority, but especially in the Driftless Region, the farms
are generally smaller and so have stayed in the couple-hundred-acre
range. Wisconsin also has a history of diversified agriculture. I feel

really lucky to have found agriculture as what to invest my life in. In some ways, I'm thankful that I don't come directly from a farming family. So few young farmers stay in farming because they saw how hard it was for their parents. [I'm] coming in without those paradigms. Seeing farming as a lever for change as opposed to something we have to perpetuate, because there are so many things that are broken. We are motivated to be engaged with policy and help change the agricultural landscape—diversify, have fair markets, and help young farmers access land and gain skills. There are so many successes and so much potential.

AB: OK, final question: Do you cook with the flour that you mill?

HW: We make bread all the time. I just made a tres leches cake with whole wheat pastry flour and rye milled on our Mock Mill. The recipe is from Sarah Owens and is supposed to be made with purple barley. I just made it with rye, and it was super delicious. Oh, that thick milky sauce! We made pretzels the other day. Yes, we cook with it all the time.

MILLING ABOUT

ROLLER MILL

METAL MILLS DEVELOPED IN EUROPE IN THE 1860S THAT SEPARATE THE ENDOSPERM FROM THE BRAN AND GERM BEFORE MILLING THE REMAINING ENDOSPERM, YIELDING A WHITE FLOUR THAT IS MORE SHELF STABLE.

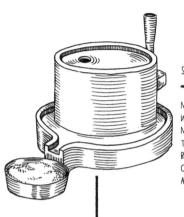

STONE MILL

MOST TRADITIONAL FORM OF MILLING, WHERE GRAINS ARE RUN BETWEEN TWO MOVING MILLS WITH GROOVES CUT INTO THEM. THE GRAINS ARE CRUSHED BETWEEN TWO STONES, RESULTING IN CRACKED WHEAT, IF LEFT VERY COARSE, ALL THE WAY DOWN TO FINE FLOUR.

BLEACH AND BROMATE

HISTORICALLY, WHITE, STONE-MILLED FLOUR WAS MORE EXPENSIVE BECAUSE OF THE ADDITIONAL STEPS NEEDED TO REMOVE THE BRAN FROM THE FLOUR. TRADITIONALLY, EVEN ROLLER-MILLED WHITE FLOUR WAS STILL A CREAMY YELLOW. TO MAKE THE FLOUR WHITER (AND THEREFORE SEEM FANCIER AND MORE DESIRABLE), A CHEMICAL PROCESS OF ADDING BLEACH (NOT BATHROOM BLEACH BUT NOT ALL THAT DIFFERENT) AND BROMATE WHITENED THE FLOUR FASTER AND MORE ECONOMICALLY. BLEACHING FLOUR IS STILL COMMON PRACTICE. BROMATING IS NOT BECAUSE IT HAS BEEN LINKED TO CANCER IN SOME STUDIES AND, WHILE IT'S NOT TECHNICALLY BANNED IN THE US, THE FDA DISCOURAGES ITS USE.

WHOLE WHEAT FLOUR

FLOUR THAT CONTAINS ALL PARTS OF THE WHEAT BERRY—INCLUDING THE BRAN, WHICH GIVES IT THE CHARACTERISTIC BROWN FLECKS, AND THE GERM, WHICH SHORTENS ITS SHELF LIFE. WHOLE WHEAT FLOUR SHOULD BE STORED IN THE FRIDGE OR FREEZER AND CONSUMED IN AROUND 6 MONTHS TO STAVE OFF RANCIDITY.

BOLTED AND SIFTED FLOUR

BOLTED: WHOLE WHEAT FLOUR THAT HAS HAD SOME OF THE BRAN REMOVED BY RUNNING IT THROUGH A SERIES OF FINER AND FINER CLOTH TUBES TO REMOVE THE LARGER FLECKS OF BRAN, LEAVING THE FLOURY ENDOSPERM AND GERM IN PLACE. THIS IS AN OLDER TERM AND A PROCESS THAT IS MAKING A COMEBACK IN SMALLER REGIONAL MILLS.

ENRICHMENT

BECAUSE MOST OF THE MICRONUTRIENTS IN WHEAT LIVE IN THE BRAN AND GERM, ROLLER-MILLED WHITE FLOUR IS LESS NUTRITIOUS. ENRICHMENT ADDS NUTRIENTS (THIAMIN, NIACIN, RIBOFLAVIN, FOLIC ACID, IRON AND CALCIUM) BACK INTO THE FLOUR. TO BE LABELED AS ENRICHED, IT MUST MEET THE STANDARDS SET BY THE FDA.

SIFTED: WHOLE WHEAT FLOUR THAT PASSES THROUGH A SERIES OF FINER AND FINER SCREENS TO REMOVE THE BRAN—ALSO CALLED EXTRACTION FLOUR. SAY YOU TAKE 100 PERCENT WHOLE WHEAT FLOUR AND RUN IT THROUGH SCREENS TO REMOVE 10 PERCENT OF THE BRAN; YOU HAVE 90 PERCENT EXTRACTION FLOUR IN THAT 90 PERCENT OF THE FLOUR IS STILL INTACT. HIGH EXTRACTION FLOUR IS DARKER IN COLOR THAN LOW EXTRACTION BECAUSE MORE OF THE FLECKS OF BRAN ARE IN PLACE. IT'S OFTEN USED IN BREAD BAKING BECAUSE YOU RETAIN THE NUTRIENTS AND NUTTY FLAVOR OF WHOLE WHEAT FLOUR WHILE REMOVING THE SHARP PIECES OF BRAN THAT CAN CUT THE GLUTEN WEB CREATED IN BREAD MAKING THAT GIVES BREAD ITS SIGNATURE HEIGHT.

wheat berries: common, kamut, kernza, rye, spelt

Wheat berries are the straight-up, unprocessed seeds of the wheat plant. Different species and varietals will look different (kamut is the largest, kernza is the smallest) and have different flavors—all ranging somewhere on the ubiquitous "nutty" spectrum.

I use wheat berries either whole, most often boiled but sometimes sprouted, or milled into flour. Adding boiled wheat berries is one of the easiest ways to get a portion of whole grain into any given meal. They add a textural difference to the most humdrum of salads. You can add them to any random soup to make it heartier. Even plain boiled wheat berries can be used as the starch portion of a traditional dinner plate, replacing noodles, couscous, or any other grain, such as rice or buckwheat.

There are a zillion ways to use wheat flour and a zillion more cookbooks out there to give you ideas, many of them coming from bakers more skilled than I. That said, I love the galette recipe on page 392 and use it all year long. Festooned with any vegetable toppings (suggestions provided of course), it is my favorite appetizer, light lunch, or party platter.

BOILED

Any sort of whole-groat, unmilled wheat can be boiled, yielding a tender, chewy grain. The thicker the grain, the longer it will take to cook—sometimes upward of 45 minutes. Soaking does not shorten the cooking time. Thankfully, all wheat berries store well after cooking and it takes the same amount of time to cook six cups as it does to cook two, so have at it.

cucumber + parsley salad w/pickle liquid dressing

This is the sort of thing that I bring to a dish-to-pass or potluck dinner. It has texture and tang and goes with anything that others will bring. Similarly, for solo dinners at home, it does well alongside any sort of grilled meat or fish, topped with an egg, piled on top of a thick slab of tomato, or all on its ownsome. I also use salads like this as a catchall for any number of grains that I cooked in other big batches—feel free to add any lentils, buckwheat, chickpeas, or tiny grains that you happen to have on hand.

1 lb [450 g] cucumbers, half-peeled (leaving stripes of green skin)

2 cups [400 g] wheat berries, boiled

10 sprigs parsley, roughly chopped

1 recipe Pickle Liquid Dressing (page 37)

Salt

Cut the cucumber into a large dice or half-moons. Combine the cucumber, boiled wheat berries, and parsley.

Dress the wheat berry mixture with half of the dressing and a pinch of salt. Stir to coat evenly and add seasoning or more dressing as desired.

continued

variations

grilled eggplant w/wheat berries, cherry tomatoes + goat cheese vinaigrette

Heat a grill. Cut 2 medium-size eggplants into 1 in [2.5 cm] thick rounds. Dress the eggplant rounds liberally with olive oil and salt, then grill over medium heat until golden brown and cooked through.

Combine 1 cup [200 g] of wheat berries, 1 lb [450 g] of cherry tomatoes, halved, and ½ cup [125 ml] of Goat Cheese Vinaigrette (page 36).

To serve, top the eggplant rounds with the wheat berry salad and several torn leaves of basil (optional).

spinach salad w/anchovy vinaigrette + hard-cooked egg

Dress 6 oz [180 g] of spinach (or a couple of handfuls per person) with ¼ cup [60 ml] of Anchovy Vinaigrette (page 35), 2 hard-cooked eggs (cut into rounds or grated on the largest tooth of a box grater), and several grinds of black pepper. To serve, sprinkle ¼ cup [50 g] of cooked wheat berries all over the top.

roasted carrots w/wheat berries, pickled cherries, arugula + brown butter vinaigrette

Cut 2 lb [900 g] of carrots into large chunks, toss with olive oil, salt, and pepper, and roast at 400°F [200°C] until deeply caramelized and tender, about 35 minutes.

While they are cooking, pickle ½ cup [150 g] of dried cherries (or cranberries) (page 57).

When the carrots are done, combine with 1 cup [200 g] of cooked wheat berries, the cherries (without their pickling liquid), ½ cup [125 ml] of Brown Butter Vinaigrette (page 35), and a hearty handful of arugula or any other tender green you have on hand. Toss, adjust the seasoning, and serve.

It is also nice to leave the carrots whole and roast them like that, then lay them on a platter and top with the salad just before serving.

FLOUR

I learned this dough from Paula Haney, owner of Hoosier Mama Pie Company, who learned it from legendary pastry chef Della Gossett. The two types of fat make the dough incredibly flaky and tender. The butter, cut into pea-size pieces, leaves little pockets as it bakes; the cream cheese tenderizes the dough as the fat insulates the gluten proteins from developing, which also means that you can reroll the scraps of this dough several times without it toughening. Because there is no water measure, this dough is also practically foolproof, as we proved to Paula over and over again, because we never messed it up!

flaky rye + three cheese galette w/asparagus salad

Any sort of wheat can be milled into flour, and any flour (whole wheat or sifted) can be used to make this versatile dough. I like to mix rye and all-purpose flour for the darker color and notes of spice, but use what is already in your pantry.

FOR THE PASTRY DOUGH

6 oz [180 g] all-purpose flour

4 oz [120 g] rye flour

¾ tsp salt

¼ tsp sugar

6 oz [180 g] butter, cut into cubes

6 oz [180 g] cream cheese, at room temperature

FOR THE FILLING

6 oz [180 g] cream cheese

6 oz [180 g] Cheddar, grated

2 oz [60 g] ricotta

1 Tbsp whole-grain mustard

½ tsp salt

½ tsp freshly ground black pepper

8 oz [225 g] asparagus, trimmed and washed

¼ cup [60 ml] Lemon Parsley Mojo (page 48)

To make the dough: Combine the flours, salt, and sugar. Rub or cut in the butter until it is in pea-size pieces. Add the cream cheese and bring together into a slightly shaggy dough. Divide in half and pat into rounds, wrap in plastic, and chill for at least 30 minutes (or freeze for later use).

To make the filling: Combine the cheeses, mustard, salt, and pepper. Adjust the seasoning as desired and set aside.

Roll each ball into a ¼ in [6 mm] thick round of dough, roughly 14 in [35 cm] in diameter. Spread the cheese filling to 2 in [5 cm] from the edge of the pastry round. Fold up the edges of the dough to form the galette and press the points of each fold to seal. Chill or freeze the galettes for at least 30 minutes.

Preheat the oven to 350°F [180°C].

Bake the galettes until the pastry is cooked through, about 20 minutes.

Shave the asparagus into thin ribbons with a mandoline, sharp knife, or vegetable peeler and dress with the mojo.

When the galettes come out of the oven, let cool for 5 minutes then slice and top with the asparagus salad.

continued

other topping ideas

w/tomatoes + basil

w/roasted sweet corn + summer squash

w/sweet + white potatoes + rosemary lemon chili mojo (page 50)

w/thinly sliced celery + bacon

w/gingered apples (page 54)

w/mushrooms + kale

w/shaved brussels sprouts + hazelnut rig (page 47)

bulgur

I've detailed the mind-numbingly long history of wheat on previous pages. The history of bulgur is similarly ancient but significantly easier to understand.

Bulgur is not a grain in and of itself; it is any wheat berry, most often durum, parboiled, dried, and then, usually but not necessarily, cracked. In addition to being easy to understand, bulgur is also easy to cook. The parboiling cuts the preparation time to a fraction of the time needed to cook a raw wheat berry.

Bulgur is often confused for couscous, which is also not a grain in and of itself but instead very small pasta balls made, usually though not exclusively, from durum flour. Think of bulgur as the ancient version of "instant rice." While it is technically a processed food, because the bran and germ are left intact, it is still a whole grain. It's the most convenient food of the whole grain world.

BOILED OR SOAKED

Bulgur has already been cooked once (by the processor). You are, effectively, just rehydrating it. All bulgur is a little bit different, so it pays to check the packaging for any specific instructions. That said, if you have only a jar of bulgur and no cooking instructions, please know you have three options. One, boil in salted water until tender and drain (remembering that it will go super quickly because it has been parcooked). Two, boil an equal amount of water to bulgur by volume. Pour the water over the bulgur and let soak until tender, about 20 minutes. Three, soak the bulgur in an equal part of cold water overnight.

seared trout w/bulgur, fennel, radish + creamy mustard dressing

Lake trout is one of my favorite Great Lakes fish; feel free to substitute any slightly fatty fish of preference. The combination of bulgur, vegetables, and dressing also makes a great salad on its own for light lunches, picnics, or potlucks. No fish required.

1 cup [150 g] bulgur wheat

5 sprigs dill, coarsely chopped

5 sprigs parsley, coarsely chopped

Salt and freshly ground black pepper

Olive oil

Neutral oil

Four 5 oz [150 g] lake trout fillets, skin on

1 head fennel (about 8 oz [225 g]), shaved thinly on a mandoline or with a sharp knife

8 radishes (about 12 oz [340 g]), greens removed and cut in halves or quarters

1 recipe Creamy Mustard Dressing (page 36)

Boil 1 cup [250 ml] of water. Transfer to a small bowl and immediately add the bulgur. Cover and let the grain rehydrate, checking after 10 minutes.

When the bulgur reaches your desired texture (I like it a bit chewy, but not stuck-in-your-teeth gritty), drain off any excess water. While the bulgur is still warm, add the dill and parsley, a pinch or two of salt and black pepper, and a healthy glug of olive oil. Set aside, uncovered.

In a large frying pan, heat a couple of glugs of neutral oil over high heat. Pat the skin side of the trout dry and season both sides liberally with salt. When the oil is just about smoking, place the fish in the pan, skin-side down, slightly pressing down to ensure good contact between the skin and pan.

Lower the heat to medium-high and sear until the skin is well crisped and releases from the pan, 5 to 6 minutes.

While the fish is cooking, toss the fennel and radishes with the dressing and adjust the seasoning as desired.

When the fish skin is crispy and released from the pan, turn off the heat and flip the fish to lightly cook the flesh side in the residual heat of the pan, 1 to 2 minutes.

To serve, spoon the bulgur onto serving plates, nestle the fish (skin-side up) next to the bulgur, and top with the salad.

variations

w/tomatoes, cucumbers, mozzarella + romesco

Combine 2 cups [400 g] of rehydrated (or leftover) bulgur with 2 big tomatoes, diced, or 1 lb [450 g] of cherry tomatoes, halved; a cucumber, half-peeled and diced; 2 balls of fresh mozzarella, cut into chunks; two or three glugs of olive oil; and a big pinch of salt. Add a handful of chopped herbs (basil, mint, parsley) and toss to combine. Dish into bowls and top with 2 to 3 Tbsp [30 to 45 ml] of Romesco (page 49) per person.

w/shaved brussels sprouts, pecorino + walnut aillade

Shave enough Brussels sprouts or cabbage to get about 3 cups [300 g] total. Combine that with 2 cups [400 g] of rehydrated bulgur, 2 oz [60 g] of pecorino shaved into ribbons with a vegetable peeler, and 1 cup [250 ml] of Walnut Aillade (page 50). Toss to coat and adjust the seasoning as desired. Dish into bowls and top with more aillade and shavings of pecorino.

w/beets + gribiche

Roast 10 or so beets, about 2 lb [900 g], any color, and cut into wedges or irregular chunks. Combine the beets and about 1 cup [200 g] of rehydrated bulgur with about 1 cup [250 g] of Gribiche (page 47). Toss to coat and adjust the seasoning as desired.

FRIED

Bulgur, like most grains and legumes, can be prepped in a larger volume than needed for the meal at hand, then used throughout the week. That said, any of them can get boring eaten the same way several days in a row. Crisping bulgur changes the texture and, often, how the grain is featured in a dish. Traditionally, rehydrated bulgur makes up the lion's share of any given salad. When it is fried, I like it more as a garnish, crispy bits scattered over a larger quantity of vegetables. The decrease in volume also means frying grains is a good way to use up that random couple of spoonfuls of whatever you cooked way back at the beginning of the week.

roasted carrots w/crisped bulgur, pistachios, goat cheese, pickled cherries + arugula

To crisp bulgur—or any grain, really—simply pan fry the grain in a healthy amount of oil. Neutral oil (any flavorless oil with a high smoke point) works better than olive oil because it gets hotter and fries the grain faster, making the outside crispy without drying out the interior. With all frying, water makes the oil pop and splatter. If I think far enough ahead, I spread the grain on a plate or baking sheet to air-dry for 10 to 15 minutes before crisping. If I don't think ahead, I'll use a grease shield or piece of foil lightly draped over the frying pan to keep it from splattering on me.

2 lb [900 g] carrots, washed and cut in half lengthwise or left whole	1 Tbsp Ras el Hanout (page 41)	2 oz [60 g] arugula, washed
Olive oil	½ cup [65 g] pistachios, roughly chopped	½ cup [150 g] Pickled Dried Cherries (page 57)
Salt and freshly ground black pepper	2 Tbsp neutral oil	2 to 4 oz [60 to 120 g] fresh goat cheese
	1 cup [200 g] rehydrated bulgur	

continued

Preheat the oven to 400°F [200°C]. Toss the carrots with a glug of olive oil and a pinch of salt. Transfer to a baking dish and roast until the outside is caramelized and the inside is tender, about 35 minutes. Transfer to a serving dish.

In a small frying pan, heat a glug of olive oil over medium heat until it begins to shimmer, about 1 minute. Then add the ras el hanout and briefly fry to bloom the flavor, about 30 seconds.

Add the chopped pistachios and toss to coat in the ras el hanout oil, then turn down the heat to low. Toast the pistachios over low heat until fragrant, 1 to 2 minutes. Remove from the heat and let cool.

Wipe the frying pan clean, then heat the neutral oil over high heat until almost smoking. Add the bulgur and a pinch of salt and pan fry, stirring occasionally, until crisp and toasty brown, about 4 minutes.

Remove from the heat, add the pistachios, and set aside.

To serve, dress the arugula with a glug of olive oil, a pinch of salt, and a grind of black pepper and heap on top of the carrots. Scatter the pistachio-bulgur mixture over the whole thing. Dot all over with the dried cherries and crumbles of goat cheese and serve.

variations

spinach salad w/smoked whitefish + creamy mustard dressing

6 oz [180 g] spinach

4 radishes (about 4 oz [120 g]), shaved thinly (optional, or use an equal amount of any other vegetable shaved thinly)

½ cup [125 ml] Creamy Mustard Dressing (page 36)

Salt and freshly ground black pepper

1 cup [200 g] rehydrated bulgur, crisped

6 oz [180 g] smoked whitefish, picked

Dress the spinach and shaved veg in the dressing with a pinch of salt and a couple grinds black pepper.

Scatter the crisped bulgur all over and toss lightly to integrate with the greens.

To serve, portion among four serving bowls and scatter the smoked whitefish all over.

braised fennel w/lemon parsley mojo

2 to 4 heads fennel (about 2 lb [900 g] total), trimmed and cut in half, keeping the core intact	½ cup [125 ml] white wine 2 cups [500 ml] stock or water 1 tsp salt	1 cup [200 g] rehydrated bulgur, crisped ½ cup [125 ml] Lemon Parsley Mojo (page 48)

In a saucepan, combine the fennel, wine, stock, and salt. Bring to a boil, turn down to a simmer, cover, and cook until the fennel is soft but not mushy. Lift the fennel from the liquid and place on a serving platter.

Combine the crisped bulgur with the mojo and spoon over the fennel.

roasted eggplant w/lemon tahini dressing + herb salad

2 to 4 eggplant (about 2 lb [900 g] total) cut lengthwise into halves or quarters Olive oil	Salt ½ cup [125 ml] Lemon Tahini Dressing (page 36)	1 cup [200 g] rehydrated bulgur, crisped 5 sprigs each basil, parsley, and mint, leaves picked and roughly torn and combined

Preheat the oven to 400°F [200°C]. Coat the eggplant liberally with olive oil and sprinkle with salt. Roast, cut-side down, until the eggplant flesh is golden brown, about 25 minutes.

Transfer the eggplant to a serving platter and drizzle liberally with the dressing. Scatter the crisped bulgur and herbs all over. Serve warm or at room temperature.

farro

As detailed on page 375, farro epitomizes the hair-pulling confusion around wheat. As common wheat gained popularity, emmer, einkorn, and spelt fell out of vogue, often being grown as a subsistence crop in areas where common wheat would not take root. One place where these three never lost favor was northern Italy. Italians use the term "farro" as a catchall for einkorn, emmer, or spelt, differentiating them only by their size—piccolo, medio, and grande. I've included it as its own section within wheat because farro is often polished, having some or all of the bran removed, which changes how it behaves compared to an unprocessed wheat berry.

The level of processing is most important in how the grain will behave in your kitchen, and as with all parts of life, there is a constant cost-benefit analysis.

Whole-grain farro is the most flavorful and the most nutrient and fiber dense, and it takes the most time to tenderize into something you can chew. The bran acts as a tough outer coating that must be broken down with time or temperature—often taking 50-plus minutes to boil or 4 days to sprout. It is darker in color and the edges of the grain will look sharper, as they have not been polished.

Pearled farro makes up for what it lacks in flavor and nutrients in its maximum efficiency of preparation time—often taking only 15 minutes to tenderize in simmering water. Pearled farro is lighter in color, as the bran has been removed and the starch of the endosperm is revealed. It also looks a bit softer around the edges—like the smooth stones on a pebbled beach, their edges worn down by tumbling in the waves.

Semi-pearled (sometimes also called polished) is that ever-sought-after middle ground. It cooks relatively quickly (usually around 25 minutes) while still maintaining some of the flavor and nutrition of the bran and germ.

BOILED

Boiled farro transitions seamlessly from a warm salad—grains pulled straight from having been drained of their boiling water—to a chilled salad using farro that was boiled last week. Fortunately, cooked farro also freezes well, so batch cook to your heart's content. Simply bring the salted water to a boil, stir in the farro, return to a boil, turn down to a simmer, and cook away. Boiling farro normally takes about 50 minutes for whole grain, 25 minutes for semi-pearled, and 15 minutes for fully pearled. When the grain is tender, drain it like pasta and either use it immediately or spread it onto a baking sheet to cool. Always allow grains to cool completely before freezing—warm grains trapped in a covered container can stay in the temperature danger zone and allow bacteria growth even if it is stored in the freezer.

For most grain bowls, I follow a simple formula of 2 cups [400 g] boiled farro + vegetable 1 (cooked) + vegetable 2 (raw) + dressing = a salad that can be a hearty lunch, a light dinner, or the perfect thing to pack the night before and bring to work the next day. If you pack it into a jar, I usually put the boiled farro and dressing on the bottom and top with the vegetables, then just shake or invert into a bowl to mix.

matrix of farro salads

Start with 2 cups [400 g] cooked farro, warm or cool up to you, and add . . .

1.	2.	3.
VEGETABLE 1 (USUALLY COOKED), AS MUCH OR AS LITTLE AS YOU WANT:	**VEGETABLE 2 (USUALLY RAW), AS MUCH OR AS LITTLE AS YOU WANT:**	**DRESSING ABOUT ½ CUP [125 ML]:**
blanched peas	shaved radishes	Brown Butter Vinaigrette (page 35)
roasted and peeled beets, cut into chunks	ribbons of radicchio	Goat Cheese Vinaigrette (page 36)
roasted broccoli florets	shaved cauliflower	Bacon Vinaigrette (page 35)
cherry tomatoes (roasted or raw)	cucumber half moons	Creamy Mustard Dressing (page 36)

4.

TO SERVE:

Toss the warm farro, peas, and warmed brown butter vinaigrette with a big pinch of salt and black pepper. Just before serving, add the shaved radishes. Note: This salad is best warm because otherwise the brown butter vinaigrette will congeal a bit.

Place the farro on a serving platter and top with the beets and a pinch of salt and black pepper. Add the radicchio and spoon the goat cheese vinaigrette all over. I like to finish this salad with a handful of toasted pepitas. Note: If you toss all of this together it will become one big magenta salad from the beets, so I prefer to build it in layers.

In a large bowl, combine warm farro, roasted broccoli, and shaved cauliflower with the warm bacon vinaigrette. Toss it all together with a pinch of salt and several turns of black pepper. Note: This salad is best served warm because otherwise the bacon vinaigrette will congeal.

In a large bowl, combine the farro with the cucumbers, tomatoes, and creamy mustard dressing. Toss to coat, taste, adjust the seasoning as desired, and serve.

continued

instructions

w/radishes + peas w/brown butter vinaigrette

2 cups [400 g] boiled
farro

1 cup [250 g] peas,
blanched

½ to ¾ cup [125 to 185 ml]
Brown Butter Vinai-
grette (page 35)

5 radishes (about 8 oz
[225 g]), shaved thinly

5 sprigs parsley, roughly
chopped (optional)

Warm the farro and peas with the vinaigrette. Add the radishes
and some chopped parsley if you have it. Serve warm.

w/beets + radicchio w/goat cheese vinaigrette

2 cups [400 g] boiled
farro

2 lb [450 g] beets,
roasted, peeled, and cut
into chunks

8 oz [225 g] radicchio, cut
into ribbons

½ cup [125 ml] Goat
Cheese Vinaigrette
(page 36)

Salt and freshly ground
black pepper

Handful of pepitas

Toss the farro, beets, radicchio, and vinaigrette together with a
pinch of salt and black pepper. Garnish with a scattering of
pepitas. Serve warm, at room temperature, or chilled.

w/broccoli + cauliflower w/bacon vinaigrette

2 cups [400 g] boiled
farro

1½ lb [675 g] broccoli,
stems and crown
trimmed into florets,
roasted

1½ lb [675 g] cauliflower,
shaved thinly and
left raw

1 cup [250 ml] Bacon
Vinaigrette (page 35)

Warm the farro and toss with the broccoli, cauliflower, and
dressing. Serve warm.

w/cukes + parsley w/creamy mustard dressing

2 cups [400 g] boiled
farro

2 lb [900 g] cucumbers,
half-peeled and cut into
thick half-moons

10 sprigs parsley, roughly
chopped

½ cup [125 ml] Creamy
Mustard Dressing
(page 36)

Toss all together and serve at room temperature or warm.

RISOTTO-ED

The risotto method works for many grains whose starch is easily accessible and released through the agitation of continuous stirring. Farro is no exception, though be sure to use either pearled or semi-pearled; whole-grain farro will take a very long time to cook with this method, and the starch never releases in quite the same way. If the farro bag doesn't specify the type, look for a chalky dusting on the grains or in the bag. If the grains are perfectly uniform and dark brown, consider boiling or stewing.

pork meatballs w/tomato farrisotto

Most of the time I can't be bothered to actually make these meatballs and instead opt for just seasoning the ground pork and browning it in the pan before making the farrisotto and crumbling it on the top just before serving. That said, when you make little mini-meatballs and nestle them into the creamy-tomatoey-slightly-chewy farro and top with a hefty grating of cheese, the care and time shows on the plate.

I add bread crumbs (and egg and cream) to meatballs to both bind them and make them feel lighter in the mouth. If not making the balls, skip all three. I generally want a bit more salt, but try this measure to start. Finally, meatballs toughen when overworked, so mix them gently, and when forming the balls don't compact them like you would a snowball to throw at your worst enemy. Cup them just enough to get them to hold their shape. Good advice for any sort of hand-formed ball, really.

continued

1 lb [450 g] ground pork

1 egg

¼ cup [60 ml] heavy
  cream

¼ cup [45 g] bread crumbs
  (optional)

1 tsp salt, plus more as
  needed

½ tsp freshly ground black
  pepper

¾ tsp herbes de Provence
  or dried oregano

Neutral oil

1 onion (about 8 oz
  [225 g]), thinly sliced

3 garlic cloves, minced

2 cups [250 g] pearled
  farro

14½ oz [410 g] canned
  ground tomato

2 oz [60 g] Parmesan or
  pecorino for grating
  (optional)

5 sprigs parsley, roughly
  chopped (optional)

In a medium bowl, combine the pork, egg, cream, bread crumbs,
1 tsp salt, pepper, and dried herbs. With your hands or a wooden
spoon, mix until slightly tacky. Pinch off a little bit and fry it to
check the seasoning and adjust as you like.

Scoop approximately 25 tablespoon-size balls onto a baking sheet,
then lightly roll to make balls that hold their shape.

In a large frying pan, heat a glug of neutral oil over medium heat
and brown the meatballs on all sides until just cooked through
(internal temperature of 165°F [74°C] or so). Remove the
meatballs and set aside.

Bring 8 cups [2 L] of water to a boil and keep it simmering.

In the frying pan with the fat rendered from browning the meatballs, add the onion and garlic with a big pinch of salt and sweat
over low heat until soft, 5 minutes or so. Add the farro and toast
until fragrant, 1 to 2 minutes.

Add the ground tomatoes and stir regularly until the tomatoes
have started to bubble and the liquid has started to absorb.

Add a ladleful of the boiling water and stir continuously until the
liquid is absorbed. Continue adding the water, a ladleful at a time,
stirring regularly, until the farro is tender but not mushy, about
20 minutes.

To serve, portion the farrisotto into serving dishes. Top with the
mini-meatballs and a hefty grating of cheese, and sprinkle with the
chopped parsley (if using).

continued

variations

w/spring pea + mint w/citrus ricotta

Make the farrisotto basic recipe—sweat some onion (maybe add a few minced garlic cloves), add the farro, add some wine, and add the water a ladleful at a time, stirring continuously, until the grain is tender.

With the last ladleful of water, add 1 lb [450 g] of frozen or fresh peas and allow to cook until bright green.

To serve, portion into serving bowls, dot with Citrus Ricotta (page 43), and sprinkle with chopped mint and parsley.

w/mushroom cream sauce + arugula

Make the farrisotto basic recipe—sweat some onion (maybe add a few minced garlic cloves), add the farro, add some wine, and add the water a ladleful at a time, stirring continuously, until the grain is tender.

With the last ladleful of water, add 1 cup [250 ml] of Mushroom Cream Sauce (page 44) and stir to coat.

To serve, portion among dishes and top with a handful of arugula dressed simply in olive oil with a pinch of salt and a grind of black pepper.

STEWED

I prefer a brothier stew to one where I can stand a spoon up in the center. If you want it to stick to your ribs a bit more, either add less liquid at the get-go or boil off the liquid by simmering uncovered for longer. Italy has a deep tradition of farro stews as well as for cooking vegetables well past the al dente crispness prized in this country. These stew ideas combine both of those traditions, so don't be concerned about the long cooking time. I find the accessible starch in the pearled or semi-pearled farro works best for these stews. I also find myself cooking them most in those few weeks when summer is turning to fall—when all the produce is still available, but the chilly evenings call for something warm and, well, stewy.

carrot farro stew w/lemon chamomile oil

My friend Annie Compercchio once sent me a jar of chamomile blossoms from her garden, which were lovely and smelled amazing but left me at a bit of a loss on how to incorporate them into my food. Somehow, I arrived at steeping them in oil with a lot of lemon zest, and the smell immediately reminded me of wild carrot flowers. Now the two flavors are permanently combined in my mind. Should you not have a darling friend to send you hand-harvested and hearth-dried chamomile, substitute any sort of chamomile tea. Simply cut open the bag and forge on.

As with all stews, cooking them on the stovetop will go faster. Cooking in the oven will take longer but requires less checking along the way.

continued

Olive oil

5 sprigs thyme (optional)

1 cup [200 g] farro

2 lb [900 g] carrots, cut into ½ in [12 mm] chunks

1 onion (about 8 oz [225 g]), thinly sliced

Salt

1 cup [250 ml] white wine

1 recipe Chamomile Lemon Oil (page 39)

10 sprigs parsley, roughly chopped (optional)

In a medium Dutch oven, heat a glug of olive oil over medium-high heat until it begins to shimmer, about 1 minute. Add the thyme and farro and briefly fry, 1 to 2 minutes. Add the carrot and onion with a big pinch of salt, toss to coat, and lower the heat to medium. Add the white wine and cook until reduced by half.

Add 3 cups [750 ml] of water, bring to a boil, turn down to a simmer, and cook, half covered with a lid, until both the carrots and farro are tender, 30 to 60 minutes depending on the type of farro.

To serve, transfer the farro stew to a serving dish and drizzle the stew liberally with the chamomile lemon oil and a flourish of chopped parsley (if using). Taste and adjust seasoning.

eggplant tomato farro stew w/harissa

Neutral oil

1 cup [200 g] farro

1 sprig rosemary

1 onion (about 8 oz [225 g]), thinly sliced

4 garlic cloves, smashed and roughly chopped

3 lb [1.35 kg] eggplant, cut into chunks

Salt

4 lb [1.8 kg] fresh tomatoes, cut into chunks, or 24 oz [726 ml] canned crushed tomatoes

¾ cup [180 ml] Harissa (page 47)

In a medium to large Dutch oven, heat a large glug of neutral oil over medium-high heat. Add the farro and rosemary and fry until lightly toasted, about 2 minutes.

continued

Add the onion, garlic, and eggplant and a big pinch of salt and toss to coat. Add the tomatoes. If using canned, rinse out the can with a ¼ cup [60 ml] of water and add to the pot.

Bring to a boil, lower to a simmer, and cook, partially covered, until the farro is tender, the eggplant has cooked through, and the tomato liquid has reduced to a savory stew, about 25 minutes.

To serve, portion the stew into serving bowls and dollop with a hefty scoop of harissa.

farro stewed w/runner beans + a lot of garlic

I like this with tongue of fire or scarlet runner beans and a 50/50 mix of water and chicken stock.

Neutral oil	Salt	3 cups [750 ml] chicken stock, water, or a mix
1 cup [125 g] farro	1 cup [250 ml] white wine	
2 bay leaves (optional)	2 lb [900 g] green or shelling runner beans, cut into 4 in [10 cm] lengths or left whole	1 cup [250 g] True Aioli (page 38)
2 onions (about 1 lb [450 g]), thinly sliced		
10 garlic cloves, smashed		

In a medium to large Dutch oven, heat a large glug of neutral oil over medium-high heat. Add the farro and bay leaves (if using) and fry until lightly toasted, about 2 minutes. Add the onion, garlic, and a big pinch of salt and toss to coat. Add the white wine, turn down the heat to medium, and cook until reduced by half and the onions start to tenderize.

Add the runner beans and stock. Bring to a boil, lower to a simmer, and cook, partially covered, until the farro is tender and the beans are soft and silky, about 20 minutes. Remove the bay leaves.

To serve, portion the stew into bowls and dollop with aioli.

zucchini + farro stew w/paprika cumin oil

Neutral oil

1 cup [125 g] farro

1 sprig rosemary

1 onion (about 8 oz [225 g]), thinly sliced

4 garlic cloves, smashed and roughly chopped

Salt

1 cup [250 ml] white wine

3 lb [1.35 kg] zucchini or summer squash, cut into 3 in [7.5 cm] long wedges

3 cups [750 ml] chicken stock or water (or a blend)

¼ cup [60 ml] Paprika Cumin Oil (page 40)

Parsley or cilantro, chopped, for garnish (optional)

In a medium to large Dutch oven, heat a large glug of neutral oil over medium-high heat. Add the farro and rosemary and fry until lightly toasted, about 2 minutes. Add the onion, garlic, and a big pinch of salt and toss to coat. Add the white wine, turn down the heat to medium, and cook until reduced by half. Add the zucchini and stock. Bring to a boil, lower to a simmer, and cook, partially covered, until the farro is tender and the zucchini have cooked through, about 20 minutes.

To serve, portion the stew into serving bowls, drizzle with the paprika cumin oil, and garnish with parsley (if using).

FLOUR

Some of the most avid pasta aficionados swear up and down that farro flour is the best choice for pasta. The structure of the starch lends a specific chew, and the wheat itself a lovely brown hue. I find that I'm often using eggs of vastly different sizes, so I have begun to rely on a hydration percentage rather than a specific egg count. If you haven't used baking percentages, don't be scared off. Note that this ratio works well for any sort of wheat flour pasta, but the more whole grain in the flour, the more the dough benefits from a longer rest after mixing, so give it a good couple of hours if you can.

basic pasta ratio

Baker's percentages are based on the amount of liquid as a percent of the weight of flour. You do need a scale. Grams is the most precise. Imperial will work.

All of my pastas are 66 percent hydration using whole egg—the weight of the egg is 66 percent of the weight of the flour. Last night, for four people, I cracked four eggs into a bowl and weighed them. The weight was 190 grams. Divide the weight by 0.66 to get the amount of flour, 288 grams.

Flour	Eggs	Salt

Add the flour to the eggs along with a pinch of salt and knead together.

Knead until the dough is stiff but silky. If it is shaggy or crumbly, add a splash of water, 1 tsp at a time. If the dough is tacky and clings to your hands like a shy toddler, add a sprinkle of flour and continue kneading. I find it best to be on the drier side than on the stickier side.

continued

Once the dough is well kneaded, cover in a bag or plastic wrap or in a lidded container and let rest. For white flour, I let it rest about 30 minutes. For a whole wheat flour, like farro, I give it at least an hour, and it prefers a luxurious 2 hours.

Then roll out the dough with a machine or rolling pin. I have found I like a slightly thicker noodle, so on my pasta roller I roll to the #6 thickness. Play around and find what you like best.

To cook, bring some heavily salted water to a boil and drop the pasta in. It will cook quickly, in 2 to 3 minutes.

I pull the pasta from the water when it is about 85 percent cooked and then transfer it to the prepared sauce to finish cooking in the sauce itself. This has two primary benefits. One, I'm way less likely to overcook the noodles. Two, the last bit of starch released from the dough in the cooking process gelatinizes the sauce, both thickening it and encouraging it to cling to the noodles themselves.

variations

w/spinach + mushroom cream sauce

Spring is rich in alliums and greens. Slice some alliums (onions, ramps, green garlic, leeks, or a mix) and sweat in a good knob of butter or glug of olive oil and a big pinch of salt until soft but not brown. Add twice the amount of roughly chopped mushrooms, any variety. Sweat the mushrooms with another pinch of salt and some black pepper. Add ½ cup [125 ml] of white wine and let reduce at least by half. Add 1 cup [250 ml] of cream and bring to a soft boil. Turn off the heat and wait. When the pasta goes into the pot, turn on the heat on the sauce. When the pasta is 85 percent cooked, add it to the cream sauce and let finish cooking, 1 to 2 minutes, swirling continuously to coat the noodles. Just before serving, stir in a handful of spinach per person and let gently wilt in the warm sauce.

w/tomatoes, creamed mozzarella + olive rig

In summer, I skip making a proper sauce and simply cook the pasta to 95 percent done and then toss it in a bowl with a good glug of olive oil and a couple of spoonfuls of the pasta cooking water. After the oil and water mix to make a light coating, I add some chopped tomatoes (say 1 to 2 lb [450 to 900 g], cut into largish chunks) and toss again. Then dish up and dot with the Creamed Mozzarella (page 43) and spoon Olive Rig (page 49) all over it. If you have some basil on hand, a few leaves torn on top would be quite at home.

w/squash purée + ras el hanout apricot almond rig

When squash is at its peak, I buy them in larger quantities, say 5 or so at a time. Cut them in half, scoop out the seeds, and roast at 375°F [190°C], cut-side down, until the flesh collapses when prodded with a probing finger, about 30 minutes. Remove from the oven and let cool until easy to handle, then blend the flesh in a food processor with several good glugs of olive oil and pinches of salt. That purée is great on any number of things, but maybe best of all as a sauce for pasta. Simply warm about ¼ cup [60 ml] of the purée per person and toss it with the just-cooked pasta and a couple of spoonfuls of the pasta cooking water to thin and coat. Then dish up the pasta and top with a hearty garnish of Ras el Hanout Apricot Almond Rig (page 49).

w/sage fried brown butter, garlic bread crumbs + citrus ricotta

Make the Sage Fried Brown Butter (page 50) in advance, removing the fried leaves to a paper towel to drain and crisp but keeping the brown butter in the frying pan. To make garlic bread crumbs, mince 2 or 3 garlic cloves and soften in a good glug of olive oil, add ½ cup [60 g] or so of bread crumbs and toast (TBH, I do this in large batches and keep on hand for sprinkling all over just about everything), then set aside. When the pasta is 85 percent done cooking, add to the brown butter in the frying pan along with a spoonful of the pasta water and finish cooking over medium heat, stirring continuously. Dish up into serving bowls. Dot all over with Citrus Ricotta (page 43), scatter liberally with the garlic bread crumbs, and then crunch the fried sage leaves on top.

freekeh

Freekeh (also called farik) is another ancient way of processing wheat that remains popular in North Africa and the eastern Mediterranean basin. Commonly, wheat ripens and dries in the field before harvesting. Freekeh are green wheat berries, traditionally durum, that are harvested before they have a chance to dry on the plant. After the green berries are cut, they are carefully set on fire. The high moisture content of the green berries keeps them from burning while the straw and chaff burn. The now-roasted wheat berries are then threshed or rubbed, giving the food its name ("farik" translates to "rubbed") to remove any remaining chaff. Freekeh is often then cracked so it resembles bulgur. Because it is not parboiled, it takes longer to cook than bulgur, and because the wheat berries are harvested when green, it often has a more vegetal flavor than other wheat products.

BOILED

Freekeh tends to be sold as cracked wheat, the wheat berries having been broken in processing, though whole kernel is available. Cracked freekeh boils faster than whole, as the water and heat can penetrate more easily, and it is texturally very similar to bulgur. Whole freekeh, like whole wheat berries, takes longer and has a chewier mouthfeel.

   Note that the following recipe and its variations would also do well with crisped freekeh. Simply pat dry and pan fry the already boiled freekeh in a healthy amount of oil until golden brown and crispy. If using crisped freekeh, I decrease the amount of boiled grain by half.

slow-cooked salmon w/freekeh + lemon tahini dressing

I hem and haw about my favorite way to cook salmon. On one hand, I love searing fillets to get a burnished, crispy skin. On the other, sliding a whole side of salmon into a low oven until meltingly tender without fear of overcooking, then serving it as a giant lovely centerpiece is pretty nice too. This recipe is written to make best use of the grill—low heat to cook the salmon and then high heat to char the green beans. Feel free to use an oven instead and then pan fry the green beans. It is also written to serve 6 to 8, big dinner party style. To serve fewer, simply decrease the amounts proportionally. Or, you know, leftovers.

2 cups [300 g] freekeh	Salt and freshly ground black pepper	1 recipe Lemon Tahini Dressing (page 36)
Olive oil		
1 side salmon (about 5 lb [2.25 kg]), scaled and trimmed	3 lb [1.35 kg] green beans, cleaned and stringed as needed	6 sprigs parsley, roughly chopped
		3 sprigs mint, roughly chopped

Bring a large pot of salted water to a boil. Add the freekeh, return to the boil, lower to a simmer, and cook until tender, about 20 minutes for cracked or 40 minutes for whole. When tender, drain and toss with a glug of olive oil and set aside.

Heat the oven (or grill) to 300°F [150°C]. Season the salmon liberally with salt and place on a foil-lined baking sheet. Bake the salmon until the flesh color changes to a lighter pink and is just cooked through, about 35 minutes.

Remove the salmon from the grill, lightly cover with more foil to trap the heat, and let rest. Increase the heat of the grill to high.

Toss the green beans in a glug of olive oil with a big pinch of salt and black pepper. Grill the beans until well charred on the outside and bright green in color.

To serve, either make a salad to serve alongside the salmon by combining the cooked freekeh, green beans, tahini dressing, and chopped herbs, or spoon the freekeh onto each plate, nestle a piece of the salmon next to it, top with a pile of green beans, liberally spoon the tahini dressing over the whole thing, and garnish with a flurry of chopped herbs. Again, options.

variations

w/delicata squash + walnut aillade

Cut 2 delicata squash (about 1½ lb [675 g]) in half and scoop out the seeds. Cut the squash halves into ½ in [12 mm] thick half-moons. Toss with a glug of olive oil and a pinch of salt and roast at 400°F [200°C] until the squash is caramelized on the outside and tender when pierced, about 20 minutes. Combine the roasted squash with 1 cup [200 g] of boiled freekeh and toss with another good glug of olive oil. Transfer to a serving plate or bowl and top with ½ cup [125 ml] of Walnut Aillade (page 50).

Serve on its own as a light meal or with any sort of grilled protein.

w/cabbage kohlrabi salad, dates, + tajín oil

Thinly slice 8 oz [225 g] of cabbage. Cut 1 or 2 kohlrabi (about ½ lb [225 g]) into matchsticks. Remove the pits from 8 (or so) dates and chop. Roughly chop 10 to 15 sprigs of cilantro (I like a lot in this salad; use as much as you like, or substitute parsley). Combine all of the above with 1 cup [200 g] of boiled freekeh, ½ cup [125 ml] of Tajín Oil (page 40), and a big pinch of salt.

Serve on its own or with any grilled protein. Also good eaten with tortillas or over polenta (page 255).

continued

w/shaved fennel + rhubarb salad w/lemon + herbed yogurt

Cut 1 or 2 fennel heads (about 1 lb [450 g]) into wafer-thin ribbons and immediately submerge in acidulated water (see page 24) to prevent browning. Cut 2 stalks of rhubarb into equally thin long pieces. Add the zest of 1 lemon to ½ cup [125 ml] of Herbed Yogurt (page 45; dill is especially nice with this combination). Combine the shaved fennel, rhubarb, and 1 cup [200 g] of boiled freekeh with a big glug of olive oil and a pinch of salt. Toss to coat and transfer to a serving platter. Drizzle with the yogurt mixture and serve.

STEWED

Because freekeh is often sold cracked, it tends to break down a bit more in the longer stewing process, which gives the finished dish both chewy texture from the grain and a thickened porridge-like quality from the starch in the grain.

stewed freekeh + chicken w/asparagus + lemon oil

Chicken leg quarters are an entire quarter of the bird—thigh and drumstick still attached. They feel somewhat decadent because of their size and the volume of skin that gets crispy when finished in the oven. With this volume of meat, I tend to have leftovers. Simply pick the meat from the bone, discarding any remaining skin, and then add the meat to the stew for ease of reheating. Stewed freekeh can be done in the oven or on the stovetop, depending on your day—just note that cooking in the oven will take a bit longer because the heat is indirect versus the direct heat of a burner. Note: Opt for the thicker asparagus stalks; they're easier to shave thinly.

Neutral oil

4 chicken leg quarters (2 lb [900 g])

Salt

1 cup [150 g] freekeh

½ cup [125 ml] white wine or hard cider

1 onion (about 8 oz [225 g]), thinly sliced

5 garlic cloves, minced

1 lemon, cut into small chunks (seeds removed, ideally)

8 oz [225 g] asparagus

¼ cup [60 ml] Coriander Lemon Oil (page 39)

Parsley, chopped, for garnish (optional)

continued

Preheat the oven to 400°F [200°C]. In a large ovenproof frying pan, heat a glug of neutral oil over high heat. Pat the chicken leg quarters dry and season liberally with salt.

Sear the chicken, skin side-down, until the skin is golden brown, about 5 minutes. Remove the chicken, add the freekeh, and turn down the heat to medium. Toast the grains in the hot oil for about 1 minute.

Add the white wine to deglaze the pan and reduce the wine by half. Add the onion, garlic, and lemon chunks and a big pinch of salt.

Add 4 cups [1 L] of water and place the chicken legs, skin-side up, on top of the mixture. Place the pan in the oven and roast until the freekeh is tender and the chicken is cooked through, about 25 minutes.

Shave the asparagus into thin ribbons with a mandoline, sharp knife, or vegetable peeler.

To serve, dress the shaved asparagus with the coriander oil and a big pinch of salt, adding a flurry of chopped parsley (if using).

Portion the chicken into serving dishes and top each with a mound of asparagus salad.

continued

variations

w/tomato, clams + romesco

¼ cup [60 ml] olive oil, plus more for the arugula

1 sprig rosemary (optional)

1 tsp fennel seed

1 cup [150 g] freekeh

1 onion (about 8 oz [225 g]), thinly sliced

5 garlic cloves, minced

Salt and freshly ground black pepper

3 lb [1.35 kg] tomatoes, cut into chunks, or 24 oz [720 ml] canned crushed tomatoes

2 lb [900 g] clams

4 oz [120 g] arugula or spinach

½ cup [125 ml] Romesco (page 49)

In a large Dutch oven or saucepan, heat the olive oil over medium-high heat until just about smoking. Fry the rosemary (if using) and the fennel seed until fragrant, about 30 seconds. Add the freekeh and fry to toast, about 1 minute.

Add the onion and garlic with a big pinch of salt and turn down the heat to medium. Sweat the onion and garlic until they are just about to take on color, about 4 minutes.

Add the tomatoes and cook until they just start to give up their juice. Cover and stew until the freekeh is 80 percent tender, about 20 minutes.

Add the clams, replace the lid, and cook the clams until they open, about 5 minutes.

Dress the arugula with a glug of olive oil, a pinch of salt, and a grind of pepper.

To serve, dish the stew into serving bowls. Top each bowl with a hearty spoonful of romesco and some arugula salad.

w/pumpkin + mint almond relish

¼ cup [60 ml] olive oil

1 cup [150 g] freekeh

1 onion (about 8 oz [225 g]), thinly sliced

6 garlic cloves, minced

Salt

¼ cup [60 ml] white wine

2 lb [900 g] peeled and cubed pumpkin or squash

14½ oz [410 g] crushed tomatoes, canned or fresh

1 cup [250 ml] Mint Almond Relish (page 48)

In a large Dutch oven or saucepan, heat the olive oil over high heat until just about smoking. Add the freekeh and fry to toast, about 1 minute.

Lower the heat to medium and add the onion and garlic with a big pinch of salt and sweat until just about to color, about 4 minutes.

Add the white wine to deglaze the pan and cook until reduced by half. Add the pumpkin, tomatoes, and 1 cup [250 ml] of water and bring to a boil. Lower to a simmer and cook until the pumpkin and freekeh are both tender, about 25 minutes.

Portion into serving bowls and top each with a couple of big spoonfuls of the mint almond relish.

w/celery root, smoked yogurt + spinach

¼ cup [60 ml] olive oil

10 sprigs thyme, tied in a bundle

2 cups [300 g] freekeh

2 onions (about 1 lb [450 g]), thinly sliced

Salt and freshly ground black pepper

1 cup [250 ml] sweet apple cider

2 lb [900 g] celery root, cut into matchsticks

1 cup [125 ml] Smoked Yogurt (page 45)

6 oz [180 g] spinach

In a large Dutch oven, heat the olive oil until almost smoking. Fry the thyme for about 30 seconds. Add the freekeh and fry for about 1 minute or until toasty and fragrant.

Lower the heat and add the onions with a big pinch of salt. Sweat the onions until softened, then add the sweet cider to deglaze the pan. Allow the cider to reduce by half, then add 3 cups [750 ml] of water.

Bring to a boil, lower to a simmer, and cook until the freekeh is tender, about 25 minutes.

Combine the celery root and smoked yogurt with a pinch of salt and a grind of black pepper.

To serve, place the spinach in serving bowls and ladle the hot freekeh over the spinach, encouraging it to wilt from the heat of the grain. Top with the celery root salad.

sources

Thankfully there are more and more grain and legume producers across the United States supported by a growing network of millers and distributors. If you are looking for places to source the grains and legumes, this is a quick rundown of regional producers and distributors who ship nationally. In addition to those listed here, local farmers markets, co-ops, and regional grocery chains are often good places to look for a new and exciting sack of seeds.

Anson Mills
Columbia, South Carolina
Since 1995, Anson Mills has led the way in growing and selling heirloom grains as a way to keep them and expand their availability.

Barton Springs Mill
Dripping Springs, Texas
Family-owned millers focusing on landrace wheats and heirloom corn.

Bob's Red Mill
Milwaukie, Oregon
Bob's Red Mill is becoming more and more widely available across the country as well as through their robust online store. BRM is my go-to source if I can't find an ingredient through a regional producer. I feel good about supporting them because they have been employee owned, through their employee stock ownership structure, since 2010, providing a strong model for other corporations to follow. Note that many grocery stores stock BRM products in several different locations: the health aisle, the baking section, and the "world food" aisle.

Breadtopia
Fairfield, Iowa
Breadtopia is my most-used resource for bread-baking equipment, but they also have a large selection of heritage wheats, both as flours and whole groats.

Carolina Ground
Asheville, North Carolina
Stone millers in North Carolina focusing on wheats grown in the South, from Virginia to the Carolinas.
They are a great resource for heritage and freshly milled flours.

DeZwaan Windmill
Holland, Michigan
A 1760s Dutch windmill, moved to the United States in the 1960s, is now stone-milling regional flours with wind power. Flours are available on site and through mail order.

Farm and Sparrow
Mars Hill, North Carolina
Stone millers in North Carolina who carry (and mill) a variety of grains and legumes, including field and chickpeas.

Ferris Organic Farms
Eaton Rapids, Michigan
This 200-acre organic farm has been in production since 1837. They now ship a variety of beans, seeds, and flours grown in the northern midwest and milled on site.

Grist & Toll
Los Angeles, California
Traditional stone milling in the heart of Los Angeles. Grist & Toll house-mill a variety of heirloom wheat and corn.

Hayden Mills
Queen Creek, Arizona
Father and daughter team in Arizona milling fresh flours, whole grains, and a variety of beans and pulses.

Janie's Mill
Ashkum, Illinois
The Wilken Family are fifth-generation farmers who transitioned to organic production in 2001. Their Danish-designed stone mill turns out a variety of heritage whole-grain wheat, buckwheat, oat, and rye flours.

Maine Grains
Skowhegan, Maine
Focused on reinvigorating rural Maine, Maine Grains repurposed a jailhouse into a gristmill while focusing on regional growers and producers to create a no-waste facility supporting economic growth.

McKaskle Family Farm
Hayti, Missouri
Steve McKaskle was the first midwestern organic rice producer. Realizing the demand, he helped his farming neighbors convert to organic and grow production, expanding to include organic corn.

Meadowlark Organics
Ridgeway, Wisconsin
The Wepking and Bickford families are working together to raise a variety of landrace grains and heritage legumes on their farm in Wisconsin. In 2020, Meadowlark finalized the purchase of the Lonesome Stone Mill and are now milling on a farm while championing vibrant, regional grain economies.

North Bay Trading Company
Brule, Wisconsin
Since 1987, North Bay Trading Company has been sourcing regional food staples and distributing for their network of producers.

Rancho Gordo
Napa, California
Steve Sando pioneered the resurgence of heirloom beans, other legumes, and grains by focusing on New World crops and expanding a cooperative network of regional producers to supply home cooks everywhere.

Sheridan Acres
Ubly, Michigan
Fourth-generation bean farmers in Michigan's thumb, Kevin Messing started growing heirloom beans in 2016.

Stokli
Santa Fe, New Mexico
Chef Marianne Sundquist pivoted from catering to ingredient distribution during the COVID-19 pandemic. Seeing the gaps in the supply chain between regional producers and consumers, she and her husband, Hans, started Stokli, a subscription-based food hub to support southwestern growers and to increase food security in their region.

Zingerman's
Ann Arbor, Michigan
Since 1982, Zingerman's has been the primary resource for high quality, artisan ingredients. In addition to hand-selected specialty grains, their bakehouse has recently started milling their own flours. Their large mail-order operation ensures it's easy (and fun) to order your sought-after ingredient.

Zursun Beans
Twin Falls, Idaho
Founded in 1985, Zursun was one of the first American companies to begin growing hard-to-find beans and legumes. Their beans are available via specialty retailers across the country or by mail order.

Yolélé
New York City, New York
Yolélé was founded in 2017 by chef Pierre Thiam to create economic opportunity for smallholder farming communities; to support biodiverse, regenerative, and resilient food systems; and to share Africa's ingredients and cuisines with the world.

acknowledgments

This book would not have been possible without the contributions and support of the following:

matt berens * jerry hebron * carl wagner * wesley rieth * rachel roche * larry gates * halee wepking * andrew harris * granor farm * adrian lipscombe *

kari stuart * ee berger * mollie hayward * lucy engelman * sarah billingsley * sara schneider * kristi hein * claire gilhuly * magnolia molcan * steve kim * tera killip * cynthia shannon * ilana alperstein * vanessa santos * cat shook * christie goodfellow * cg ceramics * laura brown * laura lou pottery * nathaniel mell * felt + fat * nicolas newcomb pottery * emily winter * the weaving mill * meredith lee * ruth and rhoda *

tim mazurek * kelsey coday * erin stanely * farm club * rose hollander * eric gerstner * laura piskor * abbi hoiles * andrea deibler * mario aranda * paul fagen * heidi joynt * molly kobelt * ellie mullins * pat mullins * emma brewster * joe lindsey * katherine miller *

and, as always, erik hall

index